Theology and Identity

Traditions, Movements,
and Polity in the United Church of Christ

Edited by
Daniel L. Johnson
Charles Hambrick-Stowe

Newly Expanded by Daniel L. Johnson

UNITED
CHURCH
PRESS®

Cleveland

United Church Press, Cleveland, Ohio 44115

© 1990, 2007 by United Church Press

11   10   09   08   07   5   4   3   2   1

Library of Congress Cataloging-in-Publication Data

Theology and identity: traditions, movements, and polity in the United Church of Christ/edited by Daniel L. Johnson, Charles Hambrick-Stowe.

p.   cm
ISBN 0-8298-0807-8
ISBN-13: 978-0-8298-1772-0

1. United Church of Christ. 2. Reformed Church—United States. 3. Congregational churches—United States. I. Johnson, Daniel L. II. Hambrick-Stowe, Charles E.

BX9885.T54   1989   89-78141
285.8'34—dc20   CIP

CONTENTS

Part 2

Polity, Ministry, and Worship Issues

Part 3

Theological Issues and Movements

CONTRIBUTORS

DONALD G. BLOESCH
Professor of Theology, University of Dubuque Theological Seminary, Dubuque, Iowa

GABRIEL FACKRE
Abbott Professor of Christian Theology, Andover Newton Theological School, Newton Centre, Massachusetts

CHARLES HAMBRICK-STOWE
Vice president and dean of Northern Seminary in Lombard, Illinois

DANIEL L. JOHNSON
Retired United Church of Christ minister, taught UCC polity and history at Yale Divinity School and Eden Theological Seminary

ROSEMARY McCOMBS MAXEY
Pastor, Mt. Tabor United Church of Christ, Rocky Ridge, Maryland
Adjunct Lecturer, Religious Studies, Western Maryland College

M. DOUGLAS MEEKS
Professor of Systematic Theology and Philosophy, Eden Theological Seminary St. Louis, Missouri

ELIZABETH C. NORDBECK
Professor of Church History, Lancaster Theological Seminary, Lancaster, Pennsylvania

ALICE O'DONOVAN
Pastor, Congregational Church, Peru, Vermont

RALPH C. QUELLHORST
  Conference Minister, Indiana-Kentucky Conference, United Church of
  Christ

SHARON H. RINGE
  Professor of New Testament, Methodist Theological School, Delaware,
  Ohio

REUBEN A. SHEARES II
  Former Executive Director, Office for Church Life and Leadership,
  United Church of Christ Pastor, Congregational Church of Park
  Manor, Chicago, Illinois

JOHN C. SHETLER
  Conference Minister Emeritus, Pennsylvania Southeast Conference,
  United Church of Christ Executive Vice-President, Mercersburg
  Society

ROGER L. SHINN
  Reinhold Niebuhr Professor Emeritus of Social Ethics, Union
  Theological Seminary, New York

SAMUEL N. SLIE
  Director, Downtown Cooperative Ministry, New Haven, Connecticut

DAVID M. STOWE
  Executive Vice-President Emeritus, United Church Board for World
  Ministries Occasional visiting professor at United Church of Christ
  related seminaries

RICHARD H. TAYLOR
  Pastor, First Congregational Church, Benton Harbor, Michigan

FREDERICK R. TROST
  Conference Minister, Wisconsin Conference, United Church of Christ

BERTRICE Y. WOOD
  Associate for Planning and Administration, United Church Board for
  World Ministries

BARBARA BROWN ZIKMUND
  Professor of Church History and Dean of the Faculty, Pacific School of
  Religion, Berkeley, California

PREFACE TO THE REVISED EDITION

In 1990, when *Theology and Identity* first appeared, it and other earlier works studied the life of the United Church of Christ at thirty and more years into its development, together with historical analyses of the four predecessor denominations. Additionally, the journals *New Conversations* and *Prism* have contributed to the self-understanding of the UCC, a church often described as "a work in progress", or as Elizabeth Nordbeck and Clyde Steckel have it, "the unfinished church". More recently a study by Randi J. Walker, *The Evolution of a UCC Style* [1], has added to the growing collection of UCC identity studies, along with these earlier published works to describe the spirit and ongoing formation of the denomination.

Style is an interesting word choice. It implies a reality more flexible than *identity or ecclesiology* would convey. In 1988 I remarked to the late Charles Shelby Rooks, my regret that the early UCC Theological Commission had not long continued in its original design and purpose. Shelby disagreed. He replied "That just wasn't our *style*."

Probably there is never a perfect time to describe the ever-developing United Church of Christ. But now at our fiftieth anniversary year, it seemed timely to present a partially updated edition of *Theology and Identity*, commenting on both some of the observations of the first edition and on some of the significant developments in the church and the world since the decades of the 1980s and 1990s.

The former Afterword (now chapter 18) is the work of Roger L. Shinn, one of the original shapers of the United Church of Christ. The Afterword was first a lecture presented at the close of a day-long theological symposium for members of the Connecticut Conference in 1985. Samuel W. Fogal and Amy Beveridge, then serving on the Connecticut Conference staff, committed valuable creativity and time to making the well-attended symposium a reality. At the end of a long and stimulating day of theological education about the past and present, Dr. Shinn provided a clear and uniquely informed glimpse into a tomorrow still to come twenty-one years after he spoke. Twenty-one years later much, of course, could now be added to his summary of pivotal events of the time. But the Afterword still looks forward with hope to what may yet become.

Several chapters of this book were lectures given at the Connecticut symposium. Several other chapters had been similar presentations, also in 1985, for the Central Atlantic Conference. Charles Hambrick-Stowe and I, working from two contrasting vantage-points, cooperated to turn these presentations into a book, augmented by other essays from invited contributors. *Theology and Identity* still functions as one resource for seminary courses in history and polity, examining historical roots, polity issues, and various matters of theology in turbulent times. It may also serve some of the needs, questions and interests, coming from other Christian communions.

It was my privilege to teach United Church of Christ history and polity, first with Joan Forsberg at Yale Divinity School and later at Eden Theological Seminary. The questions and contributions of colleagues and students in both schools helped to shape some of the priorities of *Theology and Identity*. In the years I taught those courses I attended several of the annual gatherings of UCC seminary polity teachers in Cleveland. Elizabeth Nordbeck, Clyde Steckel, and Barbara Brown Zikmund gave those meetings, organized by Lynn Bujnak, sharp focus and significant purpose. The United Church of Christ remains regionally separated with four distinct (dare I say autonomous?) historical roots and ways of worship and witness. We can be glad that those who teach students for the ministry in all the various UCC regions across the country meet regularly to "get it right" by mutual reinforcement and contrast. Such work continues to develop the UCC "style" of being Christian in this ever-unfolding world. I will gratefully comment further on this ongoing process in chapter 19.

Finally, my thanks to staff of United Church Press, for their encouragement to revise and update this 1990 commentary on the elusive identity of the United Church of Christ. I am once again foolish enough to attempt the difficult, if not impossible.

NOTES

1. Walker, Randi J. *The Evolution of a UCC Style* (Cleveland: United Church Press, 2005).

INTRODUCTION

DANIEL L. JOHNSON / CHARLES HAMBRICK-STOWE

This book had its origins in projects simultaneously undertaken in 1985 in the Connecticut and Central Atlantic conferences. The Theological Consultation of the Central Atlantic Conference commissioned six essays on selected topics and distributed them in booklet form as part of an educational effort at the conference's annual meeting in June. In Connecticut, the Department of Church Life and Leadership sponsored a symposium called "United Church of Christ Theology: Yesterday, Today, Tomorrow" in November of that year and later made the papers available informally on a limited basis. These grass-roots efforts made use of both nationally known figures and local talent to address issues of denominational importance. The two projects illustrate Louis H. Gunnemann's observation that denominational identity depends on "the growing capability of the conferences in their servicing of the local churches."[1] Marion M. Meyer, then Senior Editor of Pilgrim Press, introduced the chairpersons of the conference-level work to one another. This book is not, however, simply a shuffling together of two sets of papers. Because of overlap and a desire to explore new directions, some essays were abandoned, others revised, and many were added. The authors—pastors, seminary professors, and denominational executives—were asked to write for a general audience.

The one spirit and the many visions toward which people in the United Church of Christ live today embody sensitivity for heritage as well as for the present context. The prophets and Jesus himself stood firmly on the foundation of the ancient covenants as they witnessed to God's righteousness and voiced God's promise/warning concerning the future. In accord with this understanding, this collection of essays is organized into three sections: Roots; Ministry, Polity, and Worship; and

Theological Issues and Movements, and concludes with a provocative look to the future.

"Roots" is not intended as history for its own sake, but as an effort to uncover some of the legacies that live on in our denomination today. The four major traditions that came together to form the United Church of Christ continue to influence the church. Elizabeth Nordbeck not only traces the theological tradition of Congregationalism to its Puritan origins but follows it through nineteenth-century liberalism and the social gospel. John C. Shetler finds in the German Reformed experience, notably in its Mercersburg expression, an ecumenical theology that provides a foundation for our common work today. Ralph C. Quellhorst, in his informative essay on the Evangelical Synod, identifies pietism as an ongoing force in our denomination. Richard H. Taylor describes and celebrates the freedom of the Christian stream, and lifts up the challenge of unity in the face of pluralism. In addition to these four traditions, however, many in our denomination look to other roots as well. Samuel N. Slie explores the influence of the black experiences in our churches, pointing to its emphasis on justice for all oppressed persons. Rosemary McCombs Maxey, herself a Creek Indian, throws open the doors of Christian theology to invite in traditional religious elements of indigenous peoples.

The three chapters in the section "Ministry, Polity, and Worship" bring our traditional theological concerns to bear on the life of the church today. Reuben A. Sheares, who has been at the center of the quest for theological identity, shares his insights into the ecclesiological nature of the United Church of Christ. Barbara Brown Zikmund pursues further her seminal thesis of embodiment and empowerment as twin conceptions of ministry. And the editors of this volume have collaborated on an exploration of worship traditions, the new *Book of Worship,* and the ecumenical context of liturgical renewal.

Contemporary theological issues and movements within the United Church of Christ are given voice in Part 3. David M. Stowe introduces the main themes of process theology. Sharon H. Ringe explains how feminism has influenced our denomination. Bertrice Wood pushes our traditional theology of mission into the arena of liberation and empowerment of the poor. M. Douglas Meeks elucidates in a clear and concise way the tenets of this liberation theology. Alice O'Donovan then boldly puts forth her case for the church's openness to homosexuals in ministry. By contrast, while many of today's theological movements seem to push our faith in new and conflicting directions, Donald G. Bloesch expresses a more conservative theology of denominational renewal. Gabriel Fackre also reroots us by thoughtfully analyzing the role of doctrine in the life of the United Church of Christ. Frederick R. Trost

concludes this section of the book by examining the question of authority, with special reference to the heritage of the Evangelical Synod.
Finally, readers will especially appreciate Roger Shinn's prophetic Afterword, "The United Church of Christ Tomorrow."

We have sought to make available the thinking of persons from across
the United Church of Christ. The essays display an astonishing diversity
of viewpoints and Christian experience. Readers (the editors included)
will not agree with everything they find here. But we cannot deny the
place each group or movement occupies within the body of Christ today.
Further, not every group or concern active within the church is included,
and no slight was intended by the selection process. But we believe the
essays are broadly representative of the forces pushing, tugging, worshiping, and serving together in our church. Indeed, this book covers a
wider and more colorful spectrum of experience than any previous
presentation of views in the United Church of Christ.

Various movements express corresponding visions of what God would
have our church do and be in our generation. The problem of identity,
which has vexed the United Church of Christ as much and perhaps
more than other denominations, is thus the task of theology. Answers to
the questions, Who are we? and What shall we do? depend on our
responses to the prior question, What do we believe? The pluralism of
possible responses suggests the complexity of being Christian in the
United Church of Christ. The American religious dream of gospel
simplicity is elusive. In our own traditions, after the American Revolution, leaders of the movement that became the Christian denomination
affirmed their identity as "simply Christian." But they also stressed the
importance of personal freedom to express the faith in varieties of ways.
In a noncoercive church the range of views exemplified in this book is
not only tolerated but encouraged.

While some denominations establish their identity by inspecting the
walls for breaches and requiring those persons inside to conform to
essential standards, the United Church of Christ characteristically has
held the gates open wide and cultivated diversity. To change the image,
rather than screen out members, movements, and theological views that
are somehow not true-blue, the United Church of Christ has viewed the
rainbow as a symbol of grace and hope for the people of God. To
recognize this posture as characteristic is to see that love for those who
differ, desire to learn by dialogue, and tolerance of ambiguity are
important parts of our identity in Christ and as a church. In short, we
have emphasized the word "all" in our motto, "That They May All Be
One" (John 17:21).

To claim such an identity, and to claim it as *Christian*, is by no means
an excuse for doctrinal laziness. Indeed, the work of theology becomes

more challenging as we hold lovingly to our own history and faith expressions while in fellowship with those who, inspired by the same Bible, express the faith differently in their lives and with words other than ours. We reject the notion that the United Church of Christ can legitimately be ridiculed for an "anything goes" approach to belief. If anything, uniformity can produce a scholasticism that masquerades as theological rigor but is in fact a comfortable retreat. On the contrary, we must become theologically rigorous precisely because God calls us to understand one another, criticize and learn from one another, and stand and serve together in Christ. Pluralism in the body of Christ forces the continual rethinking of basic theological issues and their practical implications.

Unmistakable signs of mature theological activity in the United Church of Christ make these exciting days. Some of these signs are visible at the grass-roots level where pastors and lay people have engaged in lengthy, painstaking discussions of the World Council of Churches' document, *Baptism, Eucharist, and Ministry* (BEM),[2] and the Lutheran-Reformed dialogue document, *An Invitation to Action*,[3] which outlines an ecumenical convergence in sacramental theology and the nature of church and ministry.[4] Pastors increasingly took this theological discussion into their churches as attention shifted to the proposed covenant put forth in 1985 by the Consultation on Church Union (COCU) to create a Church of Christ Uniting. Association Church and Ministry Committees and local church groups study *The COCU Consensus: In Quest of a Church of Christ Uniting*[5] and *Covenanting Toward Unity: From Consensus to Communion*.[6] COCU, with its projected Covenanting Councils, forces a new sense of immediacy in local theological reflection. What will this mean in our town and in our church? BEM, the Lutheran-Reformed consensus, and COCU orient the United Church of Christ mainly (but by no means exclusively) in episcopal and more highly liturgical directions, while the covenant between the Christian Church (Disciples of Christ) and the United Church of Christ has caused some clergy and laity to wrestle with the meaning of the sacraments in the context of the traditions of American revivalism, believers' baptism, and lay authority. Also at the grass roots, adherents and sympathizers of the Biblical Witness Fellowship continue to play the role of loyal opposition within the denomination, calling the church back from liberalism to a more traditional stance. Black and other minority groups in the denomination enunciate distinctive theologies of liberation in the language of ethnicity, social context, and struggle. And members of the Mercersburg Society and the Biblical Theological Liturgical Group have sought renewal through fresh identification with living tradition.

The year 1984 heard a variety of voices within the United Church of

Christ issue the summons to greater theological clarity. Thirty-nine seminary professors signed a January 1984 document declaring this to be "a most difficult and urgent time."[7] Citing "a void in sustained disciplined reflections that can claim the assent of the church," the professors called for a "reconsideration of the historic and confessional roots of our church." Barbara Brown Zikmund of the Pacific School of Religion expressed it as looking for "sound teaching" and a "teaching consensus" not imposed from above but "growing out of natural communities of faith."[8] That same year, the Biblical Witness Fellowship followed up its Dubuque Declaration (November 1983) by publishing *Affirming Our Faith*,[9] an aggressive critique of the baleful influence of heterodoxy—in the form of process theology, liberation theology, and feminist theology—within the denomination. And 140 persons in May committed to the theological grounding of the United Church of Christ gathered on Cape Cod, at the invitation of planners from the Biblical Theological Liturgical Group and the Mercersburg Society, for the first Craigville Colloquy. Craigville I, occasioned by the fiftieth anniversary of the Barmen Declaration, demanded a new dedication to reflection on Christian action. They said that "the trumpet has too often given an uncertain sound" and "theological disarray and lackluster witness" have often undermined the work of the church. In January 1985 another group within the United Church of Christ, Christians for Justice Action (CJA), set out explicitly "to draft a contribution to the current theological dialogue" and produced an article "The Prophet Speaks to Our Times."[10] The CJA document, a meditation on Isaiah 58 including confession of sin, a call to total discipleship in the church, and a manifesto for economic justice, demonstrates the biblical rootedness of the whole church in the 1980s. At the same time, Christians for Justice Action speaks for many, and stands opposed to other calls for clarity, when it states: "God's revelation is continuous in the midst of struggle and refuses to be confined to creeds, doctrines, or statements of faith from any particular time and place."[11] It is no wonder that in the autumn of 1984, as he concluded a sabbatical during which he read theology and denominational history, Avery Post, president of the United Church of Christ, wrote of the "explosion of theological work" at many levels of the church's life.[12]

The ferment of 1984 was salutary in its effects. The United Church Board for Homeland Ministries published these documents, together with new commentary and responses by key theologians, in its journal *New Conversations* (Spring 1985). The seven closely related seminaries joined in 1985 to launch a new journal, *Prism: A Theological Forum for the United Church of Christ*. The denominational newsletter, *Keeping You Posted*, inaugurated a "Theology Forum" column, and the new publication, *United Church News,* included articles on theological concerns. Furthermore, the first Craigville Colloquy met with such enthusiastic response that it has become an annual event with an open invitation to all interested participants. Craigville II (1985) explored sources and nature of authority; Craigville III (1986) studied the ministry of the whole people of God; Craigville IV (1987) examined Eucharist; Craigville V (1988) focused on Baptism; Craigville VI (1989) struggled with the ethics of abortion. More colloquies are currently in planning stages. Theological reflection took place in other settings as well. The Office for Church Life and Leadership conducted a series of regional theological consultations with representatives from the theology committees of the conferences. The visit of theologians in 1985 from the German Evangelische Kirche der Union (EKU) with seminaries, congregations, and local UCC-EKU working groups, planned by the EKU Working Group of the United Church of Christ, sparked continued assessment of "the question of just where the common theological basis of the UCC and its witness lies."[13]

The process of theological self-identification is dynamic and dialectic, not fixed in the past or in any static symbols. The two revisions of the Statement of Faith and debate over the need for an entirely new affirmation and the development of a mission statement for the denomination demonstrate the fusion of theology and the emerging social justice agendas of the church. The need for inclusive language, for example, unthought of in 1959, is now generally recognized as both an ethical and a theological issue, involving our perceptions of God and humanity. Worship and program materials published by the Office for Church Life and Leadership, including resource booklets, the *Manual on the Ministry* (1986), and the new *Book of Worship* (1986), also reflect and draw out the church's theology. Theology in the United Church of Christ is thus more a process than a product. Even a "product" as substantial as the *Book of Worship,* ten years in the making and with the physical appearance of a book intended for long duration, is introduced as a piece of "transitional literature."[14] The United Church of Christ's reputation for trendiness is inaccurate. Many of these recent theological expressions are as fully traditional as they are contemporary, suggesting that the United Church of Christ is entering a period in which relevance to the present does not mean neglect of the past. This is indeed a happy prospect.

We hope that this book will promote theological discussion not only among pastors and seminarians but at the local level of seeking believers in adult classes and fellowship groups, for theology is not a finished product in our denomination. It is a dynamic process flowing out of our experience in the church of Jesus Christ in the world.

NOTES

1. Louis H. Gunnemann, *The Shaping of the United Church of Christ: An Essay in the History of American Christianity* (New York and Philadelphia: United Church Press, 1977), 107.

2. Faith and Order Commission, World Council of Churches, *Baptism, Eucharist and Ministry,* Faith and Order Paper No. 111 (Geneva: World Council of Churches, 1982).

3. James E. Andrews and Joseph A. Burgess, eds., *An Invitation to Action* (Philadelphia: Fortress Press, 1984).

4. See the entire issue, "Lutheran/Reformed Church Dialogue and the UCC," *New Conversations* (Winter/Spring 1988).

5. *The COCU Consensus: In Quest of a Church of Christ Uniting* (Princeton: Consultation on Church Union, 1985).

6. *Covenanting Toward Unity: From Consensus to Communion* (Princeton: Consultation on Church Union, 1985).

7. "A Most Difficult and Urgent Time," memo to the Executive Council of the United Church of Christ, January 21, 1984.

8. Barbara Brown Zikmund, memo to the Executive Council, Conference Ministers, and signatories of "A Most Difficult and Urgent Time," 26 March 1985.

9. Biblical Witness Fellowship, *Affirming Our Faith* (Souderton, Pa., 1984).

10. "The Prophet Speaks to Our Times," *New Conversations* (Spring 1985): 19–25.

11. Ibid., 23.

12. Avery Post, memo to Administrative Committee, 31 October 1984.

13. Johannes Althausen et al., "Report on the 1985 Visit with the United Church of Christ from the Evangelische Kirche der Union," p. 3.

14. *Book of Worship* (New York: United Church of Christ, Office for Church Life and Leadership, 1986), 27.

Part 1

ROOTS

1

THEOLOGICAL TRADITION OF CONGREGATIONALISM

ELIZABETH C. NORDBECK

In 1636, Puritan John Cotton called the movement simply the Congregational "Way." It has been one of the most intensely studied religious phenomena in America—in part because for more than three centuries it has remained a "way" and a "walk," never hardening into a fixed body of doctrine. From the first adherents down to the present representatives in three contemporary denominations,[1] Congregationalism has engendered a tradition of diversity and dissent, fueled alike by passion and reason. Its inherently democratic thrust contributed to the formation of the American republic. Its spiritual children represent perspectives that range across the spectrum of theological understanding.

The term "congregationalism" refers not to a particular belief system but to a type of church government that insists on the scriptural authority and autonomy of individually gathered churches. Historically, Congregationalism has always rejected adherence to creeds and confessions as pernicious and binding. The result has been a movement that, sometimes in spite of itself, has both embraced and produced theological change.

A brief essay cannot hope to deal adequately with Congregational theology. What it can do, though, is provide a broad outline for further study, first, by describing the origins of the Way; second, by indicating some of its characteristic understandings; and finally, by noting the developments that brought Congregationalism, changed but still vital, into the mainstream of American denominational life.

The story of Congregational beginnings is familiar. By 1558 in England, two distinct lines of English dissent had arisen. One group, convinced that the Anglican Church was irredeemably corrupt, were determined to dissociate themselves completely from it; these were Separatists, forerunners of Plymouth's Pilgrims. A second group, more moderate in their assessment of Anglicanism, sought simply to cleanse or "purify" the church; these were nonseparating Puritans. Between 1620 and 1640 representatives of both groups—a few hundred Separatists and more than twenty thousand Puritans—relocated to what is now New England, and out of this "great migration" Congregationalism developed.

But here the story becomes more complicated. Were the Pilgrims or the Puritans the original practitioners of "true" Congregationalism? This old debate—an issue in the mergers of 1931 (Congregational-Christian) and 1957 (United Church of Christ)—smolders even today. Our discussion, therefore, must begin with an account of Congregationalism's first parents.

Uncompromising in their separatism, convinced that the true church consists of the regenerate only, the Pilgrims left Leyden, Holland in 1620 primarily to avoid cultural assimilation. Arriving in Plymouth, Massachusetts, nearly a decade before the first boatload of Puritans debarked at Salem (Massachusetts Bay), they sought a place to worship in isolation and in peace. The Puritans, however, had a more ambitious agenda: to establish "a City upon a Hill,"[2] a society so exemplary in its religious and civil order that it might become an irresistible model for the world to emulate. With the Plymouth Separatists, the Puritans agreed that Christ's true church consists of the elect only. But for the Puritans, it was possible to understand "true church" as a nucleus within a larger, flawed whole, a church-within-a-church awaiting the separation of wheat from chaff.

The two neighboring communities in Massachusetts quickly established regular contact; and it is likely that the neophyte Congregationalists learned and borrowed from the more experienced Pilgrims as they refined their own church discipline.[3] Nevertheless, the older settlement was eventually engulfed by Massachusetts Bay. By the end of the century the two communities were one, their churches indistinguishable.

Both Plymouth and Massachusetts Bay wielded enormous influence in the development of American Congregational thought. The Pilgrims practiced a more open, pristine form of covenantal fellowship, uncomplicated by visionary social schemes. But failure to produce an aggressive leadership, educational institutions, or an identifiable body of theology all contributed to the demise of their society. The Puritans, by contrast, built a social order of extraordinary intellectual vitality and pervasive theological influence. But their need to maintain a homogeneous Christian commonwealth promoted moral rigidity and moved them at times perilously close to Presbyterianism. Thus neither group represents anything like "ideal" Congregationalism. In them, rather, we can see the twin tendencies of the Congregational Way itself—which has always resisted attempts to encapsulate it in any pure form—as it seeks the precarious balance between antinomianism and absolutism, freedom and fellowship.

THE "HOLY EXPERIMENT"

Although the Puritans were not the first practitioners of Congregationalism, they were undoubtedly its most prolific and articulate exponents. Consequently, any treatment of Congregational theology must begin with Massachusetts Bay, for virtually all the tendencies in later, evolved Congregationalism can be traced back to the Puritans' unique theocratic vision, often referred to as the "Holy Experiment."

Theologically the Puritans were Calvinists. With the great Genevan reformer, John Calvin, they had concluded that in Adam's fall, all have sinned; that redemption depends on unmerited grace; that God has determined that some will be saved, some damned. But it was not enough simply to accept these as dogmatic truths. For the Puritans, heirs of English humanism as much as English dissent, it was also critical that the scriptures be understood as reasonable. Thus their "federal" or "covenant" theology was a way of reading the Bible that enabled them to understand it as a logical and reliable guide for living. The covenant idea explained the active relationship, on the one hand, between God and individuals, and on the other, between God and God's particular people—which the Puritans were convinced they were. At its most basic level, the covenant was concerned with both divine grace and human behavior.[4]

The Puritans believed, first of all, that an inscrutable but compassionate Creator had decided voluntarily to limit divine behavior toward humankind, and so had entered with them into a compact in which the conditions of salvation were set down. In this compact, God had agreed to deal with individuals according to human conceptions of justice. But God had also established a code for human behavior. This code was not a means of attaining salvation. It was simply humanity's half of the agreement—an agreement that persons could keep, however, only through the enabling power of free grace.

The Puritans also believed that they were *collectively* in covenant with God. Therefore they were bound to live by God's commandments not only individually, but as members of gathered churches and as a body politic. But because institutions have neither hearts to be changed nor souls to be saved, this national covenant was assumed to turn on works alone: God's rewards or punishments were meted out as temporal blessings and afflictions, according to the people's just deserts.

The foregoing is a too-brief summary of a theological system that provided the foundation for a radical new way of life. Yet even in broad outline the leitmotifs of historical Congregationalism—flexibility, social awareness, realism, missionary zeal—are evident. It is important to look more closely at these themes, for over the years they have informed the spirit of Congregational theology even as its particular substance has changed.

John Cotton would probably have been mystified to hear the Way described as flexible. Nevertheless, Congregationalism was a remarkably adaptable system, open to change even within the circumscribed world of seventeenth-century New England. The reasons were both theological and structural.

For one thing, early Congregationalists were reluctant to suggest that human knowledge was in any sense reliable or complete. John Robinson's famous farewell to the departing Pilgrims—"The Lord hath more light and truth yet to break forth from his holy Word"—has been quoted by Unitarian defectors, abolitionists, and present-day Congregationalists for whom new occasions and duties have provided new scriptural insights. If the Puritans were less willing to proclaim the open-endedness of scripture, nevertheless they harbored few illusions about human certainty. To be sure, their whole system was constructed on the dictum that "sanctification is evidence of justification," that is, that behavior is a reliable index of grace. Still, no good Puritan would have assumed that final certainty of salvation (or anything else) is available this side of Jordan. If the human mind is God-given, and therefore reasonably trustworthy, it is also tainted with Adam's corruption, and so inevitably suspect.

It is also true that Congregationalism's antiauthoritarian bias engendered a certain waywardness among the saints. By removing institutional barriers between God and humanity, eschewing creeds and confessions, and placing conversion and education in their stead, the Puritans encouraged both an intellectual assertiveness and an anti-intellectual bias that, paradoxically, undercut their own presuppositions and practices. It is no accident that the dissenting New England Way itself bred dissenters like Anne Hutchinson or Roger Williams; and there is a direct line of dissent from Puritanism to rationalistic Unitarianism.

For seventeenth-century New Englanders Congregationalism comprised a reasonably cohesive theology as well as a set of actual institutions. But the principle of autonomy encouraged regional differences and rapid change, and Congregationalism early embraced a range of diversity insupportable in other systems. Even before mid-century the Congregational churches differed widely among themselves in both theology and practice. By the time he published his descriptive *Ratio Disciplinae* in 1726, third-generation Puritan Cotton Mather was able to speak casually of the many "agreeable varieties" among the churches. No doubt John Robinson would have agreed with Mather's conclusion that these were a predictable result of human imperfection, none having "the vanity to think, that their works are perfect before God."

Today the Puritans are remembered for their moral rigidity rather than for anything like social awareness. Yet the Bay settlers' conviction that they were in covenant with God habitually directed their attention outward, linked up the public and private dimensions of faith, and gave their movement a combination of pragmatism and missionary passion that remained typical of later generations of Congregationalists. In a community "knit together as one man [sic]," the welfare of individual and society must be vitally linked. Because in the Bay system only church members could hold office or vote, the entire machinery of church and state turned on the proper discernment of election. For this reason, as well as for reasons of personal piety, devout Puritans habitually scrutinized one another's behavior, carefully monitoring outward signs of inward grace. Here, in the interactions of daily life, lay both the keys of the kingdom and the fate of society.

Nor was the Puritans' agenda for that society limited to Massachusetts Bay. At first, with the settlement in its infancy, Puritan leaders discouraged migration. But by 1640, saints were trickling north into Maine and New Hampshire, establishing civil and church order in territory where, as Cotton Mather later noted, most settlers had come mainly to catch fish. Although their missions were largely unsuccessful, New England's leaders remained verbally committed to converting the "savages" (Native Americans) until nearly 1800.

CHANGES IN THE NEW ENGLAND WAY

Sixty years after the "great migration," Increase Mather returned from a trip to England with a new charter for Massachusetts that effectively transferred governmental control to the British crown. The holy experiment was over. Dependent for success on uniformity of belief and a self-renewing supply of saints, the Puritan system was the victim of a shifting population, changing economics, and transatlantic politics. But the Way had also contributed to its own demise; for its precariously balanced system had tended easily to stiffen into a religion mainly of outward profession, a situation that was itself a sin.

Symptomatic of its decline was the fact that fewer and fewer people were experiencing conversions. The Halfway Covenant, enacted by a Massachusetts synod in 1662, had attempted to deal with the problem by enabling persons of a "godly walk" to have partial privileges in the churches; but this had succeeded only in filling the pews with well-behaved but unconverted listeners.

Between 1700 and 1740, the Congregational Way experienced substantial, if vague and undefined, change. Disenchanted with the hard doctrines of Calvinism, dissatisfied with churches that kept upright citizens from the communion table, ministers here and there modifed earlier practices and ideas. As a result, disputes began over questions of increased lay control, relaxed standards of church membership, "presbyterialized" polity, and watered-down doctrine. The gulf between Massachusetts and Connecticut, occasioned back in 1636 by the departure of Thomas Hooker from Cambridge, grew wider: Connecticut clergy flirted with near-Presbyterianism and founded their own college (Yale) as a conservative antidote to Harvard's "free and catholick" spirit. The built-in flexibility of Congregationalism temporarily forestalled any serious rifts. But on the eve of the Great Awakening the lines of future development had already been drawn.

Among those who still called themselves Calvinists these lines marked a rough cleavage between liberals and conservatives, whose differences tended to be ones of emphasis rather than essentials. Liberals, for instance, were less insistent on a "conversion narrative" by prospective church members. Many of them supported church membership based on "good conversation," and a few innovators advocated communion open to all as a means for conversion. Conservatives, on the other hand, were more likely to be rigorous in matters of membership, discipline, and doctrine. While liberals dealt with the harsher doctrines of total depravity and predestination mainly by ignoring them, conservatives still actively preached them from their pulpits.

Despite these differences, most conservative and liberal Calvinists before the Awakening numbered themselves among the orthodox. A third group, however, was by the 1730s taking measured steps away from Calvinism. Called "Arminians," after Dutch theologian Jacob Arminius, they rejected the idea of an all-powerful God who forces an arbitrary will on humankind. In their most fundamental departure from orthodoxy, the Arminians insisted on people's innate ability to influence their own salvation. Later, those of Arminian convictions would enkindle Congregationalism's first great controversy, leading numerous churches into the "heresy" of Unitarianism.

Meanwhile, though, the faith of the founders was momentarily revived by a shock wave of religious excitement that swept through the colonies at mid-century. In northern New England the first stirrings had been felt in the aftermath of the great earthquake of 1727. A similar localized "quickening" took place in Northampton during the 1730s under the preaching of Jonathan Edwards. But it was not until 1740, when England's George Whitefield first toured the region, that the "quickenings" became a full-scale Awakening.

Initially, Whitefield and the itinerants who followed him won converts among the laity and supporters among the clergy. Their message was simple: the path to religious truth is experiential, not merely intellectual; and those without "heart knowledge" cannot hope to understand scripture, or claim to have true faith. By 1743, however, the emotional excesses accompanying many conversions had turned early friends of the revival against it; by 1745, its energy had petered out.

The Awakening shook the very foundations of the Congregational Way. By validating even an uneducated convert's relationship with God, it undercut New England's intellectual elite and diminished the prestige of both ministers and magistrates. "Old Light" critics and "New Light" supporters of the revival now clashed over issues of itinerancy, emotionalism, and church membership. Some converts, dissatisfied with an "unconverted ministry" and "spiritually dead" members, left their churches to form new Separate or Baptist groups.

The Awakening also brought into public prominence the man whose work was to influence Congregational theology throughout the next century. Jonathan Edwards was a supporter of the revival—though not of its excesses—and a powerful apologist for the orthodoxy of his ancestors. Trained at Yale and apprenticed at the Northampton parish of his unconventional grandfather Solomon Stoddard, Edwards even as a young man was deeply, almost mystically, religious. His own conversion—a series of encounters with the divine—overwhelmed him with a sense of God's power and humanity's dependence, and convinced him of the validity of Calvin's insights.

Living at a time when many of his colleagues "saw no discrepancy between divine justice and human reason, between God's glory and man's [sic] goodness,"[5] Edwards was a vocal opponent of theological liberalism and ecclesiastical laxity; he dared to insist that the old ways were not simply better, but literally true. In one important respect, however, he did break with the Puritan past. God, Edwards asserted, is under no obligation whatsoever to humanity.[6] A hallmark of covenant theology had been the insistence that the relationship between God and humankind was circumscribed by an agreement that placed both parties under mutual obligation. But for Edwards the covenant was dead. The church was meant to be gathered out of the world, not linked with it; and it was to be filled with men and women on whose hearts a perceptible, saving change had been wrought.

Informed as much by Paul and Augustine as by Locke and the new science, Jonathan Edwards was a complex, transitional figure, poised between the rationalism and empiricism of the Enlightenment and the piety of his ancestors. In part for that reason, his influence was limited largely to the world of speculative theology, and only minimally to the church life and practice to which his own ministry was primarily dedicated. Nevertheless, that influence was prodigious. In sounding the death knell of the covenant, Edwards infused the moribund theology of post–Puritan New England with new life, insuring the preservation of a strong theological tradition within Congregationalism for fully another century. His emphasis on the experiential dimensions of the faith and on the nature of true virtue, moreover, reacquainted Congregationalism with its roots, and moved the churches toward the day when the evangelical power of revival would be harnessed to reform an expanding America.

Edwards died in 1758, at a time when many Americans were preoccupied with nontheological matters. Nevertheless, a theme long present in Congregational theology was attracting new attention. As early as 1713, John Wise of Ipswich had argued that the principles of democratic freedom, autonomy, and covenant inherent in Congregationalism were consistent with an understanding of natural rights. Now others were moved to agree. In particular, Jonathan Mayhew of Boston confronted the looming British threat from an explicitly Congregational perspective. Anglicanism represented not only an error in polity, he argued in *A Discourse Concerning Unlimited Submission;* it threatened both the ecclesiastical developments that Congregationalism had brought about *and* the libertarian principles that accrue to them.

Recognition of the inseparable character of civil and ecclesiastical functions was an element in Puritan Congregationalism as old as the movement itself. By 1633 yearly "election sermons" were already hallowing the political process. But by the mid-1760s, a traditional Congregational emphasis on the nature of the church and right practice had developed into a model of organization that pointed toward a broader secular understanding as well. From the pens of liberal Congregationalists like Mayhew and his Boston colleague Charles Chauncy, explicit assertions of individual accountability in civil and ecclesiastical affairs now argued persuasively against British "tyranny" and for rebellion. Once revolution came, an activist clergy preached republicanism from the pulpits, served in the militia, and helped hammer out guiding documents for the new nation. More than one historian has claimed that the principles and proponents of Congregationalism were uniquely influential in promoting the patriot cause. Nevertheless, if explicit libertarianism was a logical outgrowth of the latent republicanism in Congregational polity, it was also a harbinger of the demise of New England's established Congregational Standing Order.

ONE DENOMINATION AMONG MANY

A decade after the Revolutionary War had ended, the whole cloth of Congregationalism appeared visibly unrent. Here were churches primarily in New England, regionally autonomous, locally in fellowship. But the "unity in diversity" to which Cotton Mather had once alluded had vanished. Instead, the churches constituted a group that had inexorably followed its own organizing principles and expanded far beyond its historic boundaries theologically, structurally, and geographically. By 1800, an inherited and orthodox understanding of Congregationalism no longer accorded with the experience of the inheritors. Now, however, three developments would begin to move Congregationalism into a new period of self-assessment, and finally into the era of American denominationalism.

Precipitated by the election of liberal Henry Ware to Harvard's Hollis Professorship of Divinity in 1805, the Unitarian controversy first brought these unspoken differences into bold relief. Disputes over biblical interpretation, Christology, and church membership soon led to schism, followed by the organization of the American Unitarian Association in 1825. With this defection, Congregationalism in Massachusetts now comprised a far more agreeable and theologically restricted group.

Meanwhile, Connecticut Congregationalists had begun an ecumenical experiment with Presbyterians in 1801, framing a "Plan of Union" to promote missions in the West. Although its organizers hoped for "unity and subordination of denominational preference," their scheme unfortunately tended to move both new and existing churches toward Presbyterianism. Abrogated by one faction of Presbyterians in 1837, the plan limped along until 1852 when, in a historic "first corporate action," the Congregationalists too abandoned it.

Not least significant, the religious homogeneity that had made tax-supported Congregational churches viable for nearly two centuries had virtually disappeared in the aftermath of revolution.[7] Internal divisions, competing religious groups, a changed political climate, and a growing conviction that mandatory support for religion actually dishonors God, all made change inevitable. After 1800, Connecticut, Massachusetts, and New Hampshire passed laws disestablishing the churches; by 1833, Congregationalism was one denomination among many.

As these unsettling developments moved the churches toward a more aggressive denominational stance, so too new theological currents were gradually leading them away from Calvinist orthodoxy. With the death of Edwards and Harvard's apostasy, the theological burden had fallen to Edwards's disciples at Yale. The New Divinity Men—Joseph Bellamy, Nathanael Emmons, Samuel Hopkins, and Jonathan Edwards, Jr.—

supported revivals, orthodoxy in doctrine, and regenerate membership in the churches. Their work, however, though critically important to a fellowship facing theological challenges on all sides, had in it little of the power and scope of earlier Congregational writing. Often contentious in tone, lacking both Edwards's intellectual breadth and his vital piety, the New Divinity Men extracted and elaborated on elements of Edwards's thought in an effort to interpret old doctrines to a newly enlightened age. The results were twofold. One was a kind of denatured Calvinism, its categories still intact but their meanings altered. The second was an extensive, intricate body of divinity in which morality and Christian duties subtly replaced piety and holiness as primary emphases. After 1800, when revival again shook New England, the architects of a "New Haven theology" took these tendencies even further. Arguing that sin is "original" only in its inevitability, and that humanity has "moral power to the contrary," Timothy Dwight and Nathaniel W. Taylor now departed irrevocably from traditional Calvinism. Their work provided the basis for a coherent theology of revivalism, which thinkers like Lyman Beecher and—far more radically—Charles Grandison Finney eventually refined and developed.[8]

It remained, however, for a thinker who at college had the reputation of being a doubting Thomas to move Congregationalism toward genuinely new theological insights. Horace Bushnell entered Yale in 1824, was converted, and promptly backslid. But a revival in 1831 moved him to study divinity; and in 1833 he took a church in Hartford, Connecticut, ministering to an upwardly mobile, urban congregation. Always a practical pastor more than a speculative theologian, Bushnell set out to present to his flock a theology that spoke to their needs and those of the time.

Bushnell's first and most famous work, *Discourses on Christian Nurture* (1848), demolished the traditional understanding of original sin and the necessity for a radical change of heart. Agreeing with his Yale tutors that "sin is in the sinning," he argued that it is possible for a child, raised rightly, "to grow up a Christian, and never know himself as being otherwise."[9] Bushnell's understanding that conversion is an ongoing process rather than a one-time event was corroborated in his own life: not until the year *Christian Nurture* was published did he have the profound encounter that convinced him experientially of the transforming power of Christ. In 1849, Bushnell revealed his revolutionary views on the nature of language, presented in a preface to three lectures entitled "God in Christ." Language, he asserted, is essentially imprecise and poetic. Words themselves are at best inexact, imagistic, analogical tools for understanding, and not the literal bearers of meaning that traditional approaches to scripture and creeds might suggest.

Among the Connecticut orthodox, these and other controversial views on the atonement, the Trinity, and the immanence of God raised cries of heresy. Nevertheless, Bushnell's influence was perhaps more profound even than that of Jonathan Edwards. In time many of his "heterodox" views, as well as his catholicity of spirit and his broadly organic perception of human life and faith, became cornerstones of a new, liberalized fellowship.

In the meantime, however, the viability of Congregationalism as a denomination was unclear. By 1840 its churches were floundering institutionally and theologically. Formerly, they had been held together by the cordial ties of common history, regional interests, and state support; now, faced with a geographically expanding fellowship, mission in the West, and the antislavery cause in the South, they discovered no efficient mechanism for united action. Congregationalism, moreover, lacked a binding principle, a belief or mission around which identity and a corporate sensibility might be forged. Theologically, the churches embodied a wide range of doctrinal positions. Some remained Calvinist; others were moving toward Bushnellian liberalism. Now more than ever it was difficult to identify a single, dominant stance that could be called "Congregational."

Yet it was the very theological liability of Congregationalism—a polity that had over time encouraged departures from its own foundational doctrines—that eventually provided a powerful unifying principle. This was the conviction, echoed by historian Williston Walker, that Congregational polity "had claims that could not be ignored." These claims were rediscovered, in part, by a revisionist examination of Congregational history. New books, periodicals, and a denominational library now reacquainted clergy and laity with the ideals and aims of the founders. The conclusion seemed inescapable that Congregationalism was, as John Wise had hinted years before, a kind of pure ecclesiastical embodiment of American democracy itself—or, even more, the blueprint for it. From such retrospection the Congregationalists now extracted a single critical principle. Theological unity lay not, as formerly understood, in a sectarian faith commitment grafted on and external to congregational polity. Rather it lay in a commitment to the diversity produced and embraced by that polity, the best and only sure means for discovering religious truth.

In June 1865, Congregationalists from across America gathered in Boston at their first national council since 1648. Held in the seat of early Puritanism and featuring an emotional pilgrimage to Plymouth, it was an affirmation of the unity and common heritage of Congregationalists nationwide. In the so-called Burial Hill Declaration it most clearly outlined the denomination's new direction.

The declaration was remarkable simply as a common statement of faith by Congregationalists who, twenty-five years earlier, had agreed on very little. In its commitments to the elevation of society, the regulation of education, the purification of law, the reformation of church and state, and the spread of the gospel are evident the themes of the forebears whose faith was now being reaffirmed. Yet most noteworthy is the broad ecumenicity of the document. Refusing (albeit not without debate) to identify the faith "commonly known among us" as Calvinism, Congregationalists made their theological position clear. It was as simple—or complex—as the polity that had led them to it. Those who hold "one faith, one Lord, one baptism" are in fellowship, bound to keep "the unity of the spirit in the bond of peace" despite their inevitable differences.

In the years following the Civil War, these differences gradually coalesced to shape a denomination that was both structurally and theologically distinctive. In 1871, a historic meeting at Oberlin, Ohio resulted in the formal organization of a National Council, committed to uphold the Congregational principle of self-government as well as to foster fellowship, consultation, and cooperation among the churches. At the same time, the acceptance of diversity cautiously revealed in the Burial Hill Declaration prepared the way for further theological innovation. Among the major denominations, Congregationalism now offered the "most fertile soil for liberalism," undergoing what one scholar has called a "nearly complete transformation" theologically between 1865 and 1913.[10] An impressive group of scholar-pastors, among them Theodore Munger, Leonard Bacon, and popular novelist Charles M. Sheldon, were spokespersons for the new thought. Washington Gladden, "father of the Social Gospel," was liberalism's most influential exponent.

Openness to theological diversity, optimism about history and human ability, and skepticism about the absolute nature of various traditional Christian beliefs were the hallmarks of late-nineteenth-century liberalism. To these Washington Gladden added profound social concern and a conviction that the churches must confront public as well as private, systemic as well as specific, sinfulness. The gospel itself, he insisted, calls for an end to "unbridled individualism" and economic injustice, demanding instead a society radically reconstructed on a foundation of service and mutuality. Although Gladden died in 1918, his vision of a church of broad social outreach eventually found expression in the Council for Social Action, organized in 1934 to work toward "a warless, just, and brotherly world."

Meanwhile, modern Congregationalism was emerging as a broad and catholic movement, rooted in a revered past but directed toward the future. Not quite fifty years after the historic Burial Hill Declaration, the National Council adopted a new, streamlined statement of faith, significant as much for what it did not say as for what it did. Omitting reference to human sinfulness, Christ's expiatory atonement, eternal rewards and punishments, or the sacraments, the Kansas City Statement of 1913 asserted the churches' commitment to progress, justice, peace, and brotherhood [sic], and expressed openness to the possibility of ongoing revelation. Orthodox in essence, its very generality welcomed a variety of theological perspectives, while its strongly transformational language reflected the social awareness of the time.

Nevertheless, the change in Congregationalism was undoubtedly more evolution than transformation. Indeed, the new face of the denomination was a logical development in a movement that had, from its beginning, discovered the Christian life in the tenuous balance between opposite commitments: private judgment and communal responsibility, knowledge and experience, tradition and experimentation, autonomy and fellowship. At the beginning of the twentieth century, these commitments continued to reflect both the heritage and the promise of the faith.

NOTES

1. In addition to the United Church of Christ, the Congregational Christian Church (National Association) and the Conservative Congregational Christian Conference trace their ancestry back to English and early American Congregationalism.

2. John Winthrop's famous phase is a quotation from Matt. 5:14 [KJV].

3. Just how much the Pilgrims influenced the Puritans has been the subject of much scholarly debate. Congregational historian Williston Walker assumed that the Pilgrims had virtually persuaded the Puritans to become Separatists. The Puritans are generally assumed to be nonseparating Congregationalists who had worked out at least some of the details of their practice before arriving in the New World.

4. See John von Rohr, *The Covenant of Grace in Puritan Thought* (Atlanta: Scholars Press, 1986).

5. Harold P. Simonson, *Jonathan Edwards: Theologian of the Heart* (Grand Rapids: Wm. B. Eerdmans, 1974), 155.

6. Jonathan Edwards, *God Glorified in the Work of Redemption, By the Greatness of Man's Dependence Upon Him, In the Whole of It* (Boston, 1731).

7. From the beginning of the Puritan experiment, churches had been supported by a general tax, not just through voluntary gifts. The assumption was that "orthodox public teachers of piety and morality" had a civil as well as an ecclesiastical function.

8. Both Beecher and Finney moved back and forth between Congregationalism and Presbyterianism; both groups often claim them. Beecher was born into a Congregational family, but defected to the Presbyterians; Finney eventually

came over to Congregationalism because he found its liberal polity less constrict-
ing to his radical views and activities.

9. Horace Bushnell, *Discourses on Christian Nurture* (1848; New York: Charles
Scribner's Sons, 1912), 10.

10. Sidney E. Ahlstrom, *A Religious History of the American People* (New Haven:
Yale University Press, 1972), 775–76.

2

REFORMED CHURCH THEOLOGICAL TRADITION

JOHN C. SHETLER

The body of congregations that once belonged to the Reformed Church in the United States constitutes one of the four branches of that limb of the great tree of the whole Christian church we know as the United Church of Christ. Prior to 1863 this branch was known as the German Reformed Church. On the occasion of the Tercentenary of the Heidelberg Catechism (1563), the General Synod was organized, and in order that others might recognize that the denomination had people of other ethnic backgrounds the word "German" was dropped from the name.

The great flow of German Reformed refugees to America began in the early years of the 1700s. The books they brought with them tell the story and the nature of the Reformed Church. Those who could afford books brought in their sea chests the Heidelberg Catechism and the German Bible. Some few who were pastors or schoolmasters brought the Marburg Hymnal or the Palatinate Liturgy. Nearly all the books were in the German language until the early 1800s when English translations began to appear. These books take us back to the centers of the Reformation in Europe: Heidelberg, Marburg, Strassburg, Geneva, and Zurich. Here we meet Bucer, Ursinus, Calvin, and Zwingli, as well as Melanchthon, Olevianus, Oecolampadius, Farel, Beza, and Bullinger. While the Reformed Church traces its roots to Switzerland, we do not look back as do Lutherans to one founder, but to a collegium of scholars and reformers in the first three generations of the Reformation.

The first great theologian in the Reformed tradition was Ulrich Zwingli of Zurich. His reforms began with the study and preaching of the Word of God through the Holy Scriptures, first at Glarus (1506–1515), then at Einsiedein (1516–1518), and finally at Zurich (1518–1531). In 1519 at the Grossmunster he began his famous series wherein he preached his way through the New Testament. The preeminence of the scriptures in Reformed origins is further seen in that the sixty-seven theses upon which Zwingli based his reforms, given on January 29, 1523, were based on the Bible.

John Calvin is ranked by historian and Mercersburg theologian Philipp Schaff as the ablest biblical exegete among the Reformers. His Bible commentaries are still printed and studied today. His *Institutes of the Christian Religion,* which embody the most complete theological system in Protestantism, stands firmly on biblical text and interpretation. The development of the liturgy and the introduction of congregational singing from the Psalter carried the Bible into worship in the language of the people. Reformed views spread from German- and French-speaking Switzerland to Germany and France, in particular Heidelberg and Strassburg. We may note, too, that from Geneva Calvinism reached Scotland through John Knox and that Presbyterianism and Puritan Congregationalism form another part of the Reformed family.

During the sixteenth century only Roman Catholicism and Lutheranism were permitted by state agreement in the principalities of the Holy Roman Empire, until the 1648 Peace of Westphalia ended the Thirty Years War. For a century, congregations became Reformed only while a particular prince adhered to the Reformed faith and then disappeared or existed in secret when a Lutheran or Roman Catholic prince ruled. The Augsburg Confession (1530) became the official standard for Protestant Germany. Its statement on Holy Communion was carefully written to protect the Lutheran faith against Zwinglian, and later Calvinist, errors. Lutheran theologian Philipp Melanchthon studied Calvin's position on the Lord's Supper and in 1540 attempted to alter the passage to reconcile the differing views and to remove the anathema. Frederick III, elector of the Palatinate from 1559, embraced Reformed theology and likewise sought ways to bring religious peace. He conceived the idea of a catechism and assigned the task of writing to two young theology professors and third-generation Reformers, Zacharias Ursinus and Caspar Olevianus.

Ursinus was a strategic choice, as in his theology he linked German Lutheranism and Swiss Calvinism. Ursinus studied at the University of Wittenberg and was particularly influenced by Melanchthon. He studied in Zurich, including one period with Henry Bullinger, and in Calvin's Geneva. Ursinus was acquainted with several German and Swiss catechisms and had experienced the hostility of the high Lutherans who were critical of Melanchthon for being soft on Calvinism. Ursinus's and Olevianus's Heidelberg Catechism took an ameliorating position. The basic tenets of Reformed theology underlay its teachings, but Calvin's sharpness was tempered by the uplifting Lutheran concept of grace. The spirit of the Catechism is exemplified in its famous first question:

"What is your only comfort, in life and in death?" The answer begins: "That I belong—body and soul, in life and in death—not to myself but to my faithful Savior, Jesus Christ, who at the cost of his own blood has fully paid for all my sins and has completely freed me from the dominion of the devil . . ." The Heidelberg Catechism's emphasis on justification by faith through the free grace of God in Christ, and its heavy use of scriptural texts, proclaimed that the Reformed tradition is truly evangelical and biblical. When the Reformed Church in the United States united with the Evangelical Synod of North America in 1934, the Heidelberg Catechism, along with Luther's Shorter Catechism, the Augsburg Confession, and the Evangelical Catechism, became the doctrinal standards of the new Evangelical and Reformed Church.

The Bible and the Heidelberg Catechism comprised the chief textbooks for confirmation education and young men studying for the ministry. Pastors were trained either in Europe or in rustic parsonage seminaries. In 1825, however, the Eastern Synod voted to establish a theological seminary. Begun in York, Pennsylvania, it moved successively to Carlisle, Mercersburg, and Lancaster. During the Mercersburg years (1835–1870) a distinctive theological expression of the German Reformed tradition took shape. The Mercersburg professors, notably John Williamson Nevin and Philip Schaff, wrote extensively on the Heidelberg Catechism and were leaders in the celebration of its Tercentenary. While their theology may be described as catholic or ecumenical in spirit, it rigorously subjected tradition to the discipline of the Word of God. Mercersburg Theology continues today to be the subject of investigation of scholars of Protestant and Roman Catholic background.

The principal liturgies of the Reformed Church, including those of Martin Bucer at Strassburg, the Palatinate Liturgy, and the 1866 liturgy reflecting Mercersburg influence, have embodied the Calvinist view of the sacraments. As the Heidelberg Catechism states in reply to Question 66, "What are the Sacraments?" "They are visible, holy signs and seals instituted by God in order that by their use he may the more fully disclose and seal to us the promise of the Gospel, namely, that because of the one sacrifice of Christ accomplished on the cross he graciously grants us the forgiveness of sins and eternal life." As visible signs communicate invisible grace, Calvin states, believers "form one body with Christ, so that everything which is his they may call their own."[1] One of the key components of Mercersburg Theology was the doctrine of the spiritual real presence of Christ in the Lord's Supper, put forth with vigor by John Williamson Nevin in *The Mystical Presence* (1846). At the time of its writing, the church was surrounded by sects and a revivalism that emphasized emotionalism and conversion. The emotional upheaval of the person was commonly substituted for the nurtur-

ing of the soul in Christ through Word and sacrament. With Nevin and
Schaff, the Eucharist becomes the center of the church's life and from
this center issues education, church order, and social action.

Mercersburg's emphasis on the Holy Spirit as kinetic, mystical, and
corporate in nature saved the church from shallow emotionalism. In
their celebration of Holy Communion, Reformed pastors pronounced
the epiklesis in the eucharistic prayer: "Send . . . the powerful benedic-
tion of Thy Holy Spirit upon these elements of bread and wine . . ."[2]
The Mercersburg professors' historical study of the Eastern Church and
of the St. James Liturgy here put the Reformed Church a century and a
quarter ahead of other communions in the West who only in recent
years have adequately included the epiklesis in their liturgies. The use
of the epiklesis instead of merely the words of institution also delivered
the pastor from any charge that liturgical activity bordered on magic.
The more highly liturgical movement associated with Mercersburg was,
in this way, as centered on the work of the Holy Spirit as any movement
in American religious history.

While Calvin desired the weekly celebration of the Lord's Supper in
Geneva, the Reformed Church came to observe it less frequently and
finally settled on quarterly observance. There were those who deem-
phasized the sacrament by supposing that the Word of God and the gifts
of the Spirit were received primarily through preaching. Many American
Protestants claiming to be Calvinists not only elevated the sermon but
denigrated the Lord's Supper by holding a mere memorialist view of it.
But the integral union of Word and sacrament in Calvin's thought is
clear in his statement: "Wherefore let it be a fixed point, that the office
of the sacraments differs not from the word of God; and this is to hold
forth and offer Christ to us, and, in him, the treasures of heavenly
grace."[3] The Calvinist centrality of the Lord's Supper was honored in
the development of the Mercersburg Liturgy of 1866—and its heir, the
1947 liturgy of the Evangelical and Reformed Church—by making it the
ante-communion service. The order was the same through the offertory
so that on any Sunday the service could continue with the presentation
of the elements and the eucharistic prayer. The words of the preface
and the confession of sin were more didactically related to the Eucharist
in the order for the Lord's Supper. The order and position were the
same. While infrequency prevailed, at least Calvin's intention of weekly
celebration was in this sense preserved.

Pastors who disagreed with the Mercersburg professors reflected the
general anti-Catholicism of American evangelicals in the mid-nineteenth
century. The low-church wing of the Reformed Church centered in
Ohio on the frontier and in Philadelphia, where Catholic influence from
new immigrants was feared. Complaints were registered against written

prayers and responses, the lectionary, altars, crosses, and creeds. Congregational participation in worship was often limited to singing and financial contribution. But both sides of the Mercersburg controversy relied on the Heidelberg Catechism, which proved to be a stabilizing factor. A truce was called and a new constitution with revised liturgy generally following the 1866 liturgy was approved. The 1920–1921 hymnal published with the Reformed Church in America (Dutch) was available with either the 1866 or revised liturgy. Most congregations ordered the former.

The Reformed Church, since its Zurich and Geneva origins, held to a high view of the ministry. Pastors were educated and carefully examined by the synod or classis. As with the Lutheran tradition, the doctrine of the priesthood of all believers did not in any sense denigrate the need for ordained clergy. In fact, the role of the pastor was more important because of this doctrine, since the teacher and preacher of the Word of God equipped the members for their own ministry. And part of that ministry of the priesthood of all believers involved being able to nurture those from whom God would call and appoint some to be pastors. Through the synod, classis, or council the lay members participated in approval of pastors for ordination. With such judicatories the congregation in turn called a particular pastor to serve a congregation. The pastor was the celebrant at the sacraments to insure that the administration was faithful and true to the scriptures.

The ordained ministry was always conceived to be a corporate office of the whole church, not an individual prerogative or privilege of one person or congregation. Evidence of this broad understanding is seen in the administration of the first German Reformed Communion in America at Falkner Swamp, Pennsylvania. Because no ordained minister was available from the German Reformed Church, the people requested a schoolmaster who had been preaching for several years to administer the sacrament. John Philip Boehm, who had served as parish schoolmaster, lay reader, and pastoral assistant in Germany, celebrated Holy Communion at this and other churches in 1725. The Falkner Swamp congregation, having a high concept of ministry, knew this was not according to the order of the home church in Germany, however, and sought to regularize their practice. After communication with the Dutch Reformed Church, they sent Boehm to New Amsterdam for examination. After a two-year process, the Classis of Amsterdam, Holland, authorized Boehm's ordination by the Dutch Reformed Church.

The Heidelberg Catechism teaches that the Reformed Church is part of the Holy Catholic Church. In the *Commentary of Zacharias Ursinus on the Heidelberg Catechism,* Ursinus expands upon this by calling the church evangelical, reformed, catholic, and apostolic. These words, popularized by the Consultation on Church Union, are not of recent origin but are part of our heritage.

Calvin believed that where the Word is rightly preached and the sacraments rightly administered, there is the church. As Word and sacrament present Christ to the people, the church becomes the body of Christ. This body, according to the brilliant insights of the Mercersburg theologians, is continuous through history from Jesus and the apostles to the present. It is organic in nature, able to develop, heal itself, and grow. The ordination questions in the 1866 Reformed Church service, which were used until 1947, stress this continuity: "Do you receive the confessional system of the Heidelberg Catechism as being in harmony with the Bible, and the ancient Christian Creeds?" "Do you acknowledge the rightful authority of this Church, from which you are now to receive ordination, as being a true part in the succession of the Church Catholic . . . ?"[4] The church is evangelical because it is the spiritual body of Christ who is the Word. The church which communicates the Word and sacramentally celebrates the Word actually becomes the Word. Nevin and Schaff taught that the church is a continuation of the incarnation. Of course, the church is imperfect because it incorporates imperfect human beings, but as the body of Christ it is always being reformed, that is, cleansed and renewed. In order to be catholic and apostolic, the church must always be reformed. Conceiving the church in this way as a body, Geneva, Heidelberg, and Mercersburg theologians saw all parts related to the whole and to each other. Separatism and atomism, characteristics of American religion, are destructive of the church and must therefore be overcome.

In Zurich, Geneva, the Rhineland, and the Netherlands representative church government embodied this ecclesiology. The first representative synod of the Protestant Reformation which included two lay delegates from each congregation took place in Zurich on Easter Sunday, 1528. Several words came into general use: *synod* for the large regional or national body, *classis* for a smaller area made up of a number of congregations (the Latin word *coetus,* pronounced seetus, was also used), and *consistory* for the local church council. Michael Schlatter established the first coetus in the American colonies in 1747, composed of pastors and elders of the churches, under the authority of the Classis of Amsterdam. The Dutch Reformed Church acted as a missionary sponsor for the German Reformed people because the poverty and desolation of the Palatinate had left the homeland church unable to assist. The coetus examined and ordained clergy, provided for the relief of needy pastors and widows, oversaw the work of the congregations, and discussed the concerns of the German Reformed parochial schools and their relationship to the Charity Schools of Pennsylvania (precursor of the public schools) of which Schlatter was superintendent. The coetus sought new pastors from Europe and assigned the development of new congregations. The Reformed Church, therefore, was from its origins connectional or presbyterial and practiced a representative form of government. The judicatory served as a corporate bishop. Pastors and congregations had membership in the synod or classis. Ministry was the concern of the corporate body. Connectional administration of the churches provided freedom within order through the representative process. Similarly, the confessionalism of the church provided a kind of ordered freedom, as the creeds and confessions were taught as reliable testimonies of faith and not as doctrinal tests.

As we look forward to further ecumenical developments in the spirit of recent documents published by the Faith and Order Commission of the World Council of Churches and the Consultation on Church Union, we may give God thanks for the gifts brought to the United Church of Christ by its Reformed Church tradition. Reformed doctrines and liturgies, focused by Mercersburg theology, are as fresh, vibrant, and ecumenical today as they were over a hundred years ago. The Reformed Church legacy was derived from the great church of all ages, times, and places in continuity with the apostles and with Christ the head of the church. Because the church is the body of Christ, these doctrines are living realities, as new as the real presence of Christ in the breaking of the bread and the taking of the cup at that table at which all believers will one day gather as a united body. The twenty-first century will be the great catholic century. As the church was bifurcated East and West in the century beginning with the year 1000 C.E., and again split as Roman and Protestant in the 1500s, so in the century beginning with the year 2000 the church will begin to assume its rightful nature and be the body of Christ united and whole. The Reformed Church tradition constantly reminds us that the church must always be catholic, evangelical, reformed, and apostolic.

NOTES

1. John Calvin, *The Institutes of the Christian Religion* (Grand Rapids: Wm. B. Eerdmans, 1966), IV.xvii.2 (vol. II, p. 558).

2. *An Order of Worship for the Reformed Church* (Philadelphia: Reformed Church Publication Board, 1869), 180.

3. Calvin, *Institutes*, IV.xvii.17 (vol. II, p. 503).

4. *Order of Worship*, 219–20.

3

EVANGELICAL SYNOD
THEOLOGY

RALPH C. QUELLHORST

In 1826 the American Home Missionary Society, a group of Congregational clergy and laity, worked to develop the westward expansion of English-speaking Protestants. Fourteen years later, in October 1840, six pastors gathered in a parsonage in the Gravois Settlement near St. Louis to form *Der Kirchenverein des Westens*. This meeting of clergy was the beginning of the Evangelical Synod of North America. Its first elected president was Karl Daubert, a German Reformed pastor from the Basel Missionary Society. Funded by the American Home Missionary Society of Connecticut via the Reformed Church in the United States, Daubert served as a leader of the Evangelical Synod of North America. Between 1841 and 1861 twenty-one members of the *Kirchenverein* received financial support from the American Home Missionary Society. Excepting only the Christian Connection, which had not yet found its way into western territory, one finds in these beginnings a prefiguring of the United Church of Christ to come a century later, a new denomination brought into being with four partner churches finding a rich and common heritage in Jesus Christ.

The western territories were settled by groups of immigrants. As each group arrived, the people would travel up the Miami-Erie Canal as far as construction development permitted. At that point they would start a new community, in some instances a German Roman Catholic settlement and in others a German Protestant settlement. My hometown in western Ohio was founded in 1832 by people from Bremen, Germany; in the same year they founded my home church. Here a mixture of Evangelical, Reformed, and Lutheran German Protestants began to live their life together. Within my own background, with early experience in the Evangelical Lutheran Church, training at Heidelberg College under the Reformed Church in the United States, and receiving both my M.Div.

and D.Min. degrees from Eden Theological Seminary of the Evangelical Synod, I bring together the heritages of these many different parts of the United Church of Christ.

What were the gifts brought into the United Church of Christ from the Evangelical heritage? The Niebuhrs were of this background, and in 1930 the Evangelical Church invited Dietrich Bonhoeffer to the United States. Elmer Arndt, a strong Evangelical leader and scholar, cochaired the commission that wrote the Statement of Faith of the United Church of Christ, and his daughter Jane Arndt Chittick is now one of the leaders of the Connecticut Conference of the UCC. Walter Brueggemann suggests three main Evangelical themes that enriched the life of the United Church of Christ:

1. Pietism between orthodoxy and rationalism;
2. No creed but Jesus Christ crucified;
3. The motto of Eden Seminary:
    "In essentials unity,
    in non-essentials freedom,
    in all things charity."

Let us look briefly at these three themes.

A tension exists in the life of the church between those who insist on rigid orthodoxy and those who promote rational free thinking. Lutherans often sought to settle the issue, testing whether faithfulness to a particular theological doctrine was being upheld or undermined. The Missouri Synod Lutheran Church was founded in St. Paul's Evangelical Church in Chicago when a group of members, unable to live with the freedom of the Evangelical tradition, attempted to settle the matter of doctrine. Over against doctrinal rigidity, rationalists were the forerunners of American pragmatism, open to the insights of scientific technocratic humanism.

Evangelical heritage offered another alternative: the ability to benefit from both orthodoxy and rationalism, but not to be caught in the argument between which is true and which is false. Brueggemann says:

> The pietism carved out between orthodoxy and rationalism was a strange mixture. . . . It believed in a compelling but uncomplicated faith, and it believed in a church practice which was in no way oppressive, but on the other hand was not excessively accommodating. It dared to believe in a church which had a sense of its own identity not drawn from the culture around it, but an identity shaped by devotion to a crucified Christ and therefore, a church which had the energy to order its own life and to practice a mission marked by compassion and generosity.[1]

I am convinced that the call for Evangelical pietism is still alive in the church. From my perspective the current renewal of interest in spiritual formation finds a home in the United Church of Christ through the pietism of the Evangelical tradition. However, the old categories of orthodoxy and rationalism do not fit anymore. A return of the United Church of Christ to some rigid orthodoxy would serve us no better than a radical liberalism accepting no boundaries save rationalism itself. The yearnings I hear from pastor and layperson alike are for a passionate and compassionate faith linking personal discipline and concern for the whole world in Christ-centeredness.

The seventeenth-century Pietist Phillip Jacob Spener called for the opening of the Bible in every part of the church, for the study of the Word by laity and clergy, for genuine nurture of the faith, and for the ministry of Christians to one another. Spener said that knowledge cannot save, but Christ can make all things new; where this happens, theology is reformed, for there is room alongside dogma for personal piety, prayer, and devotion. Theology done faithfully brings a change of heart, for the Word of God brings an end to confessional boundaries and opens the door to one another.

Rudolf Schade, former Elmhurst College professor, reminds us that piety was understood as *Frommigkeit,* or "warm-hearted faith that is spent in the world." Too many people today think of piety merely as an individualistic Bible-centered endeavor. The Evangelical Church was deeply immersed in the world and not interested in the individualistic faith espoused by many in our time. Pastors were called to live out their faith with full integrity. Preaching, teaching, healing, and pastoral care were the very essence of their lives. And in the ministry of both clergy and laity, institutions like the Deaconess Hospitals and Emmaus Homes throughout the Midwest continue to give themselves to the service of needs in society.

The second contribution of the Evangelical Church to the United Church of Christ is found in a noncreedal centrality of Christ crucified. Over a century ago Andreas Irion, president of Eden Theological Seminary, set the tone for the christological center of the Evangelical tradition. "We preach Christ crucified" (1 Cor. 1:23) and "For I decided to know nothing among you except Jesus Christ and [Christ] crucified" (1 Cor. 2:2) were foundational Pauline arguments in Irion's efforts to steer away from creedal formulation. Creeds were received from both Reformed and Lutheran tradition. The *Kirchenverein* in 1847 published its very important *Evangelical Catechism,* widely used until 1889 in German and after that date in both English and German. Its 219 questions and answers dealt in devotional rather than dogmatic ways with the Ten Commandments, the Apostles' Creed, prayer, and the sacraments. Where there was a difference of opinion on doctrine the Evangelical Church would simply say, "We believe in Christ crucified."

The center of our identity is rooted in this simple confession. We need to be careful not to make this confession merely individualistic in the fundamentalist manner, in which everything is slanted in terms of a personal decision. In Evangelical Church tradition, confession of faith is an act of the whole body of Christ, a body of believers who cannot be separated by diverse creeds. Christian unity is found not in individual decisions, nor in the proliferation of creeds, but rather in the basis of confession of faith in a crucified Christ.

Recovery of the passion of Evangelical tradition is needed in our time. Many congregations hardly ever hear or celebrate the message of a Christ-centered *world*. The common ground on which all may stand with Christ is at the heart of the Evangelical Church.

The third gift of the Evangelical Church to the United Church of Christ is the Eden Seminary motto, "In essentials unity, in non-essentials freedom, in all things charity." This motto, first published in 1848 by Philip Schaff in *Der Deutsche Kirchenfreund,* effectively captures the spirit of the Evangelical tradition. Early founders of the United Church of Christ such as Samuel Press and Truman Douglas surely had the essence of this motto in mind. The difficulty, of course, is always in distinguishing between the essential and nonessential in matters of faith and practice. Some always urge that a particular creed or polity structure is essential; others treat these as human creations which can function as helpful tools but are not ultimately essential. Each succeeding generation of Christians is called to make decisions about essential and nonessential matters of theology and polity.

Serving in a conference of the United Church of Christ in which all four strands of our predecessor denominations are represented, I have discovered that church structure is less and less important. What matters in polity and practice is whether or not the church expresses *charity.* I often think that too much time is spent discussing how a project is going to be implemented, with insufficient attention paid to the will of Christ. As President Avery Post once characterized the United Church of Christ, we are long on analysis and short on real help. Evangelical tradition is compassionate toward the whole world, and passionate in faith. To this day former Evangelical Churches remain generous in support of Our Church's Wider Mission and other benevolences beyond the needs of the local congregation. The *Verein* (the informal collegium of Evangelical Synod pastors) were and are still strong. The outward direction of concern for justice in the *Verein* is foreshadowed by the friendship of the father of Walter Rauschenbusch within that initial collegium of pastors that met in 1840. Allen Miller, long an Evangelical Church leader, suggests that the strong collegiality of pastors, the high view of the role of the pastor in the life of the church, together with the contribution of the *Evangelical Catechism* to the developing tradition of the United

Church of Christ are all significant gifts from the Evangelical Church background.

The United Church of Christ brings together several strands of Christianity developed historically by our predecessors. An important strand, which characterized the Evangelical Synod of North America, is the *Frommigkeit,* the warm-hearted faith that is spent in the world.

NOTES

1. Brueggemann, *Festival of the Church* (New York: United Church Office for Church Life and Leadership, 1978), 6–7.

4

CHRISTIAN CHURCH
PERSPECTIVES

RICHARD H. TAYLOR

Ask well-informed members of the United Church of Christ to tell you something about our predecessor denomination known as the Christian Church and they may be able to say that it consisted of three groups and professed six principles. They may recall a few of the early leaders and their denominational backgrounds. But that would be about all.

The Christian Connection, as adherents sometimes called themselves, is admittedly the least visible of our antecedents. They were far smaller than the Reformed Church, the Evangelical Synod, and the Congregational churches. The 1931 union of the Christian Connection with the National Council of Congregational Churches to form the General Council of Congregational Christian Churches was in some ways less a case of merger than absorption. But the Christian Connection was also the most unique of the four uniting denominations, and perhaps the hardest peg to fit into a unified plan. Unlike the others, Christians do not trace their roots to the continental Reformation. The denomination arose on this side of the Atlantic after the American Revolution as a distinctly American phenomenon.[1]

The Revolution was a political and military event, but it was born from a set of ideas and it fostered ideas. Much of that thought stemmed from the English philosopher of the Enlightenment, John Locke (1632–1704). Locke's great theme was freedom. He sought to free humankind from every form of absolute power and to envision a means by which free individuals could unite in a just society. In his *Essay Concerning the Human Understanding* (1690), Locke rejected any notion of innate ideas or inevitable behavior and put forth the idea that knowledge is subjective and born of experience. Since individuals were to be free, they held certain inalienable rights (life, liberty, property) which governments had no authority to suppress. Traditional thought had insisted that individual passion fostered tyranny over reason and intelligence and must be subjugated by divinely appointed political and religious authority. Locke, on the contrary, believed that passion is the supreme power in human nature, and that instead of being suppressed it should be freed. But to prevent anarchy, he also argued that this freedom was fulfilled and guaranteed through law agreed upon and enforced through the consent of the governed. In his *Second Treatise on Civil Government* (1690), Locke argued that just government would be an expression of this freedom. Government must be a social contract, not between ruler and people but among the people themselves. Our forebears who came to adopt the simple name of Christian disdained philosophy and even theology, so their debt to Locke's thought, as it was mediated through republican ideology during the Revolutionary era, is indeed ironic.

The first great wave of Locke's thought in America arrived through a religious event, not a philosophical debate, the Great Awakening of the early 1740s. The revival allowed people the freedom to express their passions and to channel those emotions in the unity of voluntarily following the law of Christ. Note the three Lockean themes: freedom, passion, unity through law. These ideas were all the more significant to the coming of the American Revolution. Freedom was the byword, and from the Boston Tea Party in New England to Patrick Henry in Virginia we observe the expression of strong personal passion. Finally, the diverse independent colonies had to seek a unity under law, or else their freedom would not be realized. America was in large measure an example of Locke's thought worked out in history.

With the heady victory of this republican ideology in the Revolution, citizens of the new United States broke out into a passionate independence of spirit. The goals of the Revolution were now to be achieved in every area of life. How did this way of thinking, this new way of acting, change our thought about God? How did the Revolution affect theology? On the frontier religion was utterly free to develop in radically new ways. People were on their own. Sects abounded. The staid pre-Revolution mix of Calvinists, Anglicans, and a few Quakers, Baptists, and Methodists was suddenly shattered by the appearance of Free Will Baptists, Universalists, Unitarians, now-fast-spreading Methodists, Shakers and other utopians, and assorted freethinkers.

Frontier life created new problems as settlers built homes beyond the reach of existing schools and churches. Isolation produced a kind of emotional starvation in which the passions were all the more accentuated, often in destructive and even criminal ways. There was a great desire for human contact, spiritual grounding, and some kind of law and order. The frontier did not desire expensively trained intellectual elitists from eastern schools so much as plain and warmhearted leaders with keen moral sense and toleration of the eccentricities of freedom.

In this intellectual and emotional social setting arose the three religious movements that are the subject of this essay. On different frontiers of the new United States, the groups applied themselves to the basic questions of life and came to the same conclusions. On finding one another, they melded together as the Christian movement. All three struggled to free themselves from doctrinaire ideas and hierarchies. All three found passion and emotion to be more important in religion than theory, thought, and reason. All three sought a way to be unified by channeling passion into the formation of a pious moral order.

1. In the south, a decade after the Revolution, James O'Kelly, who had been an itinerant circuit-riding evangelist, broke from the Methodist Church in opposition to its newly elevated bishops and its rigid controls. O'Kelly, a friend of Patrick Henry, stressed freedom from imposed authority. Yet he wished to continue a strong Wesleyan emphasis on the warmed heart. At first, this group went by the name of Republican Methodists, combining Jeffersonian agrarian freedom with Wesleyan emotion. But within a year they adopted the simple name "Christian," aiming for a unity beyond narrow sectarianism.

2. By the first decade of the 1800s, on the northern frontier of New England, Baptists Abner Jones and Elias Smith reached similar conclusions. They said insistence on baptism by immersion, even insistence on baptism itself, thwarted gospel freedom. Christians are free to accept or reject sacraments, they claimed. They found the name "Baptist" to be both partisan and unscriptural. They stressed piety and moral activity over doctrinal agreement. In reaction to the division of small communities into too many denominations, Jones and Smith called for believers to unite simply as Christians.

3. Barton W. Stone, a backwoods Kentucky Presbyterian, meanwhile, helped to organize the most famous camp meeting revival of all time at Cane Ridge in 1801. Between ten and twenty-five thousand people gathered for a week of exuberant preaching and often excessive religious expression. Stone encouraged the emotional power of the revival as he preached free salvation. By modifying the Calvinist doctrines of election and reprobation he was naturally in conflict with his presbytery. With other like-minded leaders he withdrew, first to form the Springfield Presbytery but then, after publishing their famous "Last Will and Testament of the Presbytery of Springfield" (1804), to affirm the Bible as their only creed and Christian as their name.

These three groups became aware of one another, wrote in one another's publications, and beginning in 1819 made regular but never fully successful efforts to unite. The Christian Connection was a pioneer in the use of mass media to communicate its ideas and hold far-flung churches together. The northern branch's *Herald of Gospel Liberty*, first published in 1808, was America's earliest religious periodical. Their radically congregational polity and the distance between the southern and the northern groups made a united Christian Connection difficult to achieve. Moreover, at a regional gathering in New England in 1844, a denunciation of slavery rendered the prospect beyond discussion until the 1890s.

However, throughout the nineteenth century the congregations tracing their roots to the three groups in both north and south never lost sight of their commonalities. The glue that held them together was their love of freedom, passion, and unity. Their sense of freedom from structure and doctrine is exemplified in their reluctance to put belief statements in the bylaws of the congregations. In fact, some churches refused to have bylaws. A few early Christian leaders were even known to burn the minutes at the end of their meetings to prevent some future tyranny of tradition. Abner Jones stated: "Every Christian should be allowed to follow the dictates of their own conscience, and Christian character rather than creedal statement or baptismal mode should be the test of church membership or fellowship. We know them by their fruits, not by the doctrines they hold." Theology and philosophy were seen as the destroyers of the church. Stone said, "Speculative theology and preaching should be eschewed and plain Scriptural doctrines and practical Christian ethics should be proclaimed and inculcated."

Christians taught that the way to Christian unity was to allow any and all variations in doctrine, and to stress a more basic unity in Christian living. If there was a unifying doctrine it had to do with the sufficiency of scripture alone. Jones insisted on "Thus saith the Lord" and "Thus it is written" as grounding for his thinking and teaching. On these grounds, early Christians had proclaimed their freedom by walking out of more rigid denominations in protest against their narrowness. They rejected creeds, bishops, Calvinism, and theology schools. They felt nothing but antagonism in the early years for New England's Congregational establishment. The liberalization of disestablished Congregationalism, together with a developing enthusiasm for Christian unity, made their eventual merger possible. The General Convention of the Christian Church was formed in 1922.

In this passionate, revivalistic Christian setting people of all backgrounds, black and white, were welcomed. They received any sincere follower of Jesus without reference to ceremonial practice or intellectual belief. Trinitarianism and early unitarianism existed side by side in the Christian Connection. But could it work? Were Bible, Christ, and ethics enough of a bond to hold a church together? The theological experience of the Christians has much light to shed on the questions we ask about the United Church of Christ today. Can a free church composed of members with varied viewpoints survive in unity?

The desire for unity drove Christians to consider merging with the Disciples of Christ, a movement initiated by Thomas Campbell, a former Presbyterian who came from Northern Ireland to the United States in 1807. The merger was firmly established by Alexander Campbell, his son, who arrived two years later. Alexander Campbell was strongly Restorationist, that is, repudiating both denominationalism and the Old Testament. He believed that he was to reestablish the New Testament church. In 1832 Barton Stone and Alexander Campbell met at Lexington and united their movements. Their agreement is the reason the denomination they formed goes by two names, officially the Christian Church (Disciples of Christ).

But the Stonite Christians were so loosely affiliated, so strongly congregational in their polity, that Stone could not carry the whole movement into the union with the Campbellites. Many Christians rejected the merger because it would not allow them enough freedom. For example, Disciples required believers' baptism by immersion, while Christians allowed any form of baptism or none at all. Christians rejected the Disciples' insistence on communion every Sunday because it was both too legalistic and too symbolic. They objected to Campbell's rule, "Where the New Testament speaks we speak, and where it is silent we are silent," as too legalistic, excluding the Old Testament, and not allowing for new revelation from God. Most interestingly, they objected to Alexander Campbell's rationalism, even intellectualism, and his admiration of secular philosopher John Locke. Campbell had studied at Edinburgh University and his Enlightenment emphasis on faith as rational assent put him at odds with the heart-oriented Christians

The 1832 question in the Christian Connection of whether to unite with the Disciples of Christ came home to the United Church of Christ in the 1980s as we debate our future relationship in covenant with that denomination. The issues have changed, as both the Disciples and the nonmerging Christians (which merged with the Congregational churches in 1931) developed over the nineteenth and twentieth centuries. The call to Christian unity, integral to the movements from their very beginnings, is heard more strongly now than ever.

But what of the freedom that has always existed within the nebulous unity of the Christian movement? Since the Christian welcomed everyone, at first everyone came. Myriads of charlatans, cheaters, fakers, and assorted Elmer Gantrys declared themselves Christian ministers. One notorious Vermont leader declared himself against bathing and soon amassed a significant congregation of the unwashed—until illness put an end to the experiment. Factions debated whether musical instruments were scriptural and soon the ethics of both sides were decidedly discordant. New ideas such as the antimission movement caught hold here and there. Free preachers denounced everything from pulpit robes to titles like "reverend." Elias Smith himself converted back and forth from Christian to Universalist several times.

Even such a free church with no creed felt the need somehow to maintain unity and identity, although they were loath to become judgmental and exclusionary. At the 1854 meeting of the northern American Christian Convention a committee was appointed to write a summary statement of what the group believed. After several days of meeting the committee came in with its report. The chairperson mounted the podium and raised a large pulpit Bible over his head. "This," he said, "is what we believe." But what does it mean to believe the Bible? Some prominent Christians took unorthodox and unitarian positions as they joined nineteenth-century debates. Other Christian leaders insisted that the Connection had always been a Trinitarian movement and must remain so. Finally the Christian Connection began to agree that there were certain principles upon which all could unite and efforts were made to write these down. Various leaders and branches of the church composed lists of principles which varied in content and in number. Most nineteenth-century lists cited five principles, not six. One list was written by Stone, another appeared in an 1827 Christian magazine. The New Jersey Conference incorporated a list of principles in its 1832 constitution. Still other versions came to be used in Ohio. Comparing these texts is like doing an exegetical study of the synoptic Gospels. And opposition continued.

When the southern American Christian Convention constitutionally adopted five principles in 1866, it was chided as being too creedal by the northern branch. When the six principles were finally published by the Christian Church nationally, they read as follows:[2]

1. Christ is the only head of the church.
2. Christian is a sufficient name for the church.
3. The Holy Bible is a sufficient rule of faith and practice.
4. Christian character is the only requirement for membership.
5. The right of private judgment and the liberty of conscience are rights and privileges for all.
6. Union of all Christ's followers is sought.

This sixth principle was added in the twentieth century. Northern historian Milo T. Morrill says it was added in the west and south; southern historian William Scott says it was added in the north.[3] From these principles we may observe that certain common strains are clear and consistent throughout the Christian Connection's thought. Three of these are crucial: personal theology, piety, and biblical authority.

Personal theology. The first strain is what we may call the unlettered personal theology of Christians. The principles of individual interpretation of scripture and of Christ as the only head of the church point in this direction. No corporate, academic, or officially taught theology bound the Christian Connection. Not one of the early leaders of the movement had formal college or theological training. It was a principle of the church that untrained people of faith were expected to express their own theology. One could say that emphasis on morality and simplicity created an anti-intellectual bias. Even in 1930, on the eve of the Congregational merger, of about 450 active pastors only 76 had both college and seminary training, 102 had college training, and the rest had neither. Among small churches, and certainly among black congregations, the model of the farmer-pastor and pastor employed outside the church persisted. Yet anti-intellectualism was not the true picture. Northern Christians attracted noted Unitarian public educator Horace Mann to start their Antioch College in Ohio. Later, noted biblical scholar Austin Craig was a denominational leader. In the southern branch, Elon College was founded in 1893. The North Carolina Colored Conference established a school to train black leadership in 1878, which became Franklinton Christian College and Franklinton Institute. Christians, then, were thinking believers but pragmatic not theoretical, practical not doctrinal. Their leaders were not theologians but preachers, educators, revivalists, editors of periodicals, medical doctors, and farmers. The lesson for the church today is that thought about God is a personal responsibility, not primarily something one learns by academic training. Further, no intelligentsia or other elitist group should set forth for the church what members should think or do.

Piety. The Christians put less stress on the mind because they emphasized the importance of the heart. The second strain in their common life is the role of piety. Character, they said, is the definition of the church. Indeed, they saw the word "Christian" itself not in terms of doctrine but of ethics and religious experience. We think this way today. If someone disagrees with us on a point of theology we shrug it off as too liberal, too conservative, or unorthodox. It is usually actions we are quick to condemn as "un-Christian." Do piety and morality define the church for us today as they did for the Christian Connection? Do Christians actually act differently from the general population? Is the ancient observation—"See these Christians how they love one another"—true? In a world that is at once secular and filled with competing religious claims, and in a society obsessed with materialism and violence, the legacy of the Christian Connection in the United Church of Christ is the call to judge and reform our behavior against the standard of Jesus' way of love.

Biblical Authority. The third strain has to do with the centrality of scripture and biblical authority. The Christian Connection never resolved the tension between the unity of holding to the Bible and the variety of encouraging individual freedom of interpretation. And neither, it would seem, must we. The Christians were biblical but not doctrinal. This kept their early leaders from falling into what would later be called fundamentalism. Their eschewing of doctrine allowed freedom to flourish. Since they were not literalists, many farmer-preachers actually expressed an early interest in biblical criticism. On the other hand, they also avoided sliding away from a christocentric position of faith. Their early alliance with the Unitarians fell apart as Unitarianism increasingly embraced intellectualism, ethical culture, and non-Christian or post-Christian religious perspectives. The Christians remained rooted in the Bible. However, as twentieth-century liberalism became increasingly secular and less biblical, some Christians began to wonder where a Bible-believing Christian was to turn if not to fundamentalism. Renewed emphasis on the centrality of scripture in the United Church of Christ is most welcome from the perspective of our Christian Connection heritage.

It seems to this author that for the most part the Christian experiment in freedom, passion, and unity failed. The stress on freedom overwhelmed the goal of unity. The movement never developed beyond the Jeffersonian agarian ideal of the isolated farmer as the truly free person. There is also a built-in suicidal tendency in a church with so little doctrine. When a geographical area became overchurched, many of the small Christian congregations simply disbanded. Even relatively strong churches resisted not only the development of a statement of common beliefs but also an adequate doctrine of covenant. Fear of institutions and an antimission streak left many churches organizationally unstable. Its intense sense of local freedom exacerbated the defense of slavery in the Christian Church in the south until after the Civil War and its lingering support of segregation and opposition to the goals of the ecumenical church in this century. Those congregations that have become vital parts of the church today have tended to be those that turned to an educated clergy, supported mission beyond the local church, accepted a semipresbyterian polity, and embraced the six principles or some substitute for them as a focus of belief.

The legacy of this important part of our United Church of Christ heritage lies in the interaction among the three common strains expressed in the principles of the Christian Connection. These three strains—personal theology, piety, and biblical authority—represented the religious application of Locke's principles of freedom, passion, and unity under law. They constituted, in this one part of our United Church of Christ, the American revolution in religion. Fortunately or unfortunately, our Christian forebears leave us with more questions than answers. Can a church allow, even encourage, the unlimited personal expression of theology? How are pluralism and unity to be held together? What is the relationship of personal faith to the doctrines of the apostolic church? What is the role of emotion in religion? Should revivals, including appeals to the masses through modern media, become part of the ministry of our church today as they were in the early days of the Christian movement? What of piety and character? Stress on ethics and character tended to institute a kind of works-righteousness in the church. How does grace operate in an ethics-oriented church?

Further, the moral sense of the early Christian Connection was influenced by a particular rural American vision of life. They accepted pluralism of thought, but rejected pluralism of life style. Beer-loving Germans and the Women's Christian Temperance Union could never embrace. Today the issues of ethics and morality are even more complex, including diverse views in such areas as sexuality and employment in the military-industrial complex. The United Church of Christ seeks to offer a home to all. If a church is held together by neither doctrine nor moral character, what is the basis of Christian unity? In the United Church of Christ today, the legacy of the Christian movement lives on, both in the common themes of our life and in the questions with which we live. While upholding in some sense the authority of the Bible, we encourage an approach to theology that is more personal and popular than elitist, more varied than uniform, and more practical than dogmatic.

NOTES

1. For full treatments of aspects of the Christian movement, see Willis Elliot, "Forgotten Legacy: The Historical Theology of the 'Christian' Component of the United Church of Christ," *Historical Intelligencer* 3(1984):9–14; J. R. Freese, *A History and Advocacy of the Christian Church* (Philadelphia: Christian General Book Concern, 1852); A. D. Jones, *Memoir of Elder Abner Jones* (Boston, 1842); Milo True Morrill, *History of the Christian Denomination in America, 1794–1911* (Dayton, Ohio: Christian Publishing Association, 1912); J. Taylor Stanley, *A History of the Black Congregational Christian Churches of the South* (New York: United Church Press, 1978); Durward T. Stokes and William T. Scott, *A History of the Christian Church in the South* (Southern Conference of the United Church of Christ, 1973); and Richard H. Taylor, "The Congregational Christian Union at

Fifty Years: An Assessment," *Bulletin of the Congregational Library* 32 (Spring/ Summer 1981):4–13.

2. From *Book of Worship* (New York: Office for Church Life and Leadership, 1986), 515. Also see, in this volume, Samuel N. Slie, "The United Church of Christ and the Experience of the Black Church," chap. 5.

3. Among the principles put forth at various times that did not make the final list, several may be mentioned. One source added a principle on ecclesiology that each local church is independent and autonomous. While this was generally true, several conferences did act under a semi-presbyterian system. Another source, in addition to the emphasis on Christian character, provided a separate principle that discipline should be based on gospel teaching. General decline of interest in rigid discipline of members pushed this out of discussion. Barton Stone, no doubt under Campbell's restorationist influence, included among his basic principles the idea that the New Testament should be the church's organizational model. Opposition to restorationist legalism in the Christian Connection eliminated this principle.

5

THE UNITED CHURCH OF CHRIST
AND THE EXPERIENCE OF
THE BLACK CHURCH

SAMUEL N. SLIE

The subject I discuss here deserves a book and not an essay, even when one's reflections are confined to one denomination, the United Church of Christ. As I have attempted to read the writings of many others on the history of the black church and its developments, I have not only come to appreciate their work but have also come to feel no need to replow ground already broken. Rather, I would like to touch upon some key points of the black experience in the UCC and its antecedent denominations that strike me as contributions to the formation, growth, and future of the UCC. These points are gleaned from the aforementioned writings and my own nurture in the Congregational Christian Church and subsequent ministry in it and the United Church of Christ.

HISTORY

Pilgrims and Puritans, colonialists and revolutionaries, immigrants and slaves, freedmen and native Americans, Hispanics and so many other ethnicities contribute to the whole of the UCC. What kind of dynamic, leaven, challenge, and contribution has the black church evidenced in that mix? Perhaps initially this could be said to have been passive, more a matter of presence in the midst of early American society, much of which claimed to be Christian, and, if Christian, thus concerned about the conversion of nonbelievers and setting captives free.

> God has sent me to bind up the brokenhearted, to proclaim liberty to the captives. (Isa. 61:1)

> And Jesus said to the disciples, "Go into all the world and preach the gospel to the whole creation." (Mark 16:15)

A. Knighton Stanley notes that in colonial America, "Even at this time the Puritans were concerned with the conversion and transformation of a people and culture that bordered and impinged upon their own."[1] He quotes Clifton E. Olmstead's observation, "The charter of the Massachusetts Bay Colony . . . depicted an Indian crying, 'Come over and help us.' "[2] Lawrence N. Jones notes that:

> Puritan theology made no provision to evangelize non-believers as practiced in contemporary Christianity. Election to salvation was God's prerogative though instruction in Christian teaching and conduct was required for all. Parents were expected to instruct their families and servants in the faith. As a consequence, most slaves who became church members were nurtured within the family context. In the family setting, the slaves retained their caste status despite the concern for their souls.[3]

Much has been written of the communities both northern and southern in which slaves were allowed to worship in the balconies of their white masters' churches. While the Christian message itself was new to slaves, the sense of religion and an awareness of God, of an all-pervading Holy Spirit, was not since most natural African religion saw every person and everything as a place where the Spirit dwelt. The word about an omniscient and omnipresent God was not news to them.

In 1966 an All-Africa Conference of Churches consultation was held in Nigeria. In a paper he presented, Stephen N. Ezeanya said: "For the African, the world of spirits is a real world. . . . It has . . . the closest possible connection with this material world . . . indeed, the world is a spiritual arena . . . [Humanity . . .] is entirely dependent upon these spiritual beings."[4]

Undoubtedly, a special contribution the black slave brought to the New World was a capacity to be religious in a total way—in mind, body, and spirit. This meant that the slave could not sustain forever the role of second-class citizen in the church. The desire of blacks to be a church community led Cotton Mather, a New England clergyman, to meet, pray, and preach with them. In his diary in 1693, Mather recorded his "Rules for a Religious Society for Negroes," and later he established a "Charity School, for Negroes in the evenings, to learn to read and be instructed in the Catechism." Yet despite his progressive form of Christian openness Mather spoke of blacks as a "miserable nation" descended from Adam and Noah and carrying the mythical curse of Ham. "Mather's arguments had their parallels from Massachusetts to Georgia. . . . They were convenient rationalizations invoked to accommodate the participation of (white) Christians in both the institution of slavery and in the Christianization of Blacks."[5]

The black presence in America not only contributed a significant mission field for the early American churches, but it also meant that a new dimension and style of faith expression emerged in what has come to be named the "black church." In many ways the incapacity of the white churches fully to absorb their black brothers and sisters made this inevitable.

The first ordained black Congregational clergyman was Lemuel Haynes (1753–1833). His contributions as a patriot and as a churchman were legendary and included service as Revolutionary War Minuteman, soldier at Fort Ticonderoga, itinerant evangelist, and pastor in Vermont, New Hampshire, and New York. Haynes was ordained November 9, 1785, in Torrington, Connecticut, and was much respected as a theological scholar among Congregational clergy. He pioneered what has become a long legacy of black Congregational, Christian, and United Church of Christ clergy.

The Christian Church had blacks, slave and free, in churches where the blacks worshiped at the back, up in the balcony, or outside. At the end of the Civil War, blacks began to form their own congregations and by 1873 had formed three conferences in the South, including ninety-one ministers and fifty-one churches. The first black Congregational church, the Dixwell Avenue Congregational Church, was organized by black freedmen in New Haven, Connecticut in 1820. Within a few years other Congregational churches were established in the North. The first black congregation in the Christian denomination (which would merge with the Congregationalists in 1931) was established in 1854 in Providence, Rhode Island.

In 1892 blacks organized within the Christian denomination an Afro-American Christian Conference. When this conference met in 1895, it included five subregional conferences, 69 churches, 33 ministers, and 18 licentiates with a membership of 6,000. The North Carolina Colored Christian Conference had established a secondary school in Franklinton, North Carolina in 1878 supported by assessments of its member churches. In 1891 the school became Franklinton Christian College and did remarkable service until the Depression caused it to close in 1930. In writing about the significant contributions of Franklinton Christian College, Percel Alston writes: "Although it never achieved the full status of college by reputable standards, it provided the essential education and training for pastors and lay leadership for the Afro-Christian Church."[6] The white college institutions of the Christian Church were not open to blacks until the merger into the Congregational Christian denomination opened all the Congregational and Christian seminaries to blacks. Only a few blacks could qualify for admission in that era, yet on the foundation of a very significant history of accomplishment, witness, and service, the Afro-American Christian churches persevered as a vital part of the Congregational Christian Church and of the United Church of Christ today.

We continue as a denomination to be influenced by the dedication of the Afro-Christian Convention's churches to the five principles of the Christian Church:[7]

1. Christ is the only head of the church.
2. Christian is a sufficient name for the church.
3. The Holy Bible is a sufficient rule of faith and practice.
4. Christian character is the only requirement for membership.
5. The right of private judgment and the liberty of conscience are rights and privileges for all.

In 1931 the Afro-Christian Conference as a part of the General Convention of the Christian Church entered into the merger with the General Council of the Congregational Church. Until the organization of the Convention of the South in 1950, black Christian churches and black Congregational churches continued with the structures they had prior to the 1931 Congregational-Christian merger.

The American Missionary Association played an important role in the development of black Congregational churches. Let us review its history. In 1839 a slave ship, the Amistad, sailed into Long Island Sound. The slaves had mutinied and forced the crew to sail there. This brought them into the purview of the American justice system. New Englanders rallied to their defense and eventually helped them to return home to Africa. An Amistad Committee whose leadership was drawn from the American Anti-Slavery Society worked on behalf of the slaves. The Committee's chief leader and organizer was Lewis Tappan, a Congregationalist and a New York merchant.

Early abolitionists led by William Lloyd Garrison did a great deal of writing and speaking about freeing the slaves, but used blacks primarily in lesser roles or as platform speakers. Even Quakers, great antislavery workers, did not admit blacks as members of Quaker meetings. Older ecumenical mission societies, such as the American Home Missionary Society (AHMS) and the American Board of Commissioners for Foreign Missions (ABCFM) continued to receive financial donations from slaveholders and thus would not take assertive positions against slavery. So Tappan and others formed the American Missionary Association (AMA)[8] with a strong plank of church involvement and commitment in abolition efforts. It "was to be an independent, non-sectarian or interdenominational, and non-ecclesiastical organization. Membership was open to any contributor to its funds who was a professing Christian of evangelical sentiments who was not a slaveholder."[9]

Support for the AMA came from the Wesleyan Methodist, Congregationalist, and Free Presbyterian churches, with major support from New

England Congregationalists. However, a majority of the Congregational churches did not support the AMA until after the Civil War. Nevertheless, it was the strongest organization in the United States with principles calling for the absolute abolition of slavery. In writing about the history of the American Missionary Association, Clifton Johnson states: "It is significant that the Garrisonites made a wholesale denunciation of the American churches and refused to acknowledge that some of the churches had adopted distinctive anti-slavery positions."[10]

By the time of the Civil War the AMA had been at work for fifteen years. It had worked in Africa, Hawaii, Siam, Jamaica, and Egypt, and among native Americans, Chinese immigrants, and poor whites. AMA missionaries followed the Union armies, starting schools wherever a peaceful situation became established. Clara Merritt DeBoer reports that: "Most important: Some of them, men and women, were black. Some, like their white counterparts, had received their higher education at Oberlin College, remarkable in its day for its acceptance of black men and women."[11] Over five hundred schools and colleges for those freed from slavery were founded by the AMA in the South (a significant number of these continue to play vital roles in education today).

After Reconstruction other denominations withdrew from the AMA, leaving it to the Congregationalists. Some of the Congregational missionaries had established churches as well as schools.

We have reviewed something of the growth of the black Christian churches in the South and black Congregational churches in the North. It was the work of the American Missionary Association in sending missionaries to found Christian schools that initially, almost as a byproduct, began to produce black Congregational churches. These missionaries were dedicated to evangelizing but not to proselytizing. They often held evangelistic services and converts were asked to choose their own church. The choice was often Baptist or Methodist. According to J. Taylor Stanley:

> It was out of the womb of this high dedication to Christ that the black Congregational churches of the south were born. . . . They were organized initially by New England-type Congregational ministers and missionaries. The first pastors were white; the first Sunday School teachers were missionaries in AMA schools. Many churches were proud to be the *First* Congregational Church in their community. . . .[12]

What proved to be most helpful for black churches was the development of seminaries and departments of religious training at the AMA colleges which were supplied students by the AMA schools. According to the AMA 66th Annual Report (1911–12):

> Numerically speaking organized Negro Congregationalism in the South is not a large thing. The churches number only about 150 with about 10,000 members. The work of the Association among them is represented by 83 ministers who serve in about 140 churches and by a fraternal and advisory relation to the whole group. . . . They are essentially the children of the schools, either located in the same communities, or in the city centers where graduates from the schools form colonies.[13]

The transition from slavery to freedom, through emancipation, Reconstruction, urban migration, and World War I did not make it easy for any church, yet the black Congregational churches persevered. In 1918 ministers and delegates from all over the South and some northern black Congregationalists gathered in Raleigh, North Carolina for the biennial meetings of the National Convention of Congregational Workers Among Negroes. Significantly, at that event, black Congregationalists undertook to commission and send forth with their support Henry Curtis McDowell and his wife as missionaries to Portuguese West Africa (Angola).[14] One of McDowell's comments about the people he served is a profound clue to the roots of black spirituality: "I could not put my finger on any separate aspect of these [African] people's lives which was without its religious side. Their religion permeated social, economic and medical fields. I found that they could not build a house, or even eat a meal without their religious ideas entering into the situation.[15]

McDowell also speaks of Samuel Bracy Coles and his wife. Samuel came from Talledega College to be preacher, scientific agriculturalist, and building instructor in the Angola mission. The McDowells and Coles over many decades witnessed not only among the Africans but also in terms of a larger comprehension of being the church at work in the world for blacks in America and for the whole church of Christ.

The United Church of Christ came into being in the era when the Civil Rights Movement and Black Power consciousness became major American issues. It was an era when blacks not only challenged America to be America (the ideal democracy its Declaration of Independence and Constitution called into being) but also challenged the church to be truly Christian, to live faithfully. The late fifties and sixties also saw increased dynamics in the ecumenical movement. The united and uniting UCC formed in 1957 was in many special ways a concrete manifestation of this movement. Louis Gunneman writes: "Religious, ethnic and racial pluralism, once expressed by separate denominational structures, became important new realities for churches to address in the ecumenical movement."[16]

Like the Congregational-Christian merger of 1931, the Evangelical and Reformed Church was itself the result of a merger in 1934. The union came after a decade of reflection and searching together, of getting to know and trust one another. Lawrence Jones notes that: "The polities of the denominational tradition which merged to form the United Church of Christ have been basically egalitarian and democratic in principle. The social philosophy articulated at the level of national structures has been often ahead of other church bodies."[17]

The Preamble of the Basis of Union of the UCC affirms that:

> We . . . believing that denominations exist not for themselves, but as parts of that Church, within which each denomination is to live and labor and, if need be die; and confronting the divisions and hostilities of our world, and hearing with a deepened sense of responsibility the prayer of our Lord "that they may all be one"; do now declare ourselves to be one body . . .[18]

Throughout the discussion there was a clear call for the UCC to be inclusive as to race and cultural background. This came to be a marked characteristic of the church nationally, but as Lawrence Jones notes: "At the level of congregational and regional judicatories, the social outlook and institutional structures have been, until recent years, reflective of regional folkways and customs."[19]

The Third General Synod of the UCC meeting in Philadelphia in 1961 adopted the Constitution and Bylaws. The document stressed a mood of reconciliation rather than compromise, but it nevertheless put strain on the black churches who had only achieved the Convention of the South a decade before. The Constitution stressing unity required that the conferences and associations of the UCC include all the churches within their geographic area, which meant the breakup of the Convention of the South, itself a very precious and precocious unity. This was the era of the "freedom movement," through which Martin Luther King, Jr., had challenged this nation, including the church, to be about the business of racial justice now. His role of leadership was consciously shaped by his understanding of the life and gospel of Jesus Christ. It was in this ethos that Benjamin Mohr Herbster, a white Evangelical and Reformed pastor, was elected president of the UCC in 1961.

At the Fourth General Synod (1963) in Denver Herbster spoke specifically to the delegates calling upon them to act "aggressively and responsibly for the racial crisis confronting the nation."[20]

This eventually produced a churchwide focus on Racial Justice Now in response to the problem of racism in our nation. The gathering of the Seventh General Synod in Boston in 1969 was a time of special self-assertion by blacks of challenge and leadership in the United Church of Christ. James Forman presented the Black Manifesto calling for support of the Black Economic Development Conference, but, even more impor-

tant in the long run, black initiative within the UCC was strongly
expressed through the synod-designated Committee for Racial Justice
Now and the voluntary gathering of United Church Ministers for Racial
and Social Justice (MRSJ). This group sponsored the candidacy of
Arthur D. Gray, Chicago pastor and former president of Talledega
College, for the presidency of the UCC. While the presidency was not
achieved, a new depth of leadership and contributions by blacks in the
UCC had been established. Major credit for visionary direction in this
period must be given to Edwin R. Edmonds, minister from the Dixwell
Church in New Haven and chair of the UCC Commission for Racial
Justice, and Charles E. Cobb, forthright first executive director of that
same body. Black lay and clergy leadership moved the UCC into active
concern with the 1960s and 1970s. The engagement of the United
Church of Christ with racial and social injustice heightened its capacity
to deal as a community of faith with the many other problems within
and without the church in that period.

TODAY AND TOMORROW

The biblical vision of divine revelation tells us that God identifies wholly
with the liberation of oppressed peoples from worldly oppression. The
whole movement of history involves human liberation. "You shall know
the truth, and the truth will make you free" (John 8:32). Coming to
know God as faithful persons and communities means confronting the
reality of worldly oppression and being committed to the certainty of
liberation. Biblically, the knowledge of God or theo-logos is not limited
to mystical contemplation or objective rational thought. Rather, it is
much more identified with God's activity in human lives and history
through faith. When one speaks of black theology, therefore, one is less
concerned with the tradition of Western European academic theology,
which has been the preeminent plumb line for all theological thought.
Rather, blacks (and some Indians, South Americans, Africans, and
Third World and Western Christians) are saying God is not fully known
by the parameters of our thoughts, but is alive, at work, and preeminently revealed in struggles for human liberation where people can
come to know God as God has been made known in the existence of
Jesus Christ.

For black Christians within and without the UCC this central perspective has come to be called black theology. The National Committee of
Black Churchmen (interdenominational) has stated it this way:

> Black theology is a theology of black liberation. It seeks to plumb the black
> condition in the light of God's revelation in Jesus Christ, so that the black

community can see that the Gospel is commensurate with the achievement of black humanity. Black theology is a theology of blackness. It is the affirmation of black humanity that emancipates black people from white racism, thus providing authentic freedom in both white and black people. It affirms the humanity of white people in that it says No to white encroachment.[21]

In this context blacks in the UCC seek to affirm that God is a God of justice for all people. They see Jesus Christ as a paradigm of liberation for all peoples. This does not deny the UCC tradition of a trained clergy and informed laity but lifts up for equally valid recognition religious experience, in this case the black experience. This linkage sees the God of the Hebrew Scriptures, the God of justice, working through Jesus Christ, the paradigm of how you live justice. In conversation with me, Benjamin E. Chavis, Jr., current executive director of the Commission for Racial Justice, said, "Theology is the preached word, the taught word and especially it is the lived word." Such an understanding is important for the United Church of Christ precisely because it is a pioneering church, an evolutionary church, a united and uniting part of the body of Christ. Chavis has noted that the fastest growing congregations in the UCC at this time are black. He feels that this is happening because its openness to pluralism does not seek to eliminate black theology, but lets the faith search of black churches be free, not patronized but respected as a contribution to the faithfulness of the whole denomination. It is called upon not to be locked into some theological era, but to continue responding to what the Lord puts before us. The UCC has no future in assuming any "laid-back" theology; its nature calls it to worship and witness to an active and dynamic God.

The work of the Commission for Racial Justice has shown what Chavis calls "an unapologetically black perspective, but it is also unashamedly Christian." It has worked to help the UCC relate to all ethnics, and to help all ethnics—black, Hispanic, Asian American, and Native American—be a part of the whole church. What is important is that ethnics should not all be put in one box. Sometimes the Commission for Racial Justice has felt itself called to be a "thorn in the side" of the UCC, because it cares so deeply that the denomination should move into the twenty-first century as the most responsibly pluralistic mainline denomination. Respect and understanding, overcoming racism and exclusivity, working for peace with the presence of justice, and growth in ethnic membership can all make the United Church of Christ a better church. In Chavis's words, "The extent to which the UCC can reflect God's creation is the extent to which we can really become the *United* Church of Christ."

Finally I would like to give special recognition to the way in which the

United Church of Christ has given positive recognition to the contribution of its black members in national leadership roles. They are more than I can mention, but certainly include Joseph Evans's service as Secretary and later President of the UCC, C. Shelby Rooks, Executive Vice President of the Board for Homeland Ministries, Yvonne V. Delk of the Office for Church in Society, Reuben A. Sheares of the Office for Church Life and Leadership, Percel O. Alston of the Division of Christian Education, Joseph T. McMillan, Jr., of the Division of Higher Education and American Missionary Association, and Valerie E. Russell's leadership in establishing the Coordinating Center for Women.

Black contributions to the life of the denomination abound not only nationally but locally. The highest per capita giving to Our Church's Wider Mission in the Florida Conference comes from the Church of the Open Door in Miami, led by Harold D. Long, and the fastest growing church is Trinity UCC in Chicago, Illinois, led by Jeremiah A. Wright, Jr. (over four thousand members).

I count it a special blessing to have been nurtured as a Christian under Edward F. Goin in New Haven's Dixwell Church; to have been a parishioner of Homer McEwen, First Congregational Church, in the years I worked in Atlanta; to have sat in meetings of the Convention of the South and visited the AMA colleges in those years; to have attended the General Synod when it was addressed by Martin Luther King, Jr., and to be at the 1987 General Synod when the Implementation Committee reported on work done under the pronouncement on full divestment of all financial resources of the denomination from all corporations doing business in South Africa.

Thank God for the United Church of Christ. Thank God that it can be a channel of grace for liberation, justice, reconciliation, and peace among all peoples. May its whole ministry continue to grow and witness for the uplifting of all of God's children. With the church, universal and eternal, may the United Church of Christ continue to give praise and glory to God through our Lord Jesus Christ.

Psalm 141

The Faithful Community

The church

the faithful community

of believers in Jesus Christ

who come together

to worship God

to confess sin

to share in everything

who come together

> to take a stand for justice
> peace and liberation . . .
> the faithful community
> the church of Christ
> continues
> to the remnant
> existing and struggling
> to reconcile the world
> unto God.
>
> —Benjamin E. Chavis, Jr.[22]

NOTES

1. A. Knighton Stanley, *The Children Is Crying* (New York: Pilgrim Press, 1979), 1.

2. Clifton E. Olmstead, *History of Religion in the United States* (Englewood Cliffs, N.J.: Prentice-Hall, 1960), 81–82.

3. Lawrence N. Jones, *From Consciousness to Conscience* (New York: United Church Press, 1976), 5.

4. Stephen N. Enzeanya, "God, Spirits and the Spirit World," in Kwese A. Dickson and Paul Ellingworth, eds., *Biblical Revelation and African Beliefs* (Maryknoll, N.Y.: Orbis Books, 1969), 30.

5. Jones, *From Consciousness to Conscience.*

6. Percel O. Alston, "The Afro-Christian Connection," in *Hidden Histories in the United Church of Christ*, vol. 1, ed. Barbara Brown Zikmund (New York: United Church Press, 1984), 28.

7. From *Book of Worship* (New York: Office of Church Life and Leadership, 1986). Also see, in this volume, Richard H. Taylor, "Christian Church Perspectives," chap. 4.

8. At the time of the Amistad incident, James William Charles Pennington, pastor of the black Talcott Street Congregational Church in Hartford, Connecticut, gathered a convention primarily of blacks, who created the Union Missionary Society (UMS). In 1842, the Amistad Committee became part of the UMS and in 1846 was joined by the Committee for West Indian Mission and the Western Evangelical Missionary Society for Work Among the American Indians in a national missionary body, the American Missionary Association (AMA).

9. Clifton Johnson, "The American Missionary Association—A Short History," in *Our American Missionary Association Heritage* (New York: United Church Board for Homeland Ministries, 1966), 21.

10. Ibid., 5.

11. Clara Merritt DeBoer, "Blacks and the American Missionary Association," in *Hidden Histories in the United Church of Christ*, vol. 1, 90.

12. J. Taylor Stanley, *A History of Black Congregational Christian Churches of the South* (New York: United Church Press, 1978), 43, 44.

13. Stanley, *The Children Is Crying,* 73.

14. Dr. McDowell was my pastor in New Haven at the end of World War II. I

wrote to him (he is 94 [1988]) as I was preparing this essay and he suggested resources he put in the archives of Hartford Theological Seminary.

15. Henry Curtis McDowell, "A New Africa in the Making," *The Hartford Daily Courant*, 29 March 1931.

16. Louis H. Gunnemann, *The Shaping of the United Church of Christ* (New York: United Church Press, 1977), 17.

17. Jones, *From Consciousness to Conscience*, 17.

18. Gunnemann, *The Shaping of the United Church of Christ*, 26.

19. Jones, *From Consciousness to Conscience*, 17.

20. Gunnemann, *The Shaping of the United Church of Christ*, 78.

21. James Cone and Gayraud Wilmore, "Black Theology and African Theology," in *Black Faith and Black Theology*, ed. Priscilla Massie (New York: Friendship Press, 1973), 112.

22. Benjamin E. Chavis, Jr., *Psalms From Prison* (New York: Pilgrim Press, 1983), 158. Used by permission.

6

WHO CAN SIT AT THE LORD'S TABLE?
THE EXPERIENCE OF
INDIGENOUS PEOPLES

ROSEMARY McCOMBS MAXEY

The purpose of this essay is to explore the place of indigenous peoples' religions within and without the diverse theological stances of the United Church of Christ. Indigenous people are those who today are called American Indians or native Americans. I intend to recall briefly the history of the Euro-American Christian movement and the indigenous peoples' responses in early "American" history, thereby creating a base for a deeper understanding of Native American particularization of their perspectives as they relate to Christian churches today. The major thrust has to do with relationships, not with classical definitions of ecclesiology as proposed by European and Euro-American scholars. Relationships link the present with past and future and link people with all creation. Theologically, environmentally, and in their holistic under-standing of human nature, indigenous people have much insight to offer to those who seem to have garnered the best seats for themselves at the Lord's Table. The United Church of Christ, which carries as its motto "That They May All Be One" and proclaims its unity in diversity, should be especially receptive to the voices of indigenous people who desire room at the table.

HISTORICAL SURVEY

Beginning with the "discovery" made by Christopher Columbus, Chris-tians have struggled with the issue of what should be done with the original inhabitants of the New World. When Columbus returned from his first voyage in 1493, a squabble arose between the kingdoms of Castile and Portugal over possession of the lands of the New World. The Pope intervened with four papal bulls in 1493 and one in 1506, in them demarcating lands, giving most of the New World to Spain, which would convert the pagan indigenous inhabitants. Other European countries denounced or ignored the Pope's bulls, but throughout the sixteenth century theologians, jurists, historians, friars, and administrators debated what to do with the indigenous people.[1] In 1550 the issue was debated by the Catholic Church's Council of Fourteen. Two theological camps emerged. Bishop Bartolomé de las Casas debated one side: that the noble savages were developed in the arts, languages, and government. They were gentle, eager to learn, and quick to accept Christianity. The other side, represented by Gines de Sepulveda, argued that these creatures were savage-like, slaves by nature, pagan, uncivilized, incapable of learning, and unable to govern themselves.[2] The issue was what to do with the aboriginal inhabitants, whether they were entitled to the soil, and what could be done to them if they refused the beneficence of "lumbre y doctrina" ("light and doctrine" or "light and teaching"). The debate ended in Las Casas's favor, but when missionaries came from Europe, the results were more closely tied to Sepulveda's argument.[3] And for five hundred years, the primary mission strategy of many mainline denominations has followed or paralleled that early approach.

Common historic interests have always existed between the indigenous people of North America and the forebears of the United Church of Christ. In 1629 the Congregationalists began efforts to include indigenous people in the Christian fold. With well-intentioned, dedicated missionaries, the general thrust was to "wynn and invite the Natives . . . [to] the onlie God and Savior of Mankinde."[4] Missionaries from that time to the present have consistently tried to make indigenous people participate in the church as acculturated Euro-American Christians. Indigenous people have resisted, reacted, and responded in a variety of ways to Christianity as presented by the missionaries. A monograph in the United Church of Christ Heritage Series, *Two Spirits Meet*, traces the process of cultural change and conflict:

> Prof. Robert Berkhofer, in *Salvation and the Savage*, demonstrated that when missionaries successfully converted part of the tribe, they set off a sequence of events through which the tribal unit frequently crumbled. Berkhofer studied Protestant mission history of the one-hundred-year period prior to the Civil War. He outlined a sequence of four stages. After missionaries converted some members of a tribal group, either the traditional or the Christian group was ostracized. The ostracized group usually moved and separated physically from the other members of the tribe. However, both groups frequently reunited physically in the face of common military threats. After they reunited and reestablished common government, political factions emerged, usually based on religion, which prevented the tribe from taking totally effective actions.[5]

The same continues to be true today.

Three patterns of participation can be discerned among the indigenous people who relate to the United Church of Christ. The first, occurring in the earliest relationships with the missionaries, was the development of native churches. Using their tribal language in worship and church polity, single tribal churches developed along family, clan, and community lines. These churches exist today among the Dakotas and the Winnebagos.

Second, in 1982, a multitribal congregation was started in Minnesota, called All Nations Indian Church. Incorporating some of the symbols of their ancestors and their native languages, this church worships and provides services to the community. The third pattern involved other indigenous people over the years who joined Anglo churches and became involved in them to varying degrees, sometimes minimizing their identity with the indigenous community, sometimes assimilating in terms of worship but maintaining an identity with the tribal community.

My own relationship with the church as a Muscogee (Creek) Indian Christian has taken me through all three relationships. Three generations of my family have been Christian in a tribal community church affiliated with the Southern Baptist Convention. The Muscogee language is spoken in worship and business. During college and seminary, and immediately thereafter, I attempted to assimilate with the Anglo churches by working in new church development. It was not until I was a member of a multiracial church in New York City that I began to question the Euro-American nature of all Christian churches and to search for a new church relationship where the attempts at pluralism were more intentional. My search ended when I moved to Westminster, Maryland, and became friends with the leaders of a United Church of Christ congregation. In the tradition of my grandfather, who said, "I will be a Baptist because I have met a real good one," I became a member of the United Church of Christ because I met some "real good ones" who shared with me convincing evidence of the United Church of Christ's genuine interest in pluralism and ecumenism.

Since joining this congregation I have been privileged to sit with those in conference and association-level consultations who are serious about theology and serious about ecumenicity. But even they are more apt to cling to investigating "the unity." With furrowed brows, members of theological consultations and study groups pour over an array of theological position papers looking for that shred of evidence that enables them to proclaim, Aha! We are alike after all! Let's celebrate our unity. The fact that the United Church of Christ cannot declare a single or at least a four-strand theological position bothers even the most progressive theologian. The nameless "they" seem to push the panic button. "Other denominations make fun of the United Church of Christ because it is too diverse to take a theological position. . . . The UCC has been accused of a murky Christology," wailed two theologians in my presence recently.

From an indigenous person's perspective, I raise some questions about the denomination's proclaimed inclusivity. One must ask, What exactly is the criteria for sitting diversely together at the Lord's Table? What conditions and limits are placed on such an invitation? Do the indigenous peoples' ways of living and believing keep them marginalized in the United Church of Christ because there is no Euro-American theological or ecclesiastical category for them at the Lord's Table?

Can indigenous people, in their diversity, and others in the United Church of Christ, in their diversity, sit side by side in wholeness to strategize and pray for a realization of an eschatology that restores the unity of a fragmented world? Can we, in our united particularities, prepare our human communities for the wholeness that is more than people, and includes the entire cosmos?

There are difficulties in addressing these questions. In the first place, there is no way of presenting a single homogeneous view of the indigenous peoples. We are as varied and diverse as the United Church of Christ claims to be. We are many tribal groups and nations who vary in culture, thought, government, and language. However, some tribal and national commonalities exist in theological beliefs about the deity, ceremonies that celebrate the relationship between the Creator and the created, the origins of humankind, and the relationship and responsibility for living within the created order.[6] We also have many symbols and rituals that are common to us and parallel those of the Christian church. We often practice parallel Christian/Traditional rituals and rites simultaneously.

The second difficulty is our loss of pure culture. What was ideal and complete culturally cannot be entirely regained. Exploitation, relocation, assimilation, loss of sacred land bases, and loss of many of our languages (our roots of understanding) hinder us from achieving our cultural and religious goals, our ways of being. Most of us have become "diaspora people" in our own homeland.

The third difficulty in presenting the indigenous peoples' perspective is the "majority" audience who will read this essay. Conveying ideas in our common language of English is incomplete and misunderstood because of our differing world views, which remain largely unexplored and foreign to one another.

The motivation for listening to each other should, however, point to our mutual need for understanding, respecting, and living with each other. Indigenous people need the help of Christian churches in advocacy for justice and survival as distinct peoples. Christian churches need the indigenous people to help the church reclaim the activity of a particularly significant and faithful community of believers. That is, Christian people need to undertake their specific mission in the world, understand their possession of a sacred history, and live out their sacred duty to humankind and to the cosmos.

Further, the church needs to hear the indigenous peoples' voices regarding place in the universe and care for the created order. The United Church of Christ is just now doing its exegetical work on environmental theology and stewardship and coming to the same conclusions that the Ancient Ones have proclaimed all along.

IDENTITY VERSUS ASSIMILATION

In December 1978, the Native American Project (now called the Indigenous Peoples Project to avoid confusion of "native Americans" as a reference to second and third generations of others who have staked a claim in "America") of Theology in the Americas worked out a position paper to describe and analyze the commonalities that exist for indigenous peoples in their religions and the effects Christianity has had on them. The uniqueness of this project lies in the sixty-five indigenous people who participated. They included Catholic and Protestant Christians and traditionalists (those who practice only their tribal religions) from urban and reservation dwelling places and represented some fifteen tribal nations.

The common beliefs or themes that emerged follow:

> We are an ancient people whose religious oral traditions declare that we have lived and evolved in these lands since the beginning of time. Examining our history, our traditions and our beliefs, we find creation stories that point to a time of birth from out of the earth and a covenant relationship with a Creator Spirit that is unique to this part of the world. We know that we have always been integral to this part of the world; we did not come from anywhere else. We know that our covenant with the Life Giving Force did not end and was not negated with the arrival of Christopher Columbus, the Mayflower or any other foreign vessel that has ever come to this continent. Many of our tribal people have clung tenaciously to the ancient beliefs and ritual ceremonies of our people even under persecution: therefore, we have survived as distinct peoples with a history and a place in the cosmos.[7]

With the introduction of Christianity to the tribes, some of our people, regardless of tribal affiliation, found the teachings of Jesus similar and compatible to the ancient moral and ethical teachings of our people. Jesus' teachings were accepted by many who did not give up their understanding of their place in the universe as taught in traditional instruction prior to missionary influence. Indigenous peoples have started churches of their own and conducted the business of the church from a tribal perspective, that is, using the same style of selecting a minister as was used in designating a chief and designing the worship according to the model of traditional religious ceremonies. Accepting "civilization" and Christianity from this orientation was an attempt to maintain separate sovereign nations in the face of Western expansion. Ultimately, the "Indian Church" did not help maintain tribal sovereignty, but it did provide indigenous expression in a Christian mode.

Assimilation attempts by the U.S. government, working in concert with the Euro-American church, have had an impact on many of our people as well. This triumphal church approach led many of us to join the Anglo church and we often find ourselves accepting Americanized Christianity as a way of believing and living. I find that, for me, this is a dangerous way to live. The different perceptions of the ministry of the church and the Euro-American's view about humankind's place in the universe and the church's efforts to universalize and impose its beliefs on all peoples of earth create difficulty and confusion for many indigenous people.

In spite of Christianity's doctrine of original sin and the virtue of humility, the European perception and attitude about their place ("a little lower than the angels") is quite lofty. This is the irony of a pessimistic view of sinful humanity. The contradictions between stated beliefs and the actual life style leave one to compromise and compartmentalize daily living into incompatible units. The belief that Jesus came "that all may have life" and the actual practices of genocide to indigenous peoples are strange bedfellows indeed!

Granted, the United Church of Christ has adopted an impressive and new missiology. It has become common to affirm that "the gospel is in the people and we go to them and discover the gospel in their lives." Evangelism has become more of a witnessing/inspecting mechanism to see the gospel at work and respond with awe. Is this another name for "fact-finding missions" where the church checks to see *if* God is at work and is surprised to find out that it is so? This missiology may have been slow in coming, but it does make way for cultural diversity within the church and may be welcomed by indigenous people who are outside the church.

Those indigenous people outside the church who maintain their tribal religious ceremonies and ways of being are referred to as the traditionalists. Indigenous people within the church who adore their heritages must express gratitude to those who in the face of adversity have held to the ancient beliefs of our peoples. It is through the efforts of the traditionalists that indigenous Christians stand a chance of regaining identity as a distinct and covenanted people. We must reconsider our old values if not our old practices, even as we take our places at the Lord's Table.

To promote greater understanding and cross-cultural exchanges, traditionalists have invited Anglos to share in ceremonials such as the Vision Quest and Sweatlodges. Recently, some of our brothers and sisters in the United Church of Christ have explored these experiences of Native Americans. Ordinarily, one would welcome these cross-cultural opportunities but two suspicions arise. These ceremonials are about the essence of survival as a covenanted people. When nonindigenous persons bypass the hardships of reservation life and what it means to be Indian in this country and move into the ceremonials for filling a personal spiritual void, are they not exploiting the religious experience for personal gain? What are they contributing back to the survival of a people and our beloved Mother Earth? Another question concerns people like those in the New Age movement. The New Age movement people who have explored Native American spirituality have turned a nice profit by writing and lecturing on Native American spirituality.

I find it odd/interesting that while some Anglos learn and experience Native American roots of spirituality, the United Church of Christ affirms and supports indigenous Christians in their efforts to learn about scripture, tradition, and reason in order to provide leadership for indigenous peoples' church community. Such engaging issues are prime topics for opening dialogue for all of us. Consider Josh. 24:25–28, where God made a covenant with the tribes of Israel:

> So Joshua made a covenant with the people that day, and made statutes and ordinances for them at Shechem. And Joshua wrote these words in the book of the law of God; and he took a great stone, and set it up there under the oak in the sanctuary of the Lord. And Joshua said to all the people, "Behold, this stone shall be a witness against us;   lest you deal falsely with your God.

Some of the psalms likewise speak of God's power in created nature. Psalm 96 says, "Sing to the Lord, all the earth! Let the heavens be glad . . . let the sea roar . . . let the field exult, and everything in it! . . . the trees of the wood will sing for joy."

PERCEPTIONS OF THE DEITY

In the Muscogee (Creek) language, the name of the creator-spirit deity is *Hesaketvmese,* that is, "Breath Holder." Other meanings include Creator (earth), Sustainer (air), Redeemer (water), Intervener (unexpected events), Lover, Intimate Confidant, and Fun-Loving Friend (gentle breezes and small whirlwinds). The deity is accessible and present throughout the entire cosmos.

The scriptures, in remarkably similar ways, attest to the presence of the deity in what are considered by the Euro-American to be inanimate objects. In the Gospel according to Luke, when Jesus was making the triumphant entry into Jerusalem amidst the palm waving and praise, the Pharisees in the crowd spoke to Jesus, saying, "Teacher, rebuke your disciples." He answered, "I tell you, if these [disciples] were silent, the very stones would cry out" (Luke 19:40). Passages such as these resonate vibrantly in the essence of indigenous peoples.

In the history of the church there have been a few individuals, Francis of Assisi, St. Anthony, and Julian of Norwich, for example, who have been especially spiritually alive to the Creator in the created world. In the indigenous peoples' history Black Elk is recorded as a spiritual holy man attuned to the created order, and there are many others, including women, who are known to us by oral tradition.

But greater than the enchantment of mystery in the created order and stones that shout is the recognition that nature is an active participant with human beings and has feelings. Nature may have immortal and inexhaustible qualities, but it can die and it can die at the hands of human beings if human beings are not attuned to the voices and feelings of nature.

Indigenous people call for the recognition of the Breath Holder who through the act of creation permeates all life forms. Native thought has always embraced the philosophy enculturated through our oral traditions that all of the created elements are to be revered as an elder and nurtured as a child. What creation provides is to be cared for and used by all.[8] All of creation is sacred.

PERCEPTIONS OF HUMANKIND

The stories of many tribal nations concerning the creation of human beings are not unlike the Genesis account (2:4a–23). We are created from the earth, made last, not as a hierarchical culmination, but in a more humble position. The human being is considered the weakest of creation, entirely dependent on all other created life forms for mere existence. Gratitude, nurture, and equality are to be accorded all creation.[9] The Genesis story of the fall from grace and expulsion from Paradise (Genesis 3) should humble us, not make us proud and possessive. Christian faith aims to restore the state of grace with God and creation but Christians have alienated themselves too far from nature, making reconciliation in universal wholeness difficult.

Only in recent biblical scholarship have theologians begun to see that the Hebrew words for dominion (radah) and subdue (kabash) are antithetical to universal harmony and order.[10] Some ancient manuscripts can be read as either *radah* or as *mashal*. Could it be that substituting the Hebrew verb *mashal* for *radah* would clarify human beings' place in the created order? While the root word of *mashal* is difficult to trace, one of the verb's meanings is "to pattern one upon the other" as in speaking in parables. If humankind could pattern its relationship to the created order in the way the Creator is related to creation, humankind could be cocreators with God in God's world. God-likeness would generate harmony and order rather than dominion and subjugation.

Contrast that to the Euro-American distortion of the concept of "man" naming, subduing, and having dominion over the earth. This forces the earth to produce rather than allowing the earth to flourish under the rhythm of life. Western European technological arrogance has jarred the harmony of the cosmos and thwarted the Creator's intention. The drive to possess the land, rather than act as God's cocreators, further adds to the imbalance. Christianity's influence in this regard affects all humanity. The earth and every living entity have been objectified, depersonalized, and made inanimate. The concept of humankind being patterned after God, the Breath Holder and Gardenkeeper, is lost.

The United Church of Christ has exhibited concern for the environment and a desire to uphold a theology of stewardship rather than dominion. It seems, then, that one of the areas that indigenous peoples have in common with the United Church of Christ is the goal of restoring harmony with each other and the natural order. But how do we overcome our diverse perceptions of what that means?

I had the privilege of attending the first Theodore Roosevelt Environment and Conservation Symposium (Fall 1986) sponsored jointly by Grace Reformed Church in Washington, D.C., the United Church Board for Homeland Ministries, the Central Atlantic Conference of the UCC, the UCC Office for Church in Society, the Stewardship Council, and the National Wildlife Federation. While the goal of preserving creation was common to all, the contrast in approach between the United States Forestry Service and the United Church of Christ was interesting. The theological approach was that the problem is people taking over the function of God instead of recognizing that God is at home in God's world, and that God has shared God's home with nature and humankind alike as a household. The Forestry Service representative called for persons to exercise their responsibility to be God's stewards and use and renew resources as appropriate to the technology that has been developed by humankind. In other words, to him it seemed that people have found a way to care for the world in God's absence.

The perspective of the UCC theologian is in harmony with indigenous peoples' goal of restoring and maintaining harmony with each other and the natural order. But we have a lot of work to do to overcome our

diverse perceptions of what that means. Over a century ago, Chief
Seattle spoke of the indigenous peoples' perspective of our human
relationship to earth and the environment, the indigenous sense of
harmony, and the problem with the Euro-American world view. In
1854, at a time when the president of the United States was trying to
negotiate a treaty, Chief Seattle said,

> So we will consider your offer to buy our land. But it will not be easy. For
> this land is sacred to us. . . . We may be brothers after all; we shall see. One
> thing we know, which the white man may one day discover, our God is the
> same God. You may think now that you own him as you wish to own our
> land, but you cannot. He is the God of man, and his compassion is equal
> for the red man and the white. This earth is precious to him and to harm
> the earth is to heap contempt on its Creator. Continue to contaminate
> your bed, and you will one night suffocate in your own waste.[11]

A PERCEPTION OF HARMONY

> For God so loved the world that God gave God's only Son, that whoever
> believes in him should not perish, but have eternal life. (John 3:16, RSV
> adapted)

This famous verse that the missionaries taught us, but often neglected
to analyze or assess for themselves, contains real truth in the word
"world." The Greek word is *kosmos,* or universe. The intention of the
deity seems to be to offer salvation to all of creation. The offered
salvation is not limited to the people in the church, to those who have
strands of unity, but salvation is opened to the entire cosmos. Cosmic
balance, harmony, and longevity belong to all of the created order in
their particularities and even when there seems to be no common thread
among them! Justice, ethics, and morality flow from the intertwined,
interdependent, and intimate relationships of Creator and created.

Genocide, extermination, exploitation, pollution, contamination, oppression are the acts that most upset the natural order and upset the
deity. When harmony is disrupted, the Creator is sad, hurt, angry, and
vengeful (in the sense that the disrupters must suffer the natural
consequences of their deeds). Sometimes the deity turns away from,
does not favor, those who are disruptive. Sometimes, in a manner
reminiscent of Jesus' Beatitudes, the deity intervenes with those least
likely to appear worthy and orthodox.

Learning the lessons of restoring harmony involves individuals and
their community as they participate in the ceremonies of the tribe. It is
in the seasonal, temporal, geography-centered, rigidly followed ceremonies that one learns the ways of worship, gratitude, and well-being.[12]
Ceremonies always begin with prayer. Many tribes use a sacred pipe

filled with special tobacco. First, offering the pipe to the four directions, then to the sky and the earth, then to "all my relatives" symbolizes the inclusion of all creation. Then, the smoking of the pipe by every person in the circle symbolizes communion and accepting the gift from the Creator and Mother Earth. Dances, such as the hoop dance of the Ojibwe, represent the circle of the universe. Other dances remind the tribe of its dependency on and relatedness to the Creator and the created.[13] In the ceremonies harmony is restored and perpetuated for the future. In the ceremonies indigenous nations express their connection with primordial time and space, with cosmic reality.

Yet the very ceremonies that ground our beings were hindered and outlawed with the arrival of Europeans. The attacks on our ways of life are unparalleled in human history and our ability to regain and restore these ceremonies in their fullest sense is all but lost.

WHAT CAN WE DO AT THE LORD'S TABLE?

Vine Deloria, Jr., says, "Tribal religions have a very difficult time advocating their case (in the courts) . . . They may have to wait for the radical changes now occurring within Western religious institutions to take root and flourish before much progress can be made. Protestantism is increasing its ceremonial/ritual life, and Catholicism is becoming more secular, so that behavior comparable to tribal ceremonial behavior among Christians may not be far off."[14]

The United Church of Christ is noted for its diversity within the Euro-American theological tradition, in its historic pluralism and flexibility, its ecumenical interest, and its being on the cutting edge of social issues as a prophetic voice in the world. If this church can relinquish its defensive power posture and assume a listening posture, then we can sit at the Lord's Table as I believe God intends us to do. Let the United Church of Christ forthrightly say, We don't see one strand of commonality on which to base our unity, but let's be our unique selves at the Lord's Table. At the Lord's Table there is room to be, to be included, to be fed, to be forgiven, to be acknowledged, and to be at home in God's world.

At the Lord's Table, there is a theology of listening toward mutual hearing. Our various voices, the voices of all creation, and the voice of the Creator can speak and be heard. In mutuality, we can examine our motives for listening, our motives for hearing, our motives for talking— if we can risk being heard. Indigenous peoples' ceremonies and ceremonial grounds and the worship centers of the United Church of Christ have community-building opportunities that are mandated by our sacred histories and sacred obligations.

Each of us, indigenous peoples and the United Church of Christ, must learn how to authenticate our relationships with our own people. It is one thing to stand on the side of justice in Central America, South Africa, the Philippines, and the "uttermost parts of the earth" (Acts 13:47), but it is quite another to do justice with the victimized of our own people and the contamination of the environment in which we are blessed to dwell. Community building and living requires rebirth and relinquishment in the present in this place as well as in other lands and in the future so that "all may have life" at the Lord's Table. Paulo Freire wrote,

> Those who authentically commit themselves to the people must re-examine themselves constantly. This conversion is so radical as not to allow ambiguous behavior. To affirm this commitment but to consider oneself the proprietor of revolutionary wisdom—which must then be given to (or imposed on) the people is to retain the old ways. The [person] who proclaims devotion to the cause of liberation yet is unable to enter into communion with people, whom he [or she] continues to regard as totally ignorant is grievously self-deceived. Conversion to the people requires a profound rebirth. Those who undergo it must take on a new form of existence: they can no longer remain as they were.[15]

May it be so.

NOTES

1. J. Letch Wright, Jr., *The Only Land They Knew* (New York: MacMillan Free Press, 1981), 29.
2. Ibid., 30–33.
3. Vine Deloria, Jr., *God Is Red* (New York: Delta Books, 1973), 3.
4. Stuart Lang, *Two Spirits Meet*, Heritage Series, ed. Edward A. Powers (Philadelphia: United Church Press, 1976), 3.
5. Ibid., 18.
6. Position paper of the Native American Project of Theology in the Americas, 475 Riverside Drive, New York, N.Y., 1978.
7. Ibid.
8. Ibid.
9. "Recalling, Reliving, Reviewing," a report on a religious dialogue sponsored by the Native American Theological Association and the Minnesota Humanities Commission, October 1979.
10. David Jobling, "Dominion Over Creation," in *Interpreter's Dictionary of the Bible*, supp. vol. (Nashville: Abingdon Press, 1976), 247–48.
11. The words of Chief Seattle were quoted by Adam Cuthand, in "The Spirituality of Native Americans," a speech given at the Toronto World's Future Conference (July 1980).
12. Deloria, *God Is Red*, 262ff.
13. Ibid.

14. Vine Deloria, Jr., "Indians and Other Americans: The Cultural Chasm," *Church and Society* (Presbyterian Church U.S.A.) (Jan.–Feb. 1985):11–19.

15. Paulo Freire, *Pedagogy of the Oppressed* (New York: Seabury Press, 1969), 47.

Part 2

POLITY, MINISTRY, AND
WORSHIP ISSUES

7

A COVENANT POLITY

REUBEN A. SHEARES II

There are four major ways in which the United Church of Christ has been characterized and classified over the years. I want to mention and discuss them briefly. As otherwise useful as they have been, they have contributed to confusion and distortion about the polity of the church.

One set of confusions and distortions has resulted from efforts to fit the United Church of Christ into a typology of traditional polities, in spite of the intentions of the founders to the contrary. When trying to fit a traditional polity, it is generally concluded that the United Church of Christ is "Congregational" in polity. Others would say it is "Presbyterian." Few, if any, have been found to argue that it is "Episcopal."

In support of the "Congregational" contention, reference is usually made to paragraph 7 of the Constitution, which states: "The basic unit of the life and organization of the United Church of Christ is the local church." This statement is quite true; paragraph III-A of the *Basis of Union with Interpretations* carries the same affirmation.

However, the conclusion that the United Church of Christ is "Congregational" in polity, while true, is not true enough. That conclusion is a reductionism that obscures as much as it reveals. It is inadequate. It does not do justice to the influence nor the presence of elements from the other traditional polities on and within the life and polity of the United Church of Christ.

If reference to traditional polities is to be made at all, it would be well-placed within this observation of Douglas Horton, minister and general secretary of the General Council of the Congregational Christian Churches at the time of the union negotiations:

> The United Church of Christ is: *Presbyterian* in its legislative functions, since it works through representatives of presbyters; *Episcopal* in its admin-

istrative system, since here it works through superintendents or episcopi; and *Congregational* in its judicial branch, since the congregations and several groupings make their own decisions and have no judge over them but Christ and the decent respect they have for all . . . in Christ.[1]

Horton's observation helps us to see that the United Church of Christ does contain elements of traditional polities within it, without being any one of them, or without being reduced simply to any one of them. Horton's observation also helps us to see that "a neat and distinctive way" of even talking about them has not been found.

While some helpful insights might be derived from the categories of traditional polities, they contribute to much confusion and distortion. They may actually retard—if not prevent—the discovery of a more adequate understanding of the polity. Consequently, some have advocated either abandoning or moving beyond the categories of traditional polities in describing the United Church of Christ.

A second set of confusions and distortions is related to the first, but I believe it to be worthy of separate mention. It derives from confusion about the nature of Congregationalism itself—or the Congregational principle. Obviously, this was one of the issues in the litigation around the union. There it became clear that widespread disagreement existed about the nature of Congregationalism, the Congregational principle, and surely the Congregational polity. Much of that diverse understanding, if not outright disagreement, exists up to the present in the United Church of Christ. Even when the Congregational label can be legitimately applied in the United Church of Christ, there is the danger or possibility that the "wrong" understanding of Congregationalism will be applied. This contributes to confusions and distortions. Consequently, the Congregational principle and polity need clarification.

Congregationalism itself is a term—principle or polity—applied to so wide a range of denominations that the differences can and do outweigh the similarities. Consider the diversity and variety among several denominations that are ostensibly of Congregational polity, including the Churches of Christ, the Southern Baptist Convention, the American Baptist Churches, the Christian Church (Disciples of Christ), and the True Light Holy Rollers. Whatever else the United Church of Christ is— and however else the word Congregational can be applied to it—it is clearly not Congregational in the sense that the Southern Baptist Convention is. Nor is the United Church of Christ Congregational even as some of the former Congregationalists understood the term.

One way in which some would state the Congregational principle is to assert that the local church is the only church or the only valid expression of the church. Some denominations accept that understanding and perhaps there are those within and among the United Church of Christ who would also make that claim. But that assertion seems to me to be a far cry from this affirmation contained in paragraph 7 of the *Constitution and Bylaws of the United Church of Christ:* "The basic unit of the life and organization of the United Church of Christ is the local church."

The difference between the two statements—between the "only" versus the "basic" unit—has to do with the integrity and existence of the other units of church life and their own legitimacy. They have significantly different implications. Much confusion and distortion have resulted from the diverse and conflicting understandings of the nature of Congregationalism or the Congregational principle.

A third set of confusions and distortions has resulted from efforts to characterize and classify the United Church of Christ in terms of autonomy. That word has probably been as dominant, prevalent, and valued in discussions about the United Church of Christ as any.

In support of the autonomy perspective, reference is generally made to paragraph 15 of the Constitution, which states: "The autonomy of the local church is inherent and modifiable only by its own action . . ." Indeed, for some people, references to autonomy become synonymous in meaning with the autonomy of the local church.

There are those, though, who also refer to paragraph 45 of the Constitution which, in describing the powers of the General Synod, declares that "No power vested in the General Synod shall invade the autonomy of Conferences, Associations and local churches . . ." At times reference is also made to the language of "free and voluntary relationships" in paragraph 3. And of course note is taken variously of the recognized instrumentalities—"free and independent"—within the life of the United Church of Christ. In the latter instance, there are those who lament the autonomy principle of the national instrumentalities, as if it could be said that autonomy applied to the local church is good, but applied to the national instrumentalities (or to "them") it is bad or undesirable.

Thus confusions abound even around the autonomy principle. But at its best autonomy is celebrated in the United Church of Christ. It is a principle that needs to be understood and applied. It is indeed a characteristic of the system as a whole. There is freedom and autonomy under the headship of Christ.

But the accent on freedom and autonomy can be a reductionism, especially when they are left standing in isolation or when understood essentially as "freedom from" versus "freedom for." There are rights involved, but there are also responsibilities and accountabilities. There is the need—and provision—for what the founders called "fellowship," lest freedom become license.

Thus it has become more common now even in discussions of the autonomy of the local church to note that paragraph 15 of the Constitution, the radical autonomy statement, is placed between paragraphs 14 and 16, which accent mutual accountability and fellowship. The notion that in the United Church of Christ everyone is free to do his or her own thing is probably true, but it is also a distortion of the autonomy principle and a perversion of the polity.

The fourth and last set of distortions and confusions to be mentioned here results from what I call, for lack of better terminology, the "predecessor bodies view" of the United Church of Christ. Much benefit has been derived from reviewing and recalling the four traditions of the predecessor bodies, knowing and appreciating the sense in which the United Church of Christ has affinity with the Evangelical, the Reformed, the Congregational, and the Christian.

In the absence of a more compelling description, it has proven to be quite helpful to a new church to be able to locate itself in the stream of Christian history and, in that sense, to know and to be able to say to others that one has roots. The "predecessor bodies view" allows the United Church of Christ, though new, to claim a heritage, to know that it has mothers and fathers.

Yet this has contributed to some confusion and distortion over time, in much the same way that allusion to the traditional polities has created confusion. For while this "predecessor bodies view" tends to point to continuities between the predecessors and the new church, that very perspective tends not to differentiate sufficiently nor to give enough sympathetic attention to the discontinuities. It suggests somewhat that to know the parent is to know the child, which is never quite true enough. And, further, it seldom articulates and elaborates the ways in which the United Church of Christ is different from either one or all of the predecessor bodies.

Thus many use the "old," the predecessor, as the norm by which the "new" is to be evaluated and judged. In different times and places, the United Church of Christ has been lamented because its ways have been different from the old ways.

A further complication is that the focus on the four predecessor bodies can ignore the fact that the United Church of Christ is much broader and more inclusive than the predecessor bodies in its composition and membership. Even though the four traditions were dominant during the negotiation and consummation of the union, it is quite clear that over the years the United Church of Christ has been enriched by a broader diversity. Indeed, many of our contemporaries never belonged to any of the four predecessor bodies.

I, for one, am grateful for the heritage of the predecessor bodies and affirm an appropriate study of their histories and traditions as part of the background for understanding the United Church of Christ. But I recognize the limitation in the "predecessor bodies view." To be or become a member of the United Church of Christ, one does not first have to become either Evangelical and Reformed or Congregational Christian. There is a need to move beyond the "predecessor bodies view" of the United Church of Christ. The kinship in Christ we acknowledge includes but is broader than the precedessor bodies.

These descriptions, then, illustrate that a neat and distinctive way of characterizing and classifying the polity of the United Church of Christ has not been found. They further illustrate some of the confusions and distortions that have resulted, often from the very descriptions and metaphors that have been developed and used with much benefit.

Perhaps what is involved here is not so much that the description be neat or distinctive as much as it should be apt. It is what my colleagues in the Office for Church Life and Leadership have called the need and the quest for an apt metaphor, out of which concern this whole endeavor has come. An apt description or an apt metaphor would be adequate, and perhaps accurate, in characterizing and classifying the results, with compelling, consensual, and unitive powers.

The various descriptions mentioned earlier, as well as many others, have not passed the aptness test, the test of adequacy and accuracy. And we generally know that aptness in our bones. There is something inherent in either the psyche, soul, spirit, or experience of the United Church of Christ that knows that the classical metaphors do not fully apply nor adequately represent our reality, as helpful as they might otherwise have been.

Over the last several years, I have noticed with much interest the resistance in the church to many of the inadequate descriptions. The whole matter of autonomy, for example, has been augmented or counterbalanced. First, the words "congenial" and then "collaborative" began to be used descriptively alongside the word "autonomy." It has also been interesting to note how long it took before the word "covenantal" emerged and settled in as an apt metaphor.

And so it has gone. A new style of church life and organization did evolve from the dreams of the founders. They did not give it a neat or distinctive characterization and one has not readily been found over the years. The United Church of Christ is indeed in need of an apt metaphor.

In "Order and Identity in the United Church of Christ," Louis Gunnemann wrote:

> When the United Church developed its Constitution and Bylaws on the
> Basis of Union principles it did in fact develop a principle of order new in

the American scene of denominationally organized church life, based
upon principles of Reformed ecclesiology. The new element was a covenanted relationship of autonomous units of church life—a relationship
delineated but not regulated by a constitution and bylaws.[2]

The polity of the United Church of Christ may well be described as a
"covenanted relationship of autonomous units of church life." Else-
where, Gunnemann referred to the polity as "a covenant of mutual
accountability." And yet, in each instance, there is more that must be
said in order for the understanding to be full. The covenanted relationship does have context, content, and norms. It is a covenanted relationship "delineated but not regulated by a constitution and bylaws."
Therein lies a basis for the mutual accountability.

But it must be acknowledged that the term covenant can also lead to
confusion and distortion, especially when informed solely or principally
by social contract theories and organizational behavior theories, especially hierarchical views. Covenant can also lead to confusion when
understood essentially in horizontal terms: between "us."

The covenanted relationship, then, is delineated by a constitution and
bylaws. But preeminently, it is a covenantal relationship between and
among parts of the Body of Christ within the covenant that God has
established and maintains in Jesus Christ, the head of the body, the head
of the church. Perhaps it is best described as a covenant within the
covenant.

Gunnemann's discussion of the polity of the United Church of Christ
provides us with a metaphor—a description that needs to be tested for
aptness. Is it an adequate and accurate description of the polity?

To deal with that question, Gunnemann points us to the Basis of
Union with Interpretations and the Constitution and Bylaws. The polity
of the United Church of Christ is predicated on Basis of Union principles
as translated and articulated in the Constitution and Bylaws. Therefore,
grappling with the polity of the United Church of Christ may require a
more intensive grappling with the Constitution and Bylaws than many
have been inclined to do. An apt metaphor for the United Church of
Christ may not be neat, especially if by neat we mean simple or an easy
label. For here we have a mouthful that can only be shortened with
much loss: "A covenanted relationship of autonomous units of church
life . . . a relationship delineated but not regulated by a constitution and
bylaws."

The Basis of Union with Interpretations included the following principle in section III, paragraph F:

> The government of the United Church is exercised through Congrega-
> tions, Associations, Conferences, and the General Synod in such ways that

the autonomy of each is respected in its own sphere, each having its own rights and responsibilities. This Basis of Union defines those rights and responsibilities in principle and the constitution which will be drafted after the consummation of the union shall further define them but shall in no wise abridge the rights now enjoyed by Congregations.

In the Constitution and Bylaws, the term "government" per se did not survive. Yet it may be necessary to see more explicitly that the Constitution speaks generally about principles of governance, especially in paragraphs 3 and 5. Governance flows out of ordering and ordering reflects governance.

Thus when read from the perspectives of the Basis of Union with Interpretations principles or intentions, it is possible to see that the four (paragraph 5) or five (paragraph 3) components of the United Church of Christ are, in fact, elements or components of its government or system of governance; there is a distribution of power or authority or responsibility to and among the various components—"each is respected in its own sphere, each having its own rights and responsibilities"; and each has autonomy or each is autonomous—and that autonomy in each instance is respected, perhaps affirmed, by the others and exists for or is to be used in service of its responsibilities.

So, the various articles of the Constitution—especially IV (Local Churches), VI (Associations and Conferences), VII (the General Synod), VIII (Instrumentalities), and IX (Bodies other than Instrumentalities)— do further define the respective rights and responsibilities of the autonomous units as the Basis of Union with Interpretations had hoped. And, in each instance, except for the local churches, there is further elaboration in the Articles of the Bylaws. (While local churches per se are not treated in the Bylaws, there is a section within the Article on "The Ministry," paragraphs 116–25, pertaining to the local churches on "Calling, Installing and Terminating a Pastorate.")

In these sections of the Constitution and Bylaws, the respective spheres are established and bound. In language that has become more commonplace in our time, each autonomous unit is given its "mandate." The labor is divided and assigned, with appropriate delegation of authority. The Constitution and Bylaws tells who is responsible for what and, in the process, enables each part of the body to know what can be expected of the others—as well as what the others can expect from it.

Thus it seems to me that the provisions of the Constitution and Bylaws do delineate the relationship between autonomous units of church life. And perhaps it should be noted that each of these autonomous units is also described as a "body" (see paragraphs 28, 29, 31, 32, 37, 44), language I take to be intentional and appropriate for life together under the headship of Christ. Yet each autonomous unit or body is but a

member thereof. Thus each body is first and always accountable to Jesus
Christ and is endowed with freedom in Christ to follow and obey its
head.

In addition, the Constitution and Bylaws is itself a covenant within the
covenant. It is the covenantal document of a people who have been
drawn to one another because they have found a unity in Christ Jesus
and who now would order their lives and their ways "to express more
fully [their] oneness in Christ . . . to make more effective their common
witness . . . and to serve His kingdom in the world . . ." (paragraph 1).

The Constitution and Bylaws describes the relationships among the
partners or the parts of the body. It defines and establishes relationships
and procedures "to enable them more effectively to accomplish their
tasks and the work of the United Church of Christ" (paragraph 3).

The Constitution and Bylaws, as the covenantal document, is a covenant within the covenant of grace and the action by which God calls us
into the church and binds into covenant faithful people of all ages,
tongues, and races.

Of course, the partners do participate in the system on a free and
voluntary basis (paragraph 3) and continue in it on a free and voluntary
basis. Yet the decision to belong—especially for the local church, of
whom the most radical statement of the autonomy principle is asserted
(paragraph 15)—creates and involves a covenanted relationship with the
other partners. This relationship, delineated by the Constitution and
Bylaws, is a covenant of mutual accountability.

It is interesting to note that paragraph 11—which identifies the local
churches that either compose the United Church of Christ or may
subsequently become members of the United Church of Christ—initially
predicates local church status upon the approval of the Constitution. Of
course, once the Constitution was declared in force, that question
became moot and the decision for local churches became whether or
not to unite with the United Church of Christ.

There is no need to rehearse here the various patterns of voting by
which local churches became part of the United Church of Christ or by
which the two uniting bodies came together. The patterns of votes by
Evangelical and Reformed Synods and Congregational Christian
Churches are well-known. But, in either event, the crucial vote was on
and about *The Constitution and Bylaws of the United Church of Christ.* That
issue of voting resulted in the different listings of churches in the *United
Church of Christ Yearbook,* including Schedule I and Schedule II churches.
Schedule I churches voted to become part of the United Church of
Christ; Schedule II churches either had not voted or decided not to vote
on becoming a member or approving the Constitution. And, so, paragraph 13 provides a way by which an Association or Conference could

"admit, or continue into fellowship with" a local church that is not a member of the United Church of Christ. It also describes the limitations of such a local church and its members in relation to the United Church of Christ.

Thus it seems to me that the Constitution and Bylaws is the covenantal document. It delineates the relationship between autonomous units of church life, even as it regulates the General Synod and those instrumentalities related to it.

The covenantal relationship, as delineated or described, is highly interactive between and among the components: the local churches, Associations, Conferences, and the General Synod. Initiatives can be taken by any of the units. All have direct or indirect access to one another. Indeed, each can and does seek to influence the others. Each one is to be seriously considered by the others. Dynamic interaction characterizes the relationship these various components "sustain with the General Synod and with each other" (paragraph 3).

The essence of the covenantal relationship is summarized in paragraph 14, which, while pertaining to the local church, articulates a core value of the system as a whole:

> The local churches of the United Church have, in fellowship [covenant], a God-given responsibility for that Church, its labors and its extension, even as the United Church of Christ has, in fellowship [covenant], a God-given responsibility for the well-being and needs and aspirations of its local churches. In mutual Christian concern and in dedication to Jesus Christ, the Head of the Church, the one and the many share in common Christian experience and responsibility.

That of course is augmented by paragraph 16, which affirms:

> Actions by, or decisions or advice emanating from, the General Synod, a Conference or an Association, should be held in the highest regard by every local church.

It is in the light and spirit of these paragraphs that one can best understand the provisions of paragraph 152 (Associations) and paragraph 156 (Conferences) and the Associations' and Conferences' right to petition or overture the other and the General Synod. This understanding also applies to paragraphs 151 and 155, in which the responsibility of an Association or a Conference to receive and act on business, requests, counsel, and references from local churches, Associations, General Synod, and other bodies is affirmed.

The relationship between the parts is highly interactive. It is a system of cross-initiatives and cross-influencings. It is free, open, responsive, and responsible. And while the wording is different in the various paragraphs, the spirit, meaning, and intention seem comparable: each of the parts is to hold in "highest regard" actions, advice, or decisions emanating from the other parts of the church. In mutual Christian concern, the one and the many share in common Christian experience and responsibility.

The covenantal relationship, as delineated and described, is also bound. The relationship is bound by the mandates of the various spheres. It is bound by the respective responsibilities—in full awareness of being a part of the whole, a member of a larger body. And beyond that, the relationship is bound significantly by the terms, conditions, and provisions of the Constitution and Bylaws itself—by the covenant.

The explication of this point involves a couple of affirmations. On the one side is the fact that the Constitution and Bylaws assumes and, indeed, grants to each of the autonomous units a large measure of freedom for use in pursuing and fulfilling its responsibilities. That is a part of the sense in which relationships are more "delineated" than "regulated." Only the broad contours of the life of the whole—and the particular roles and responsibilities of the various components—are defined, described, or delineated there.

If the Constitution and Bylaws tells who is responsible for what, it largely leaves the how to each of the entities, even though the Bylaws tend to be more specific about the hows than the Constitution is. But in the main, each Association, Conference, or local church could essentially order its own life and work, using creatively the freedom it has in Christ. Therefore, the Constitution and Bylaws asserts, to some degree, that each unit is free to go about its work as best it can.

At the same time, the Constitution and Bylaws establishes limits or boundaries. Indeed, this is the essential boundary. Beyond the radical autonomy principle for the local church (paragraph 15) which is bound, though loosely, by paragraphs 14 and 16, there are explicit limiting provisions in the covenantal document. Associations (paragraph 33), Conferences (paragraph 39), and established instrumentalities (paragraph 48) are bound by the provisions of the Constitution and Bylaws. In the case of the recognized instrumentalities, the matter is negotiated, since paragraph 49 provides that "the General Synod shall determine the conditions under which it will recognize an existing agency to serve . . ."; within that, however, such a recognized body "shall administer its own program and financial affairs, and establish its own bylaws and rules of procedure."

We have been pursuing the description of the polity of the United Church of Christ along the lines suggested by Gunnemann:

• A Covenanted Relationship
• Of Autonomous Units of Church Life
• Delineated but Not Regulated by a Constitution and Bylaws

There appears to be evidence in both the Basis of Union with Interpretations and the Constitution and Bylaws to support this description—as reflecting the intentions of the founders and the reality of the product as it has unfolded and evolved.

To be sure, it was not easy for the founders to move from their intentions to the realization or embodiment of their hopes and dreams. The United Church of Christ came into being and took shape under conditions that were often adverse, surely frustrating. James E. Wagner, the copresident of the United Church of Christ, gave expression to much of that in a speech made to the adjourned meeting of the Second General Synod in Cleveland, Ohio in 1960:

> Moreover, it should not be forgotten that after all these years we have arrived at the point where we are under circumstances of more than ordinary difficulty. Ours has not been the task merely of finding a way to unity for two peoples of historically diverse traditions. That would have required only an exercise of Christian grace and a reasonable modicum of intelligence on the part of the negotiators and the peoples they represented. Rather, and infinitely more exacting, we have had always to labor under a shadow which was not a healing shadow, a shadow of dissent, of doctrinaire opposition, of litigation and the threat of litigation, so that the framers of the Basis of Union and as well the Commission to prepare a Constitution have never been free to ask the simple, pure, basic question, What provision, what formulation will enable the United Church of Christ to best express and serve the mind and purpose of her Lord in this generation? Instead, recalling a scripture about being "wise as serpents and harmless as doves" they have had to exercise a serpentine wisdom and at each step ask the additional distracting, debilitating question, How can we formulate the provision we are agreed upon in such a way as to offer the least risk of vulnerability to those who are ready to resort to the civil courts since they have not been able to sustain their cause within the fellowship of the churches? The necessity of continual recourse to this question has had the one major effect upon the peoples of both constituencies, and on their representatives in union negotiations and planning, of heightening sensitivities to differences which would never have arisen to harass them if they had not had to labor under the constant haunting of this ill-dispositioned spectre of the litigious spirit.[3]

Perhaps in spite of, maybe because of, and possibly independent of it all, the union came. A "principle of order new in the American scene" emerged. It is aptly described in these words: A covenanted relationship of autonomous units of church life . . . a relationship delineated but not regulated by a constitution and bylaws.

NOTES

1. Douglas Horton, *The United Church of Christ* (New York: Thomas Nelson & Sons, 1962), 190.

2. Louis H. Gunnemann, "Order and Identity in the United Church of Christ," *New Conversations*, Vol. 4, No. 2 (Fall 1979): 15.

3. From the Statement of Copresident James E. Wagner to the Adjourned Meeting of the Second General Synod, Cleveland, Ohio, 1960, *Minutes*, 72.

8

EMPOWERMENT AND EMBODIMENT: UNDERSTANDINGS OF MINISTRY IN THE UNITED CHURCH OF CHRIST

BARBARA BROWN ZIKMUND

The United Church of Christ states in its constitution that every member is called to participate in and extend the ministry of Jesus Christ by witnessing to the gospel in church and society (paragraph 17). Through baptism the ministries of all Christians are "authorized." However, the constitution also states that "the United Church of Christ recognizes that God calls certain of its members to various forms of ministry in and on behalf of the church for which ecclesiastical authorization is required by the church" (paragraph 18). Ecclesiastical authorization, through ordination, commissioning, and licensing is one of the ways in which the UCC undergirds the ministry of all members by nurturing faith, calling forth gifts, and equipping members for Christian service.

In the history of the church ordination has been, and remains, the primary rite whereby the UCC "recognizes and authorizes that member whom God had called to ordained ministry, and sets that person apart by prayer and laying on of hands" (paragraph 19). "An Ordained Minister in the United Church of Christ is one of its members who has been called by God and ordained to preach and teach the gospel, to administer the sacraments and rites of the church, and to exercise pastoral care and leadership" (paragraph 20).[1]

What does it mean to set apart someone in this way? How does this action continue general historical patterns for authorizing leadership in Protestant churches? Does the United Church of Christ have any special ways of understanding ordained ministry? What are the forces that continue to shape ministry in the UCC? These are important questions for the future of the United Church of Christ.

HISTORICAL ROOTS

All discussion of ministry in the United Church of Christ must begin by recalling its roots in the sixteenth-century Reformation. The thinking of

the Protestant Reformers shaped and continues to influence UCC definitions of ministry. The seventh article of the *Augsburg Confession* declares that the church is "the congregation of the saints in which the
gospel is rightly preached and the sacraments are rightly administered."[2]
Calvin defined the church as "where the preaching of the gospel is
reverently heard and the sacraments are not neglected."[3]

Furthermore, the United Church of Christ is a denomination that
refuses to separate theology and polity. Reformed history, from which
all streams of UCC history flow, regards the polity of the church as
divinely instituted. Ministers of the church, according to Reformed
tradition, have God-given responsibilities to protect right Christian
teaching and pure doctrine. In 1562 Henry Bullinger wrote in the
Helvetic Confession: "Only such persons are qualified to become ministers
who possess adequate and holy learning, pious eloquence, and simple
prudence and are persons of moderation and honesty."[4]

Calvin wrote that the significance of the ordination ceremony was "to
admonish the person ordained that he [or she] is no longer his [or her]
own master, but devoted to the service of God and the Church."[5]
Deviation from established ecclesiastical order was considered heresy
and one could be removed from office for blasphemy, drunkenness,
playing prohibited games, and dancing. Such things were irreconcilable
with Christian ministry. Furthermore, in Geneva ministers were admon-
ished to avoid arbitrary exegesis of scripture, presumptiveness, preoc-
cupation with speculative problems, indolence in the study of scripture,
tardiness in the denunciation of vice, avarice, irascibility, cantankerous-
ness, and unseemly dress.[6]

Zacharius Ursinus, remembered in the United Church of Christ as
one of the authors of the *Heidelberg Catechism* (1563), stated his reasons
for the institution of the ministry: it was for the glory of God, as an
instrument for conversion, to teach and to provoke godliness, praise,
and worship, so that God might show divine mercy by committing to
humanity "that great work, the ministry of reconciliation, which the Son
of God (himself) discharged." Ursinus concluded that the ministry exists
so that the church may be visible in the world, so that "the elect may
know to what they ought to attach themselves, and that the reprobate
may be rendered perfectly inexcusable" in all attempts to make God's
call ineffectual.[7]

In the earliest German Reformed churches there were five offices:
evangelist, pastor, teacher, healer, and deacon. According to Ursinus
their duties were:

1. A faithful and correct exposition of the true and uncorrupted
   doctrine of the law and gospel, so that the church may be able to
   understand it;

2. A lawful administration of the sacraments, according to divine appointment;
3. To give the church a good example of what constitutes a Christian life and godly conversation;
4. A diligent attention to their flocks;
5. To give proper respect and submission to the decisions of the church;
6. To see that proper respect and attention be given to the poor.[8]

In later German ecclesiastical history Evangelical churches had similar concerns. However, the German Evangelical Synod of North America came to speak of ordained ministry as even more essential to the work of the church. If the "mission of the church is to extend the Kingdom of God," to lead humanity "to Christ and to establish Christian principles in every relation of life," the pastor is the means whereby the church carries out its mission.[9] Where the pastor is, there is the church. Lutheran and Evangelical understandings of clergy emphasized ministry as servanthood, and refused to become preoccupied with credentials or duties.

By way of contrast Congregationalism developed a somewhat different understanding of ministry. Puritan views remained grounded in Reformed theology, but they were increasingly influenced by voluntary church polity. The *Cambridge Platform* defined the church as "a company of saints by calling, united into one body, by a holy covenant, for the publick worship of God and the mutuall edification one of another, in the Fellowship of the Lord Jesus."[10] The form and matter of the church exists in the local gathered community. Although officers were not deemed essential, they were there for the "well-being" of the faithful. Leadership was exercised by preaching and teaching officers, known as Pastors and Teachers, and by ruling officers, known as Ruling Elders and Deacons.

> The Pastors special work is, to attend to exhortation: and therein to Administer a word of Wisdom: the Teacher is to attend to Doctrine, and therein to Administer a word of Knowledge: and either of them to administer the Seales of that Covenant . . .[11]

Congregationalism was always eager to insist that the essential church existed with or without its officers. It was helpful to choose officers, "tryed and proved" leaders, but it was not essential. Furthermore, the power of all officers came as a result of being freely elected by the church members. Ordination remained a secondary rite, confirming an already held election. For this reason, the duties and responsibilities of ordained ministry were not immediately transferable beyond a local community.[12]

Among the Christians, the small denomination of Christian independents on the American frontier that eventually joined the Congregationalists, ordained ministry was more expendable. The Christians embraced a simple faith consistent with the "republican" zeal of American independence. A Virginia elder wrote, "We have no reverend, nor right reverends among us, no masters—we are all brethren *[sic].*"[13] The Christians believed that God would guide the churches to find fitting leadership.

THE UNITED CHURCH OF CHRIST SYNTHESIS

The United Church of Christ in the late twentieth century is an interesting mixture of polities, peoples, and principles drawn from scripture, Reformation history, colonial experience, frontier practice, democratic ideology, and personal piety. Out of these various pieces it has created a distinct way to define and justify "authorized or set apart ministry" in the contemporary world.

On the one hand, in an effort to preserve the importance of the laity and the ministry of every Christian, the UCC has downplayed the specialness of ordained ministry. Ordination authorizes an ordinary church member to be a Christian leader for the whole church. This argument may be called an *empowerment* justification for ordained ministry.

On the other hand, in an effort to recognize the fact that God has blessed certain individuals with gifts to enrich the church, the UCC continues to acknowledge the specialness of ordained ministry. Ordination authorizes a gifted leader to serve church and society in the name of Jesus Christ. This argument may be called an *embodiment* justification for ordained ministry.

Both of these views of ministry begin with the conviction that God alone calls the church into being. Both of these perspectives insist that the whole church is engaged in the ministry of Jesus Christ. Both of these traditions claim that Jesus Christ is the sole head of the church. Both of these viewpoints proclaim that every follower of Jesus Christ is called into ministry through his or her baptism. Both of these approaches to leadership agree that the ultimate source of authority for ordained ministry will always rest with the whole church.[14]

Yet within the United Church of Christ the tension between *empowerment* and *embodiment* understandings of ministry provides a creative energy. By examining the differences between these two perspectives it is possible to appreciate the unique synthesis that informs and justifies all authorized ministry in the United Church of Christ.

EMPOWERMENT

In those regions of the United Church of Christ rooted in Congregation-alism and the free church traditions of American life there is an *empowerment* view of ministry. This view is also congenial with certain Evangelical Synod traditions on the midwestern frontier.

The empowerment view believes that ordained ministers are called out of the community of the faithful and "empowered" to carry out the functions of preaching, teaching, and administering the sacraments. A minister is no better, no more holy, no more powerful than any other Christian. He or she simply has the gifts and graces needed in that community at that time. Words like "enabler" and "facilitator" describe the minister.

This view of ministry reminds the church that all Christians are called to ministry. Ordination occurs only when there is a need in the church for the services of an ordained person "to preach and teach the gospel, to administer the sacraments and rites of the church, and to exercise pastoral care and leadership."[15] Logically, this understanding of ministry always relates ordained status to function. Authorization is only valid in a specific place, and it is only appropriate for as long as it is needed.

The faculty at Eden Theological Seminary describes this functional view of ordination by pointing out that the authority for ordination is operative only in relationship to specific tasks and responsibilities within the life of the community of faith. "The function of ordained ministry is for the formation, enhancement, discipline, empowerment, and ref-ormation of the Christian community in its life of worship and mis-sion."[16] This position rejects all "substantialist" definitions of ordination, which center on the nature of the person to be ordained rather than on the function of the office to which a person is being ordained.[17]

Liturgically, an empowerment view of ministry approaches the ordi-nation service as a covenant service between the individual and the gathered community. It does not ask for, need, or recognize wider authorization. It does not expect other clergy to be present, except to "extend the right hand of fellowship." When the people elect their pastor, offer prayers, and lay on hands, the person is ordained. In early Congregationalism the one who was being ordained preached at the ordination service. In an inaugural sermon he (they were all men) affirmed and accepted the call to that congregation. When and if the relationship between a particular congregation and a pastor came to an end, the process began again. The pastor could not "take" that ordina-tion to authorize service in another congregation.

One of the benefits of this view of ministry is that it reminds the people that they are not dependent upon ordained ministry in order to be a church. When two or three are gathered together the church exists. Jesus Christ is its head. This view of ministry moves away from sacerdotalism and hierarchy, and it keeps strong lines of accountability between clergy and laity. However, it also creates some problems.

Empowerment views of ministry focus upon the clergy as intellectual leaders, preaching and teaching for the upbuilding of the church. This can lead to less emphasis upon sacramental life and pastoral gifts. Because clergy hold membership in the congregation they serve, this can sometimes result in narrow parochialism. An empowerment understanding of ministry diminishes and even erases the idea that a church vocation demands any special calling from God. In the name of common discipleship, clergy are congregational "functionaries" who may fail to have any vision beyond organizational maintenance. Finally, it can be argued that prophetic witness sometimes weakens with a functional view of ordained ministry, because it is too risky to offend those who create and sustain one's job.

All of the problems mentioned thus far occur when a congregation chooses to empower one person for ministry. There are also problems that develop when an individual feels a call to ministry, is obviously gifted, but for various reasons the church chooses not to ordain that person. Sometimes the church community does not believe that there is an ecclesiastical need for ordained authority. Sometimes the church decides not to entrust its authority to that particular person.

EMBODIMENT

In those regions of the United Church of Christ rooted in the European traditions of state churches and strong pastoral leadership, there is an *embodiment* view of ministry. Indeed, this more "substantialist" view of ministry has largely prevailed in the history of the Christian Church and it continues to be the normative view in ecumenical discussions on the nature of ministry.[18]

This view of ministry begins with the recognition that throughout the history of the world there have been people in every community who have religious or spiritual gifts. Anthropologists study this phenomenon; they document the work of the shaman, the priest, the medicine woman, or others who represent and are in touch with the "holy," or the "numinous." Although such religious leadership is difficult to define, in all cultures there are ways in which people "know" that some persons have a "presence" that marks them for ministry.

In its most extreme form the previously described empowerment view of ministry denies this reality. It insists that there is radical equality in Christ Jesus and equal potential for authorized ministry in every Christian. When the community sets apart some persons as clergy, they are not considered to be "holier" or more in touch with God than anyone else. Yet often one "empowered" by the community rises to the challenge. Stories abound of unlikely persons who have been elected to leadership and rendered remarkable service.

The embodiment view of ministry does not reject this possibility, but it does acknowledge that some persons already possess gifts for ministry. The primary task of the church is not to "empower," but rather to discover and release what already exists. Within the United Church of Christ this view of ministry is strongest within those congregations historically linked to our German Reformed roots. Like the empowerment view, the embodiment view of ministry has its dangers and benefits.

Basically, an embodiment view of ministry insists that there is a unique quality to Christian ministry which is more than professional competence or entrusted faithfulness. Clergy are in touch with mystery. Clergy have a special relationship and responsibility to God.

Luther's influence is significant here. He wrote that "to rule souls through the Word of God . . . is the highest office in the church."[19] For centuries, people have considered ministry a "higher profession."

The German word *Pastorenkirchen* points toward an embodiment understanding of ministry. It means that where the pastor is, there is the church. It insists that ordained clergy are necessary for the church to be fully constituted through Word and sacrament.

Probably the strongest example of the embodiment view of ministry in UCC history found expression in Mercersburg theology, a "high church" movement in the nineteenth-century German Reformed Church. The 1866 Mercersburg ordination service states, "The office is of divine origin, and of truly supernatural character and force." Ministers represent God's authority and function as "ambassadors" of God's grace. Furthermore, the ordained "are charged also with the government of the Church, and with the proper use of its discipline, in the way both of censure and absolution."[20] John Nevin argued that ministry comes from God to the church, "downwards and not upwards, from the few to the many and not from the many to the few." Ordination is the "veritable channel" of institutional apostolic succession through which "is transmitted mystically, from age to age, the supernatural authority in which this succession consists."[21]

This view of ministry upholds a strong sacramental and priestly role for the clergy. Education is advised to prevent "dumb reading" of the liturgy, but not necessarily for preaching. Ecclesiastical authority is not located in the gathered congregation, but vested in the ministry of teaching and ruling elders. These clergy and lay leaders represent the best interests of the congregation and govern the church through "consistories" or representative "councils."

Liturgically, from an embodiment perspective, the ordination service is most fittingly held in the home church of the person being ordained. It is more than a covenant service with the congregation where the person will eventually serve. At the ordination the local family of faith, which has produced and nurtured the gifted leader, hosts the service, but the leadership of that congregation is not in charge. Rather, the clergy in the area, authorized by regional bodies of laity and clergy, lay hands upon the candidate to "pass on" the authority entrusted to them and to honor God's call for that particular life. Ordination understood this way is timeless, global, and indelible. Clergy are ordained to the whole church of Jesus Christ and not simply to one particular congregation. For this reason, in the Evangelical and Reformed Church clergy belonged to the synod, never to a local church. It is argued that because one is ordained to ministry within the universal church in all times and places, an embodiment understanding of ministry allows greater freedom for prophetic witness, unencumbered by the prejudices of local congregations.

The dangers in the embodiment view of ministry are obvious. Such a lofty view of ministry creates a great gap between clergy and laity and can limit lay leadership. It creates dependencies and leads to clergy overload. It feeds professional elitism and, if it loses contact with its sacramental source, it degenerates into idolatry. At the same time it is also an important way to distinguish the church from other social organizations and to celebrate ministry as God's gift.

EXPRESSIONS OF
EMPOWERMENT AND EMBODIMENT IN
UNITED CHURCH OF CHRIST POLITY

With the recent publication of the new *Manual on Ministry*, the United Church of Christ has become more self-conscious about its procedures and its justification for authorized ministry.[22] Building upon 1983–84 constitutional amendments, the *Manual* exhibits more directly some of the ongoing inconsistencies and tensions in UCC theology and practice around the authorization of ministry. Critics of the *Manual* point out that there are no faith qualifications for ministry in the United Church of Christ. Furthermore, the stipulation that there will be periodic and special reviews of clergy raises some question about the autonomy of the congregation protected in other parts of the constitution. Finally, there is concern that the conduct of "disciplinary hearings" could lead to clergy trials subject to great abuse and error.[23]

Empowerment and embodiment understandings of ministry continue to shape all authorized ministry in the United Church of Christ. Constitutional provisions, implementation procedures suggested by the Office for Church Life and Leadership, and ambiguous attitudes among clergy and lay people stand as evidence. This creative tension in UCC polity is expressed in the following ways:

- Ordination in the United Church of Christ is for life, an unrepeatable act similar to baptism, yet it is possible to lose ministerial standing and cease to be a minister in the UCC.
- Ordained ministers in the UCC are members of local congregations, but hold ministerial standing in the association.
- Ordained ministers in the UCC are usually ordained in their "home" church and installed in the church where they will serve.
- Ordained ministers in the UCC must be educated at an accredited seminary and "good preaching" is the single most important quality considered by committees seeking pastors; yet normally it is impossible to be ordained without a call "recognized by the Association" which necessitates opportunities to "administer the sacraments and rites of the church."
- Ordained ministers in the UCC like to think of themselves as enablers and facilitators, no better than committed laity in the churches, yet clergy tax benefits, congregational expectations, and peer pressure assume that ordained persons have special privileges and burdens.

The United Church of Christ refuses to embrace a single unified justification for authorized ministry. Empowerment and embodiment thinking are both necessary to describe what is going on when the church sets apart one of its members to ordained ministry by prayer and laying on of hands.

On the one hand, the UCC holds to a functional view of ministry. Yet within the church "functional" can have two important meanings. First, it refers to particular tasks carried out by the clergy. But second, to speak of a functional ministry is also to recognize that ministry is a function of the gospel, that is, having no independent status, but only an agent of its source.[24]

On the other hand, the UCC also recognizes the representational character of ordained ministry. Within the church "representational" can have two meanings. The sacramental leadership of clergy has a representational responsibility to stand before the church on behalf of that event remembered and reenacted which makes the church the church. At the same time the clergy always stand for the church and within the church, representing the people.[25]

When the United Church of Christ authorizes persons to become ordained ministers for the church, empowerment and embodiment thinking are evident. The church is lifting up someone who is quite ordinary to serve the community. The church is also recognizing someone who is extraordinary to serve God's purposes. Both things need to happen. Within the church of Jesus Christ Christians authorize ministry to sustain the church in the world, and to serve the world through the church. The history and polity of the United Church of Christ provide unique resources for the task.

NOTES

1. *The Constitution and Bylaws of the United Church of Christ,* 1984 ed. (New York: Executive Council of the United Church of Christ).

2. "The Confession of Augsburg," in *Documents of the Christian Church,* Henry Bettenson, ed. (New York and London: Oxford University Press, 1943), 298.

3. John Calvin, *The Institutes of the Christian Religion* (Philadelphia: Westminster Press, 1960), IV.1.10.

4. Quoted by Wilhelm Pauck, "The Ministry in the Time of the Continental Reformation," in *The Ministry in Historical Perspective,* H. Richard Niebuhr and Daniel D. Williams, eds. (New York: Harper & Row, 1983), 138–39.

5. Calvin, *Institutes,* IV.3.16.

6. Summarized in Pauck, "Ministry in the Time of the Continental Reformation," 143.

7. Zacharias Ursinus, *The Commentary of Zacharias Ursinus on the Heidelberg Catechism,* trans. F. W. Willard (1852; reprint, Grand Rapids: Wm. B. Eerdmans, 1956), 571.

8. Ibid., 572.

9. *Evangelical Catechism* (St. Louis: Eden Publishing House, 1957), question 92.

10. "Cambridge Platform," in *The Creeds and Platforms of Congregationalism,* Williston Walker, ed. (Philadelphia and Boston: Pilgrim Press, 1960), II:6.

11. Ibid., VI:5.

12. Ibid., IX.

13. Quoted in D. T. Stokes and William T. Scott, *A History of the Christian Church in the South* (Elon College, N.C.: Elon College, 1973), 39.

14. An earlier treatment of this typology appears in Barbara Brown Zikmund, "Minister and Ministry in a Covenant System," *New Conversations* 4 (Fall 1979):23–28.

15. *UCC Constitution,* para. 20.

16. Walter A. Brueggemann et al., *A Perspective on Ordination* (St. Louis: Eden Theological Seminary, 1983), 7.

17. Ibid., 8.

18. Ibid.

19. Quoted in Roger Hazelton, "Ministry and Sacraments in the United Church of Christ," *Encounter* 41 (Winter 1989):98.

20. *An Order of Worship for the Reformed Church* (Philadelphia: Reformed Church Publication Board, 1869), 215–16, quoted in Charles Hambrick-Stowe,

"The Nature of the Ministry: The United Church of Christ and *Baptism, Eucharist and Ministry,*" *Prism* (Fall 1985): 26–44.

21. James H. Nichols, ed., *The Mercersburg Theology* (New York and London: Oxford University Press, 1966), 359–61.

22. *United Church of Christ Manual on Ministry* (New York: Office for Church Life and Leadership, 1986).

23. James N. McCutcheon, "Pastor's Response to New Ministry Document," *The Witness* 7 (December 1986):1, 3.

24. Brueggemann et al., *Perspective,* 7.

25. Hazelton, "Ministry and Sacraments," 101.

9

WORSHIP AND THE
ECUMENICAL CONTEXT

DANIEL L. JOHNSON / CHARLES HAMBRICK-STOWE

The theological imperatives of the 1980s have had a profound impact on our church's worship. While liturgical uniformity has never been either a reality or a goal, the movements and concerns represented in this volume have swept across the spectrum of our worship life. Indeed, the *Book of Worship* (1986) is a litmus that reveals the influence of feminist, liberation, ecumenical, and liturgical renewal movements.

ECUMENISM IN PLURALISM

The denominations that united in 1957 carried various worship traditions into the United Church of Christ. The terms of the merger honored and protected these histories, with no suggestion that one should predominate or that liturgical uniformity should be sought.[1] We differ markedly, for example, from the new Evangelical Lutheran Church in America, in which a common book of worship helped pave the way for the organic union in 1988 of several Lutheran denominations. Because of the pluralistic character of the United Church of Christ, uniformity would not have been an achievable goal in any case. One could not imagine much common ground between the plain spontaneity of worship in the Christian Connection and the high-church aspirations of Mercersburg theology and liturgy. Similarly, the elevated central pulpit of the Congregational meetinghouse embodies a theology at odds with the sacramental centrality of many congregations of the Evangelical and Reformed Church. Nor should differences within these congregations be minimized. A young teacher raised in the Evangelical Synod of North America in Illinois who moved to the Baltimore area in the early 1950s was astonished at the "catholic" liturgy in the German Reformed-background congregation she joined. The United Church of

90

Christ would have been impossible without its explicit provision for the preservation of these many traditions.

In the formal ecumenical dialogues presently taking place, it is often difficult for other denominations to comprehend how the United Church of Christ can maintain such diversity in worship and theology and yet hold together. The answer is rooted in the fact that worship in the United Church of Christ can only be understood within this very ecumenical context. Experience with other united churches—in Canada, Japan, North India, and South India—and with the National and World Councils of Churches led church leaders to envision a new, inclusive denominational life. The ecumenical movement sparked interest in and deepened respect for other, often older, ways of worshiping God. As Louis H. Gunnemann states in *The Shaping of the United Church of Christ*,[2] it was nothing other than the ideal of Christian unity that enabled the churches to persevere with negotiations until the new church came to birth. God *requires* that those who follow Christ be one, and that there be room for all within the body of Christ.

It is deeply significant that the first unitive act of the new denomination, even before the adoption of the Constitution (1960), was the drafting and acceptance of the Statement of Faith (1959). This statement was never meant for sectarian identification, but was intended to be a modern affirmation of the biblical faith composed by a united and uniting church on behalf of the whole church of Jesus Christ. Further, the Statement of Faith was meant not for the judicial use of determining orthodoxy but for use in worship—to celebrate life in Christ and the mission of the church. This is evident above all in the statement's poetic language and style. Gunnemann asserts that while the Uniting General Synod had formalized the merger in 1957, the "sealing" of the union "occurred in the unifying experience of a liturgical act—the recitation of the Statement of Faith the synod had voted to approve." The synod's "most dramatic moment" came after the delegates approved the statement by unanimous vote, as they broke into a spontaneous singing of the Doxology.[3] The Statement of Faith offered to congregations a testimony that could both help establish denominational identity and express in new form the faith each predecessor body treasured. Predictably, its use was met with suspicion in some congregations which had long resisted creedal formulations. But continued insistence that the statement was a testimony (that is, for worship), not a test of faith, together with the contemporary resonance of its wording, gradually won its acceptance and widespread use. Unfortunately for the possibility of its widespread, enthusiastic use in the 1980s, inclusive language was not yet an issue when the Statement of Faith was composed. The two adaptations (one by Robert Moss, one in the form of a doxology[4]), while helpful, are less than poetically satisfactory.

The ecumenical movement has continued to influence the worship life of the United Church of Christ in the years since 1960. The Second Vatican Council opened the door to unprecedented Catholic-Protestant understanding and heralded dramatic liturgical reform in the Roman Catholic Church. On the surface it may have seemed that Catholics were simply becoming more "protestant," with free-standing altars, services in modern English, and a new emphasis on scripture and sermon. But deeper reflection showed that Catholics were engaged in a liturgical renewal movement that was not only contemporary but also authentically traditional. The United Church of Christ joined in this movement in a variety of ways. With the ecumenical transformation of theological education in Protestant and Catholic theological seminaries, students for the ministry experienced a multiplicity of worship styles during their training. And not long after the birth of the United Church of Christ, a sermon by a Presbyterian minister in an Episcopal pulpit led directly to the creation of the Consultation on Church Union (COCU), in which nine Protestant bodies continue a difficult pilgrimage toward visible unity.[5] In 1968 COCU published *An Order of Worship for the Proclamation of the Word of God and the Celebration of the Lord's Supper,* which enjoyed wider influence than its limited use in congregations would suggest. The World Council of Churches, after fifty years of negotiations within the Faith and Order Commission, published its milestone document *Baptism, Eucharist and Ministry (BEM)*[6] in 1982. Consensus on the theology of the sacraments and the ministry reflect common understandings of the ways and means of worship among the churches. The Eucharistic Rite of Lima [Peru], written by Max Thurian of the Taize Community in France, embodies many of these understandings.[7]

Some of the denominational fruits of this ecumenical context include the Presbyterian *Worshipbook* (1970), the new Episcopal *Book of Common Prayer* (1977), and the *Lutheran Book of Worship* (1978). In the 1980s these were joined by the United Methodist *Book of Services* (1984), our own *Book of Worship* (1986), and the Christian Church (Disciples of Christ) *Thoughtful Praise* (1987). The similarities among these books testify to the common influences of the ecumenical and liturgical renewal movements.

The history of worship materials in the UCC is ecumenical and eclectic. First, with the merger, Congregational Christian and Evangelical and Reformed denominational resources became common property. The long history of liturgical development in the Reformed Church in the United States and the Evangelical Synod of North America culminated in the excellent *Book of Worship* of 1947.[8] The Congregational

Pilgrim Hymnal in its 1912, 1931, and 1958 editions included orders of worship, service music, and prayers. The inclusion of much traditional service music, liturgies, and emphasis on the seasons of the church year demonstrates that a liturgical renewal movement influenced Congregationalism early in this century. The *Book of Worship for Free Churches* (1948) was a valuable resource similar in format to the Evangelical and Reformed *Book of Worship.*

Once the United Church of Christ was formed, *The Lord's Day Service* (1964) was published as a suggested format for congregational worship. Effectively combining the two major denominational traditions, it boldly set forth the new idea, gained from the ecumenical liturgical renewal movement, that weekly celebration of Holy Communion along with the preaching of the Word should be the norm. The complete set of *Services of the Church* (1966) was published by the United Church Board for Homeland Ministries in pamphlets held together in a ring binder. While the materials enjoyed widespread use, the format also suggested the evolutionary nature of worship in the new denomination. Other worship aids, such as *Worship: Inclusive Language Resources* (1977), were published by the Office for Church Life and Leadership.

Twenty years after the 1957 union, the Eleventh General Synod (1977) called for a decisive step in denominational consolidation and ecumenical exploration—the development of a book of worship for the United Church of Christ. Test documents were made available in 1982 for congregational use, study, and critical response. Receptivity among pastors was indicated by the fact that the supply was soon exhausted and worship leaders had to beg, borrow, or steal copies. The Office for Church Life and Leadership, the instrumentality charged with the responsibility for development of the book, made many improvements in the services based on feedback—including ecumenical responses before publishing the *Book of Worship* in 1986. All these materials have had to win acceptance on their merit, for no ecclesiastical structure exists in the United Church of Christ for mandating their use in the congregations.

Similarities between the United Church of Christ *Book of Worship* and those of other denominations begin, on the surface, with the use of newly designed symbols at the head of each section which are strikingly akin to those in the *Lutheran Book of Worship.* Although there are nowhere near as many rubrics for singing or chanting as in the Lutheran services, the new United Church of Christ services present more opportunities for musical participation than in its predecessor denominations. And, while the *Manual on the Liturgy* that accompanies the *Lutheran Book of Worship* contains meticulous drawings instructing priests where to stand, how to move, and when to make various liturgical gestures, the *Book of*

Worship states in a general way that "the use of gesture and movement" is an ancient element of worship that we should recover.[9] In keeping with our less regimented style, the *Book of Worship* describes the processional as a "dance" and recommends liturgical dance and other efforts at creative movement.

Special services previously unknown in our traditions have been acquired from ecumenical partners. Among these are the Order for Foot Washing, adapted from Church of the Brethren practice, and the Easter Vigil, based on services from the Eastern Orthodox and more liturgical Western traditions. Generally excellent brief introductions to all the services set them in their biblical, historical, and ecumenical context.[10] Other new services, such as the Order for Recognition of the End of a Marriage and the Order for Times of Passage: Farewell, have no precedent in traditional worship books, but are attempts to bring the gospel of penitence, grace, and abiding love to the contemporary world of transiency and change. Resources for Ascension Day, which the *Lutheran Book of Worship* rightly urges congregations to celebrate, are sadly lacking in our new book.[11]

Some new worship books, such as the *Lutheran Book of Worship* (1978), profess to take the issue of inclusive language seriously but they stop with language about human beings, usually (but not always) replacing "man" with "humankind" and addressing the congregation as "brothers and sisters." The *Book of Worship* is the first to address the deeper issue of God language. But perhaps even at this date only the United Church of Christ would dare to produce an official service book with gender-inclusive language for God. Indeed, the original 1977 mandate for the book was motivated largely by this issue. The introduction to the *Book of Worship* states:

> The Eleventh General Synod explicitly instructed that *Book of Worship* be characterized by language that is truly inclusive with respect to God and to human beings. Although the generic use of masculine terms may have been acceptable in the past, it excludes and offends many sensitive people of faith today. Further, the use of only masculine nouns and pronouns for God and of masculine generic terms for humankind has hidden the rich feminine imagery for God and God's people in scripture. The rediscovery of the complementarity of female and male metaphors in the Bible and the literature of the early church forbids Christians to settle for literary poverty in the midst of literary riches.[12]

In general in the *Book of Worship*, terms like "Creator" and "Holy One" replace "Father" and "Lord" respectively in reference to the first person of the Trinity, while "Savior" replaces "Lord" in reference to Jesus Christ. The most significant exceptions are the use of "Our Father" in the Lord's Prayer (designated "Prayer of Our Savior") and the traditional language in the Sacrament of Baptism and the Order for Confirmation. In these two services Jesus is professed as "Lord and Savior" and in Baptism the sacrament is administered "in the name of the Father, and of the Son, and of the Holy Spirit." To have substituted other language at these points would have separated the United Church of Christ from the very ecumenical movement which has in other ways so deeply informed our liturgical renewal. Much theological work remains to reconcile Trinitarian orthodoxy with the need to overcome male bias in the wording of ancient formulations.

The Office for Church Life and Leadership clearly feels that any controversy among members who take issue with such a thoroughgoing use of inclusive language is worth the struggle. Certainly conservative critics have a point in that the relational nature of the terms "Father" and "Son" are lost when "Creator" and "Savior" are substituted, to say nothing of the fact that Jesus himself used these words. The question of whether the persons of the Trinity can be named in innovative ways without essentially altering the apostolic confession is far from settled.[13]

But "Father" is only one name among many for God, and Christians are free to find many appropriate contemporary metaphors to express their faith. Who would maintain that God or Christ is imprisoned in the precise recitation of a classic formula? The United Church of Christ has chosen a leadership role among denominations by treating the language issue as one of ethics and social justice. It may be observed that in general the *Book of Worship* employs inclusive language that is biblically sound, poetically graceful, and spiritually compelling. Use of the new book over the years will no doubt melt some of the resistance, and familiarity will actually endear it to the constituency.

The *Book of Worship* follows the 1964 *Lord's Day Service*—and the Presbyterian, Episcopal, and Lutheran books of the 1970s—by insisting that the Service of Word and Sacrament was normative in the early church and for the Reformers and must be recovered today. The two Services of Word and Sacrament are put forth as the denomination's wish for weekly worship in the congregation. Yet a simpler Service of the Word is also offered, which may convey an impression that these alternative orders were included as an accommodation to congregations reluctant to change. What does it mean that, after more than twenty years of being told that a weekly service with both preaching and communion should be the norm, so few congregations have embraced the practice? The sixty-minute worship limit is probably one factor. Pastors are reluctant to reduce twenty-minute sermons every week, especially when biblical and theological illiteracy is a major problem among church members. The free-church tradition has always elevated the sermon as the time for edification and moral guidance. Moreover, there is no way to move through the Service of Word and Sacrament in an hour if we include a fully developed sermon, concerns of the church, prayers of the people, and anthems. Another factor slowing the movement to a weekly Service of Word and Sacrament may be the predominance of the Baptist and revivalist tradition in American culture today. While the Catholic tradition sees the Eucharist as the culmination of the service of worship, in much of American evangelicalism worship culminates after the sermon with a new or renewed decision for Christ, exemplified in baptism. Finally, there is the oft-heard argument that quarterly or monthly communion emphasizes its specialness, while too-frequent repetition breeds lethargy not liturgy. But those who participate in weekly (or even daily) communion testify that this is far from the case, that weekly gathering at the Table of Christ is the real center of the church and a much-needed nourishment of spirit and community.

Our partnership with the Disciples of Christ, a denomination in the baptistic and revivalist traditions that also practices every-Sunday communion may bring fresh insight into the debate. Meanwhile, there must be ways that congregations can move toward the ecumenical ideal of more frequent communion. For example, churches with quarterly communion could celebrate it monthly or the first Sunday of every season in the church year plus World Communion Sunday. Or the sacrament could be celebrated, for those wishing to attend, at a brief service before or after the hour of worship.

In the orders for the communion services themselves, the influence of other liturgies on the *Book of Worship* is unmistakable. Phrases such as "This is the joyful feast of the people of God," "The gifts of God for the people of God," and the proclamation of the mystery of faith ("Christ has died. Christ is risen. Christ will come again.") echo through many contemporary liturgies. Following the wisdom of *Baptism, Eucharist and Ministry*, the *anamnesis* (remembrance) of the sacrificial death of Jesus is expanded to include anticipation of the heavenly banquet with the risen Christ. The *epiklesis* (invocation of the Holy Spirit) takes place as prayers of thanksgiving for the Holy Spirit and also as an explicit invocation and prayer of consecration. Perhaps inspired by the *BEM* document, which calls the Eucharist "a constant challenge in the search for appropriate relationships in social, economic and political life,"[14] the Communion Prayer asks that by the Holy Spirit the "universal church . . . may be the champion of peace and justice in all the world."[15] The *Book of Worship* voices the social and political implications of Holy Communion more clearly and forcefully than any other denominational liturgy.

While other liturgies pray that "we and all who share in this bread and cup may be united in the fellowship of the Holy Spirit,"[16] the *Book of Worship* strongly emphasizes the communal as well as the personal nature of the sacrament. One prayer option boldly asks God by the Holy Spirit and "through this meal [to] make us the body of Christ."[17] Christ is truly present in the Eucharist according to the *Book of Worship*. The prayers of thanksgiving all rejoice in "the presence of Christ."[18] Mere memorialism is banished to the scrap heap of the history of rationalism. Thanks to the theological agreement stated in *Baptism, Eucharist and Ministry*, old controversies over the real presence are rendered obsolete.

A seminary dean recently commented that it has become difficult sometimes to distinguish one denomination from another on the basis of local church worship. Orders of worship, use of the *Common Lectionary*,[19] liturgical colors and vestments, and congregational participation all demonstrate remarkable convergence. Cooperation and convergence bring many blessings as we share traditions and celebrate fellowship.

The convergence is often not only verbal but visual. The Lutheran *Manual of the Liturgy*, in setting forth the alb as the standard garb for worship, states that this white robe "is becoming a kind of ecumenical vestment, worn by Lutherans, Episcopalians, Roman Catholics, Methodists, Presbyterians, and others."[20]

Among the "others" are many pastors in the United Church of Christ. What does it mean that such traditionally Catholic vestments are slowly replacing the academic gown in our churches? What is the rationale for symbolic clothing? In fact, the academic gown was first adopted by Protestant preachers during the Reformation not as a sign of ecclesiastical position but because it was the everyday street attire of those in the learned professions, such as lawyers and teachers. Now that suits and dresses have become ordinary clothing for such people, what are the implications of continued clerical use of clothing that sets clergy apart from the laity precisely at a time when increased attention is focused on the ministry of the laity? Surely, it is time for us to develop, ecumenically, a new understanding of vestments and their use.

Along with vestments, we may consider the use of the lectionary for which the *Book of Worship* argues forcefully in its introduction. The reasons for use of the lectionary are obvious, including ecumenical fellowship, the discipline of pastors to address a variety of texts, and strong emphasis on the seasonal liturgical cycle. Ecumenical commentaries on the *Common Lectionary* mean that pastors in many denominations may study the same material in their sermon preparations. There is also the danger, however, that pastoral creativity, responsiveness, and leadership in the local setting, and the rigors of individual disciplined scholarship may be diminished. While many pastors and churches enjoy the fruits of weekly use of the lectionary readings, the system remains for us one available approach among many. Uniformity has never been considered a blessing in the United Church of Christ, and unity based on outward conformity has usually been seen as oppressive.

These pictures of worship practices in the United Church of Christ illustrate part of the theological ferment current in the denomination and indeed throughout the whole church. Once-settled patterns and unquestioned habits are challenged by new urgencies and the movement toward Christian unity. Traditional variety among the colors of our rainbow, including the many "hidden histories" in our spectrum, continue to be present. Other denominations are often puzzled by a polity that thwarts centralized authority at every turn and yet somehow maintains denominational vitality. We live our way toward the Christianity of the future, sustained and renewed by worship and service in the name of our faithful Savior.

NOTES

1. See "Basis of Union of the Congregational Christian Churches and the Evangelical and Reformed Church with the Interpretations," in Louis H. Gunnemann, *The Shaping of the United Church of Christ* (New York: United Church Press, 1977), 207–25; and *The Constitution and Bylaws of the United Church of Christ,* IV. 15.

2. Gunnemann, *Shaping of the United Church of Christ.*

3. Gunnemann, *Shaping of the United Church of Christ,* 68–70.

4. See *Book of Worship* (New York: United Church of Christ Office for Church Life and Leadership, 1986).

5. Eugene Carson Blake preached his pathbreaking sermon at Grace Cathedral (Episcopal), San Francisco, 1960. The nine participating denominations are: African Methodist Episcopal Church, African Methodist Episcopal Zion Church, Christian Church (Disciples of Christ), Christian Methodist Episcopal Church, Episcopal Church, International Council of Community Churches, Presbyterian Church (U.S.A.), United Church of Christ, and United Methodist Church.

6. Faith and Order Commission, World Council of Churches, *Baptism, Eucharist and Ministry,* Faith and Order Paper No. 111 (Geneva: World Council of Churches, 1982).

7. See Max Thurian and Geoffrey Wainwright, eds., *Baptism and Eucharist: Ecumenical Convergence in Celebration* (Grand Rapids: Wm. B. Eerdmans, 1983), 241–55.

8. See J. M. Maxwell, *Worship and Reformed Theology* (Pittsburgh: Pickwick Press, 1937).

9. *Book of Worship* (New York: United Church of Christ Office for Church Life and Leadership, 1986), 17.

10. Unfortunately, the introduction to foot washing in our opinion misses the mark by interpreting Jesus' symbolic act of humble service in the Upper Room (John 13:1–17) in the light of domestic hospitality customs. Jesus supposedly washed feet during the meal because no one had done so upon arrival. This

view ignores the Passover setting of the Last Supper. What Jesus actually did was to take the basin of water and towel during one of the ritual hand washings, drop to his knees, and instead of washing his own hands washed Peter's feet. Just as Jesus transformed the Passover bread and wine into the elements of a new sacrament, so he changed the hand washing into an example of service to others. Reference here to the Jewish Passover seder would have been helpful.

11. See the essays on the *Book of Worship,* in *Prism* 3 (Spring 1988).

12. *Book of Worship,* 8.

13. See Chalmers Coe, "The Services of Word and Sacrament: A Theological Commentary"; and esp. Paul S. Minear, "The Bible and the *Book of Worship,*" *Prism* 3 (Spring 1988): 32–39, 48–55.

14. *Baptism, Eucharist and Ministry,* 14.

15. *Book of Worship,* 48.

16. *Lutheran Book of Worship,* Ministers Desk Edition (Minneapolis: Augsburg; and Philadelphia: Lutheran Church in America Board of Publication, 1978), 223.

17. *Book of Worship,* 71.

18. Ibid., 52, 74.

19. Consultation on Common Texts, *Common Lectionary: The Lectionary Proposed by the Consultation on Common Texts,* © 1983, James M. Schellman. Available from Church Hymnal Corporation, 800 Second Avenue, New York, NY 10017. A lectionary is a table, following the church year, of prescribed readings for each Sunday.

20. Philip H. Pfatteicher and Carolos R. Messerli, *Manual on the Liturgy* (Minneapolis: Augsburg, 1979), 159.

Part 3

THEOLOGICAL ISSUES
AND MOVEMENTS

10

PROCESS THEOLOGY IN
THE UNITED CHURCH OF CHRIST

DAVID M. STOWE

Our theology—our thinking about God, Christ, the church, and our human situation—is bound to be shaped by the questions we feel life is hurling at us. The concerns and preoccupations of feminists, social activists, ethnic groups, and others reflect significant and even burning questions. They shape influential theological perspectives—feminist theology, political theology, black theology, and the like. But who in the world is concerned about process theology?

A WORLD IN PROCESS

Whether or not we *feel* a concern about "process" the fact is that the world within which we live and upon which we depend *is* a process. The most meaningful part of our universe is the life within it, and that life consists of processes of fantastic beauty and complexity These marvelous change processes most visibly distinguish cells from dust particles, crabs from stones, living persons from wax figures. But the dramatic processes of life are set within a dynamic universe which is through and through pervaded by evolution, development, growth, and decay—all processes, slow or fast, marked by differing degrees of order. Even a seemingly inert stone boulder reflects change through geological time, just as does the mountain range from which it originally came. At the most fundamental levels studied by physical science the realities are constantly changing fields of force, patterns of energy, which act and interact in infinitely complicated relationships. In short, we live within a beautiful, infinitely complex and mysterious change process; and we ourselves *are* a mysterious and complex change process.

Christians, then, may be interested in process theology because they are determined to relate the God of their faith to the real world in which they live and of which they are an integral part. A world so pervaded by processes of change and development testifies to the nature of its Creator, and to God's ways with humankind.

THE LIVING GOD

Concerns for the universal secular experience of a world and a self in process are linked with a concern to take very seriously the Bible as the resource and standard for our Christian faith. The most fundamental affirmation of the Bible is that God is a "living God." Any concordance will show how often that very expression is used. The Bible characteristically refers to God as acting, working, loving, judging, feeling, willing, purposing, even suffering[1]—all the earmarks of life as we experience it. Surprisingly, many theologians have not taken this biblical testimony very seriously. They have been more interested in proclaiming something absolutely fixed and unchanging at the heart of the universe than in the live-liness of God. At the center of some classical theologies one discovers a God who is unmoving, eternally unchanging both in being and in decree—a fixed stillness, like death itself.

A hunger for permanence amid change, for stillness amid confusion, for something utterly solid and reliable within all the swirling energies and anxieties that dominate our experience, is entirely understandable. If God is not "our dwelling place in all generations" (Psalm 90), then life lacks foundations and religious faith is a poor resource. Later on we must deal with this need and the reality to which it points. But a *biblical* theology cannot begin there, because both the character of the creation and the testimony of scripture stress that God is a living God. A sensitive human being is more "lively," caught up in a more complex flow of changing perceptions, thoughts, feelings, and actions than a stone or even a bird. The Bible testifies to a God who is "lively" like ourselves (for it tells us that we are made in God's image; Gen. 1:27), but in a much higher degree. God creates and responds to the *whole* universe in all its parts, loving, judging, listening, and speaking to every person (and taking note of every sparrow; Matt. 10:29). God participates in the whole cosmic process, everlastingly. All that transpires in a dynamic universe is included in the experience of the living God.

Perhaps, then, a better name than "process theology" would be "theology of life." Or even "biblical theology," because it takes the fundamental testimony of the Bible with radical seriousness. That testimony affirms a living God and God's ever-developing relations with the evolving world. Especially is God involved with human beings in their pilgrimage through their individual life stories and through the history of humanity as it emerges within the evolution of planet earth and of the cosmos itself.

A CONCERN FOR RELATIONSHIPS

The living God of process theology is no remote Ruler in the heavens but a creative Spirit intimately involved with every last part of the creation. We have emphasized an obvious meeting of "process" in terms of change and development through time—a dynamic view of the world and of the God who continually creates it. But a no less fundamental meaning is *relatedness,* a sense of the interconnectedness of all things. The twentieth-century philosopher Alfred North Whitehead provided much of the philosophical background for process theology. The title of his best-known book was *Process and Reality.* But his own favorite term for his comprehensive world view was "philosophy of organism." He thought the universe to be so intimately interactive in all its parts as to have the same kind of comprehensive internal relationships as the entities we normally call organisms.

Hence a process theology of the living God is deeply concerned about relationships—God's relationships with the world and relationships within God's world, especially relationships of human beings with each other and with the natural world around them. The Bible speaks of that web of relationships in many ways, beginning with an affirmation of the universal being-present of God. " 'Am I a God at hand, says the LORD, and not a God afar off? Can a man hide himself in secret places so that I cannot see him? says the LORD? Do I not fill heaven and earth?' " (Jer. 23:23–34). This divine omnipresence becomes a personal experience for the psalmist:

> Where shall I go from your Spirit?
> Or where shall I flee from your presence?
> If I ascend to heaven, you are there!
> If I make my bed in Sheol, you are there.
> If I take the wings of the morning
> and dwell in the uttermost parts of the sea,
> even there your hand shall lead me,
> and your right hand shall hold me.
>
> Ps. 139:7–9

The New Testament echoes and reinforces this theology of the living presence of God who is the binding, relating power in all things for in God "we live and move and have our being" (Acts 17:28). This is the great theme of the great passages that interpret Christ as the primary mode of God's activity in the world: "For in Christ all things were created, in heaven and on earth, visible and invisible. . . . Christ is before all things, the one in whom all things hold together" (Col. 1:16–17). According to John's Gospel the deepest form of this divine relatedness is expressed in those deeply committed to the divine will and purpose, in Christ and in Christ's faithful disciples: "I am the vine, you are the branches: He that abides in me, and I in him, he it is that bears much fruit, for apart from me you can do nothing" (John 15:5). "You, Father, are in me, and I in you, that they also may be in us" (John 17:21).

The characteristic and central Christian teaching of God as Trinity may perhaps be best understood within this relational emphasis of process theology. Not only is God actually involved in an infinity of relationships, but God's own being is intrinsically relational. There is no single solitary God. The symbolism of Father/Son/Spirit is a way in which the church has pointed historically to the profound truth that God not only acts characteristically through social process but that God's own being is eternally and essentially relational.

THEOLOGY, SCIENCE, AND PHILOSOPHY

The conviction that God's life is all-embracing is taken so seriously by process theology that it makes an effort to understand *how* all things are related to God. The Middle Ages had magnificently comprehensive theologies interpreting God's relation to the world and the ways of the world's working within the divine sovereignty. These were framed in terms of the then-scientific world view, primarily Aristotle's philosophy. But in recent centuries such matters have received little attention in Protestant theology. The Reformers virtually set aside questions about the relation of faith to the attempts made in science and philosophy to understand the world. This was partly in reaction to what they felt was an overly rationalistic Catholic theology. Great philosophers of nature like Newton, Descartes, and Leibniz had important theological interests, but their thought made little explicit contact with the working theologies of the churches and the piety of most Christians. Yet they were not without influence. Their views affected profoundly the assumptions about reality by which most people of the West, including Christians, came to live from the seventeenth century on. These assumptions were in some ways seriously in contrast with the assumptions proper to an authentically biblical theology.

Now, in the twentieth century, it has been dawning on Christians that a theology that does not take the world with utmost seriousness and attempt to understand how God is related to it and active within it is no *theo*-logy at all. *Theos* means God, and to speak of God only in prescientific terms and uncriticized conceptions is not to speak honorably of the Maker of Heaven and Earth and the directing and living Spirit of the cosmos. Drawing upon such scientists and philosophers as Whitehead, William James, Teilhard de Chardin, Charles Birch, and Charles Hartshorne, process theology attempts to correlate the insights of biblical faith and religious experience with the best contemporary understandings of the cosmic process.

AN ECOLOGICAL THEOLOGY

All this means that process theology takes the natural world very seriously. This concern for the creation, the natural process within which we live and upon which we depend, is in contrast with much traditional theology, which often seems bounded by the human story as if that were the only story in God's world. Even more limiting is the frequent focus upon those few bits of the human story that tell of ancient Israel and the peoples of the West. A different kind of narrow fence is placed around the Providence of God by some influential current theologies that focus sharply on a limited range of political or "liberation" events and issues within an exclusively human history.

Sometimes an effort to relate theology to the process and problems of the natural world, on this planet and beyond, is alleged to be in conflict with a proper Christian concentration on human life and human problems. It is true that Jesus said, "You are of more value than many sparrows" (Matt. 10:31). But we have been learning from both the insights of science and looming threats to our environment that our fate and the fate of sparrows and fish and plants have been bound up together by the Creator of all. How can we understand or deal constructively with human problems and concerns without seeing them in the context of the natural order upon which the quality of all human life depends?

China's revolution provides a striking theological lesson. Mao Tse-tung encouraged population growth, saying that "labor creates the world," not God. The more labor power China could mobilize, Mao proclaimed, in a society with socialized ownership of the means of production and an equal sharing of wealth, the more prosperous it would be. The result was a huge population explosion that has now forced China into the most drastic program of birth limitation the world has ever seen: One child per family! Idolatrous faith in a communist social system led to disaster when it ignored the realities of the natural order within God's creation. Christian faith cannot rest in anything less than a holistic vision of God's purposive presence in nature as well as in human culture and a recognition of God's claim for reverent and thoughtful stewardship of the creation.

Walter Rauschenbusch, a founder of the social gospel movement and a lifelong crusader for social justice, once put in perspective the interrelationship of the individual, the society, the cosmos, and God:

> The wind that blows, the birds that sing, and the crimson flood of life and nourishment that throbs in our pulses are all part of the great cosmic life. . . . In the ocean of the universe floats the little bark of human personality, part of it all and yet an entity in itself. It knows, it wills; it is conscious of itself over against the world, and even over against God. More and more clearly the thoughts of God are mirrored by the reflecting intellect of man, illuminated by God's own mind, the light of God in the soul of man.[2]

Process theology would complete that beautiful affirmation by adding its obverse, as Rauschenbusch has already implied: The life of humankind in the soul of God. God is the larger and more embracing reality for in God "we live and move and have our being" (Acts 17:28). Our lives, together with the whole creation, are realities within the everlasting life of God. This is not "pantheism," meaning that "God is all," or "All is God," as some religious perspectives affirm. Rather it is "pan-en-theism"—"All is *in* God," an expression particularly developed by Charles Hartshorne.

THE SPIRIT AND THE
FORMS OF LOVE

Those words are the title of a major book by Daniel Day Williams, an influential United Church of Christ process theologian. The language of love is a natural and appropriate way to translate theologically many of the insights of process philosophy. Whitehead spent the last quarter-century of his life developing foundations for process thought as a professor at Harvard University. As we have seen, he preferred to speak not of "process philosophy" but "philosophy of organism," stressing the living interconnectedness and reciprocal relationships among all realities. Charles Hartshorne, perhaps Whitehead's most influential follower, spoke of his deepest "conviction that a magnificent intellectual content, far surpassing that of such systems as Thomism, Spinozism, German idealism, positivism (old and new), is implicit in the religious faith briefly expressed in the three words, God is love."[3] Hartshorne is quoting, of course, from the New Testament (1 John 4:16). The reconciling, uniting, creative power we know as love is the fundamental moving force and determiner of destiny in the universe. As we experience and express that love in our own lives we experience communion with God, who is a loving, creating, relationship-making power everywhere, but is most fully known by loving human beings.

BUT WHAT ABOUT EVIL?

If God is all-loving, how do we understand the bitter condemnations and threats of divine judgment and punishment we find so liberally scattered throughout the Bible? And if God is Creator of the world, where do all the conflict, pain, and sadness of the world come from, if not from God?

These are questions with which Christians (and others) have always wrestled and for which no theology can provide easy and agreed answers. So far as judgment and punishment are concerned, the critical texts for process theology are those that emphasize first of all that God is not primarily interested in keeping a moral balance sheet and punishing evil. Rather, God's primary concern is for salvation, the redemption and fulfillment of every human life and all creation as far as possible. "If anyone hears my sayings and does not keep them, I do not judge that person; for I did not come to judge the world but to save the world," says Jesus in John's Gospel (12:47). Many of Jesus' most distinctive and important teachings and actions underline and apply this promise. Think of the prodigal son, the lost sheep and coin, the dealings with "sinful" women and tax collectors. On the cross Jesus said it with final authority, to be echoed within the year by the first disciple to follow him in a martyr's death: "Father, forgive them, for they know not what they do" (Luke 23:34; cf. Acts 7:60).

Second, judgment is not so much something imposed from above, a punishment meted out by an external authority, as it is an intrinsic penalty that evil brings in and of itself. "This is the judgment, that the light has come into the world, and men loved darkness rather than light, because their deeds were evil" (John 3:19). "He who rejects me and does not receive my sayings has a judge; the word that I have spoken will be his judge on the last day" (John 12:48). Or in a slightly different key, "Do not be deceived; God is not mocked, for whatever one sows, one will also reap. For whoever sows to their own flesh will from the flesh reap corruption; but whoever sows to the Spirit will from the Spirit reap eternal life" (Gal. 6:7–8). The process of the universe is intrinsically a moral process, because it is continually created and guided by a God who is love. There is judgment in it, but the judgment is by love and for love, and self-condemnation is a significant part of whatever condemnation there is. Wrongdoing is essentially self-punishing; and if that is not apparent in this life it becomes more evident in the perspective of that eternal life of which biblical faith speaks.

But beyond the question of human moral evil is the enveloping question of cosmic evil, the immense pervasiveness of predation, parasitism, pain, and death in the world. If we begin with the conviction that Christ is the clue to God's nature and intention we are impelled to believe that no matter what appearances are, "God is light and in God is no darkness at all" (1 John 1:5). We cannot deal with the reality of evil by ascribing it to God. We must do so by thinking clearly about the meaning of God's power, and of the relation of God's power to freedom in the creation.

Christians have often addressed their prayers to "Almighty God," and some theologies have taken that quite literally to mean that God is "omni-potent"—that God is all-powerful. But what "*all*-powerful" means is a complicated and difficult question. Taken literally, it seems to mean that God has a monopoly of all influence on the course of events. Literally everything that happens is the direct result of a specific and intentional exercise of that power. God is entirely responsible for all that happens, both evil and good. Such an all-powerful God means an all-powerless human being, and a lack of real spontaneity anywhere in the universe. But very few Christians really believe that, and almost none act on that basis. Christians, like nearly all healthy human beings, assume that they are themselves responsible, at least in large measure, for their decisions and actions. They therefore must assume that they have freedom to respond or not to God's leading while engaged in the unending series of decisions that make up their lives. In practical fact, a literally "all-mighty God" in the sense of a deity who totally monopolizes all power is unbelievable.

Sometimes the idea of divine omnipotence is modified to mean that although there are other centers of genuine power in the universe—such as human beings with free will, or physical entities exemplifying the laws of gravitation—yet God can and does do anything and everything God may choose to do, regardless of the decisions of other living beings or the momentum of inanimate objects acting in accord with the natural laws that are the habits of the universe. This seems to protect the greatness of God while allowing some space for the exercise of freedom and spontaneity in the created world. God is not literally "all-mighty"—there are other places where power is exercised, but only with the stipulation, so to speak, that God does not choose to override that exercise. Most Christians probably have more or less consciously understood in this way the "almightiness" of the God they worship—a deity who can do whatever God will but who allows considerable freedom to the creation in its functioning. God is then no longer fully and directly responsible for all evil as well as all good, as in the monopoly view of omnipotence. God is responsible for evil only by refusing to override it by exercising the divine capacity to do anything whatsoever.

However, process theology would prefer to deal with these crucial questions by starting from quite another point than "Almighty God," even while recognizing the importance of that expression in the devotional and liturgical life of Christians.

THE NATURE OF GOD'S POWER

From our undeniable experience of being responsible and exercising at least some freedom, and also from the biblical affirmations that God is love, that "God is light and in God is no darkness at all' (1 John 1:5), process theology develops its understanding of the meaning of divine power. The central clue is Jesus Christ, in whom all our thinking about God and the world and ourselves ought to center. Jesus' life and death exhibit not only the nature of God, but also the major mode of God's acting. Jesus said, "And I, when I am lifted up from the earth, will draw all people to myself" (John 12:32). The persuasive power of Jesus' life and speech and person drew people to him in Galilee and Samaria and Jerusalem. These together with the supreme power of Jesus' death and the evidences of his resurrection continue to draw into discipleship hundreds of millions of persons all over the world. Christians affirm that Jesus Christ is God incarnate—God made visible, tangible, a living human embodiment of who God is and how God acts. From Jesus we learn that the supreme power God does indeed exert within every part of the cosmic process is not a coercive omnipotence but the pervasive everlasting power of God's loving and creative intention. Whitehead once wrote, "The power of God is the worship [God] inspires."[4] "Worship" should be understood in the broadest possible sense as the response, sometimes conscious in faithful human beings but also unconscious in all beings, to the lure of what the most famous theologian of the Congregational tradition, Jonathan Edwards, called the "excellency" of God.

Cosmic process is replete with freedom. God is "sovereign" in that divine power is supreme; there is none to match it. But that supremacy of divine power resides in the way in which God has the first word about the possibilities available to each creature at every moment, and the last word with respect to its place in the ongoing life of the world. It is not possible to think away the problem of evil. Friction and discord and waste and pain seem to be inescapable aspects of a world of real freedom and adventurous creativity. The ancient story of the fall in the Garden of Eden and the historic doctrine of original sin are ways in which Christians have pointed to something characteristic of human life and the world in which we live. But there is a *moral* answer to the problem of evil in the realization that God shares both the responsibility and the suffering implicit in the real "fallen" world. And there is a *practical* answer to evil in a fallen world: the constant possibility of a more perfect response by every creature to God's call and purpose, and the redemption that pain and tragedy may receive in the larger harmonies and more creative adventures that God is constantly making possible. The Bible speaks of such redemption in texts like these: "With his stripes we are healed" (Isa. 53:5); and "We preach Christ crucified . . . the power of God and the wisdom of God" (1 Cor. 1:23–24).

"OUR DWELLING PLACE IN ALL GENERATIONS"

These words from Psalm 90 point back to something we noted early on, the deep and powerful impulse to seek some final and abiding center for life, an ultimate assurance that at the bottom of things there is something—Someone—unfading, unchanging, absolutely trustworthy. We saw that this instinct for the eternal is not well served by making God lifeless, that is, by banishing the divine to an unmoved stillness remote from intimate involvement in the evolving processes of creation. But now we are in a position to see how the Living God is also the Eternal God. Because God's experience encompasses the whole of the universe and its processes, all the life of the creation is held within the life and mind of God. God is especially sensitive to our human lives, because at least on this planet we are the beings who most fully bear God's image. God's ever-growing experience is everlasting. It does not fade nor dim. Within it all the values achieved in the perpetual appearing and perishing of ourselves and all the world's actualities are conserved, forever. Whitehead cites the familiar words of a hymn as a profound statement of this reality: "Abide with me; fast falls the eventide." The fall of evening reflects the perpetual perishing of all things; God is the abiding reality in whose ongoing life all find their eternal home.[5]

A correlative meaning of the Eternal God arises from what we might properly call God's *character* as contrasted with God's *experience*. We are familiar with this distinction in ourselves (as made in the image of God). We experience a never-ending flux of feelings, perceptions, motives, ideas, actions, and reactions. But persisting throughout this flux—at least in the best of us—there is a stable core of personality whose quality and intentionality does not change. That is our character. We define the character of a person by the way in which a style, purpose, habit of faithful action, persist amid all the changing external and internal situations of life. The God of Christian faith is preeminently reliable, "the Father of lights with whom there is no variation or shadow due to change" (James 1:17). It is to this God whose very character is love, revealed in Jesus Christ, that Christians entrust their souls and bodies, in life and in death.

THE CHURCH AND MISSIONARY ACTION

An important document reflecting current thinking within the United Church of Christ about the meaning and shape of the church speaks of the denomination as having a "polity in process."[6] Both the faith of the church and its polity are understood as reflecting their context in human society. This is precisely congruent with the stress upon the relational quality of all existence which is characteristic of process thought. The very structure of the church is a multiform network of relationships which is continually being shaped and reshaped. This implies both a dynamic and a "high" view of the church since Christian existence is understood as necessarily lived in community.[7]

With its major emphasis on freedom as well as relationships, process thought naturally leads toward a covenantal understanding of this essential community of faith. It is founded on and lives by a commitment that draws into living and ever-developing relationships all those who seek to live their lives in organic continuity with the life of Jesus—"members of the body of Christ" in the deepest, strongest sense.

Because God is so intimately involved with and deeply concerned about each person, those who would follow Christ must likewise be involved with and concerned about the needs and potentials of all human beings. It is terribly important that they all have a chance to know the good news about this God of creative love and to experience the presence and purpose of God in their lives. Missionary action in both gospel word and serving deed, as well as in liberating struggle, is an imperative.

One important aspect of mission, the communication of the gospel to those of other faiths, is of particular interest to process theology. Since God has from the beginning been so involved in the lives of all persons, one is bound to believe that there has been significant response in all cultures to God's active presence. Hence we should approach those of other faiths expectantly, seeking to learn in honest dialogue how God may have spoken and acted with them as well as seeking to present the special good news understood in Christian faith. Some remarkable similarities are discernible between aspects of process thought and Chinese Taoism and Neo-Confucianism, devotional (*bhakti*) Hinduism, and some types of Mahayana Buddhism, as well as with the primal religions of Native Americans and many tribal peoples. Christian mission

should press ahead hopefully with dialogue, confident that as the
meaning of these convergences is more fully understood, along with the
significance of the very real and important differences, the one truth
about the one God and the one world history in which we all live will
become more clear and more persuasive to us within the Christian
community as well as to those outside it.

To the pressing and often agonizing mission issues of human liberation and social justice, process theology brings distinctive imperatives.
Whitehead believed, quite rightly, that much traditional theology has
imaged God not only as an "imperial ruler" but also as a "ruthless
moralist," smashing wrongdoers with catastrophic punishments while
rewarding the good with unfailing well-being.

Jesus' emphasis is different. Deeply concerned for righteousness and
justice, his God operates slowly and quietly by an inclusive, loving
concern to draw all persons into a creative harmony that will continually
correct and complete imperfect and often brutally exploitative social
patterns. To be merely conservative, to cherish the status quo, is literally
to fight against the dynamic universe envisaged by process thought. But
to pattern the future in terms of any rigid formula of revolution or
reform is to risk usurping the creative, persuasive sovereignty that
belongs to God alone. Action for justice and liberation begins with
searching, patient, courageous discernment of where the Spirit of God
is leading a complicated global society within a complex and vulnerable
natural world. It calls for wholehearted and sacrificial commitment to
the imperatives that emerge from that enlarging discernment. It is often
easier to identify injustice than it is to envisage what justice would look
like. Christian activism, like other activisms, sometimes fights the bad
more effectively than it envisages and builds the better. Both the
dismantling of the old bad and the constructing of the better new are
necessary, but the former without the latter may do more harm than
good. Jesus suggested this in his parable of the demon expelled from a
house. When left empty that house was soon filled with seven more
demons, each worse than the first. Mission must strive beyond moralistic
condemnation and simplistic utopianism to search out the complicated
creative ways in which love may become more fully effective.

BUT DOES IT SING?

A valid and fruitful theology ought to have not only intellectual integrity
but it should lead on to worship and be expressible in prayer and song.
Process theology offers rich perspectives for devotional life. Many
psalms express this vision of God. Our hymnals are full of great
"process" hymns. A short sample from the As in the index to the *United*

Church Hymnal is illustrative: "Abide with me"; "All beautiful the march of days"; "All creatures of our God"; "As ancient sunlight reaches"; "Awake, awake to love and work." One of the best of the new hymns has been written by Ruth Duck from an explicit process perspective:

> God whose care the world embraces,
> God in whom we live and move,
> Whom all ages, tongues and races,
> Know as vast creative love:
> You have come to us in Jesus,
> Sharing in the life of earth,
> Calling us to be your partners
> Bringing life and love to birth.
>
> Light of Light, within life's darkness,
> Hope of Hope, within life's pain,
> Flow through us, creative Spirit,
> Work through us; reveal your reign!
> Search our hearts, our thoughts and actions;
> Show us what our lives can be;
> Hold us in your heart forever,
> Nerve us with your energy.[8]

One of the most characteristic and powerful elements of worship in the life of the United Church of Christ is its Statement of Faith. It was not written as an explicit expression of process theology. Yet its perspective, mood, and style are deeply expressive of many principal emphases of that theology. The use of present tense throughout situates us in a dynamic ongoing history, with the divine action constantly present and persuasive. It begins with the cosmic vision: God "calls the worlds into being." It concludes with God's presence "in trial and rejoicing," in all things and everywhere. And at its center it points to Jesus Christ, the man of Nazareth, in whom we see with the clarity of revelation how God is always coming to us to share our common lot. In Jesus' cross and resurrection we see how God conquers sin and death; and for all who trust God there is the promise of eternal life in God, participation in a reign "which has no end."

NOTES

1. At least hinted in Isa. 42:14, where God cries out like a woman in labor; and in Jer. 45:4, where God refers to the ruin of what God has built and planted. The pathos of God's betrayed love is poignant in Hosea 1—2.

2. Walter Rauschenbusch, "Religion: The Life of God in the Soul of Man," in

Walter Rauschenbusch, Selected Writings, ed. Winthrop Hudson (New York: Paulist Press, 1984), 132–33.

3. Charles Hartshorne, *Man's Vision of God* (New York: Harper & Brothers, 1941), ix.

4. Alfred North Whitehead, *Science and the Modern World* (New York: Free Press, 1967), 192.

5. Alfred North Whitehead, *Process and Reality* (New York: Free Press, 1969), 241.

6. *Toward the Task of Sound Teaching in the United Church of Christ* (United Church of Christ Office for Church Life and Leadership, [1977], 4.

7. Philip Schaff, the great Mercersburg theologian who did so much to strengthen a high view of the church for his Reformed denomination, believed that "the actual church is a process . . . always looking and pressing for completion." Quoted in Louis H. Gunnemann, *The Shaping of the United Church of Christ: An Essay in the History of American Christianity* (New York and Philadelphia: United Church Press, 1977), 188.

8. Second and third stanzas of "God of Endless Life Unfolding." Copyright © Ruth C. Duck. Set to beautiful original music; available from Box 100, Cascade WI 53011. It may be sung to Beethoven's "Hymn to Joy," No. 13 in *United Church Hymnal;* No. 8 in the *Pilgrim Hymnal*; No. 21 in *The Hymnal.* Used by permission.

11

FEMINIST THEOLOGY AND
THE UNITED CHURCH OF CHRIST

SHARON H. RINGE

Feminist theology appears to have come of age. One clear indication of that fact is the diversity of theological methods and agenda that currently bear that label. Gone are the days when one could claim with assurance to have addressed all of the significant works in the field, or when our internal insecurity about the emerging discipline demanded an uncritical echo from each woman engaged in the field. In fact, today the label "feminist theology" covers a range of perspectives from the post–Judeo-Christian position of a Mary Daly or spokeswomen for the "womanspirit" movements, to the "revisionist" position of many of us who know ourselves to be firmly rooted in some denomination of the biblical faith. Professionally, feminist theologians approach our task as anthropologists, psychologists, historians, ethicists, biblical scholars, ministers, and theologians.

In the midst of this diversity, it is clear that the United Church of Christ and other parts of the Christian church have been most directly influenced by those of us still in some fashion within the fold: the "Christian feminists."[1] Those of us who acknowledge such a label, however, are genuinely re-visioning and not simply tinkering with the tradition insofar as our own vision has been stretched by the more radical expressions of women's experience of the transcendent. (An analogy might be the way in which the radical statement of the black experience presented by Malcolm X has joined with the explicitly Christian perspective of Martin Luther King, Jr., to ground present-day expressions of black theology.[2]) To attempt a definition of feminist theology to give at least a minimal common ground, I would propose the following statement from Rosemary Radford Ruether:

> The critical principle of feminist theology is the promotion of the full humanity of women. Whatever denies, diminishes, or distorts the full

humanity of women is, therefore, appraised as not redemptive . . . [and] must be presumed not to reflect the divine or an authentic relation to the divine, or to reflect the authentic nature of things, or to be the message or work of an authentic redeemer or a community of redemption.

This negative principle also implies the positive principle: what does promote the full humanity of women is of the Holy, it does reflect true relation to the divine, it is the true nature of things, the authentic message of redemption and the message of redemptive community.[3]

What this means, first of all, is that feminist theology represents a critique of "patriarchy." By patriarchy we mean not merely a history in which men have been dominant and women subordinate. Instead, we use this term to summarize systems and attitudes of dominance that result in the structures and ideologies of racism, sexism, classism, and militarism. In the second place, our opposition to such systems of dominance is related to our sense that the image of God in which humankind was created (Gen. 1:27) and to which we are called (Matt. 5:43–48) gives us a quite different picture of the nature of power and the value of human beings. This God whom we have come to know at times in the midst of the traditional church and at times on its edges, draws us toward models of participation, mutuality, and solidarity with those most deeply hurt by the institutions and structures of this world. These models are the proper locus (what theologians of liberation call "praxis") of both Christian confession and Christian life.

Without pursuing further the complexities of feminist theology or spending time in retrospective consideration of the history of feminist theology (and, one might add, of feminists) in the United Church of Christ, let us consider directly the intersection of this movement with the current stress points in the theological task and vocation of the United Church of Christ.

PLURALISM

When the formerly voiceless find a voice, it should be no surprise that there is a backlog of things to be said that others may not ever have noticed. Again, to use an analogy, feminist theology is the "women's studies," "black studies," or "peace studies" part of the reform of a school curriculum, in which new priorities and agendas are introduced. As important as it is to begin to fill these significant gaps in the curriculum, such individual courses are finally no substitute for the integration of these concerns and perspectives into the rest of the curriculum. It is similarly appropriate to expect that the various theological movements included in this book will have something new to say to concerns at the very heart of the present theological ferment. We might well find ourselves revisioning the very questions being asked about our theological identity.

One might think, for example, that the historic pluralism of the United Church of Christ would account for an openness to perspectives of feminist theologians. Indeed, that is the case. However, our style of pluralism as a denomination leads to what is often only an apparent openness. We welcome "add-ons," and as with barnacles on a ship, there is usually room for one more. Also like barnacles, however, these various add-ons rarely affect the core structure of the vessel or its course. We who are added on—in this case, feminist theologians—are taken along for the ride, but it may well not be the journey on which we intended to go. The experience of various caucuses and interest groups within the denomination has been one of overt hospitality, but often of minimal influence.[4] The agenda of feminist theology challenges the very images of God at the core of our theology and worship, as well as the system of patriarchy by which our society and church are organized. The questions posed by feminist theology go to the very heart of the church's life. The prevalent style of pluralism may indeed muffle that voice in the very process of allowing it a place.

Feminist theology is at its heart contextual theology. Because of our affirmation of the importance of women's experience and the particularity of women's contexts, feminist theologians tend to be suspicious of any expression of "classical orthodoxy." Our style of theological reflection is often to begin not with the content of a particular doctrine or expression, but with questions about the circumstances that gave rise to it: political and social issues, social and economic context, and the social location of the principal actors or speakers. Not only do we regularly assume the historical and cultural relativity of expressions of classical orthodoxy, but we also recognize that what passes for orthodoxy now was originally highly controversial, and indeed the position only of the winners in disputes. Even while asking what made these positions persuasive, we would listen too for the other voices in the discussion, which also represented a portion of the community of faith.

ECUMENISM

The perspective of feminist theology similarly challenges the ecumenical involvements of the United Church of Christ, and prompts three affirmations. First, where there is a choice to be made between advocacy for justice and sensitivity to our ecumenical partners, a feminist perspective would tend to place priority on justice. For example, the issue of the ordination of women is reduced to little more than a footnote in the World Council of Churches statement on *Baptism, Eucharist, and Ministry*

(1982), partly in the hope of broadening the consensus around the document. A feminist critique of that document would not accept such a rationale. A second affirmation is that a feminist critique recognizes the historical and cultural roots of the issues that have historically divided the church. In fact, it is precisely in their political vitality that their theological significance becomes clear. Again, we would find ourselves needing to listen to the various voices in the debates, not only to those of the winners in each of the resultant groups. The consequence of the feminist challenge is a more broadly "ecumenical" methodology, more fully attentive to the universal church in its diversity and to the wider *oikoumene*.

Finally, we hold out to the church the challenge of recognizing that the ecumenical "pie" is now being sliced in new ways around issues that are of theological significance at least equal to those that resulted in the historical divisions and unions. Instead of focusing on such issues as the nature of the Trinity or Christ's "presence" in the Eucharist, the ecumenical theological issues today tend to relate to the nature of the Christian life. Struggles around issues of racism, sexism, classism, and militarism, for example, have given birth to both new expressions of unity across historical divisions and new divisions within denominational and confessional families.

In the United Church of Christ the desire for unity and the reality of divisions and pluralism have recently sparked a call for "sound teaching" or "teaching consensus." The methodological suspicion of feminist theology becomes significant as it recalls us to fundamental questions of meaning and underlying authority for our theological reflection. From where does the definition of sound teaching come? And what are its assumptions about how one knows God and discerns the social consequences of such knowing and relatedness? What is the canon of sound teaching, and what interpretive keys allow us to move between various expressions of the faith?

LANGUAGE

Cutting across every theological issue that faces the church today is the problem of the language by which theology is expressed and by which the life of the church is carried forward. Inclusive language is clearly a concern of feminist theology insofar as it requires the reform of all language that excludes, diminishes, stereotypes, or otherwise hurts people because of their gender, racial or ethnic identity, social circumstances, or physical condition. In addition to the obvious concern with language referring to people, language referring to God and Christ is also at issue.

The biblical witness itself calls us to accountability on the issue of language. Faithfulness to the biblical story draws us into dimensions of inclusiveness which our human anxieties would lead us to shun, in response to a God whose passionate concern is always for the outcast and oppressed, and whose own vision of the covenant always transcends human envisioning of its limits. Inclusive language involves precisely the linguistic expression of that vocation. We learn about God in the Bible primarily from accounts of God's activity, and rarely in visual images. We do learn, however, that the biblical claim is of humankind in all its variety created in God's image, and not of God made in ours. Any human pretext for naming or invoking God is met with warning, and in fact early in Israel's history, the name of God written in the text ceased to be pronounced aloud (a decision underlying the common occurrence of the word LORD to refer to God in most English translations). In short, we learn from the Bible that faithfulness demands of us both a commitment to inclusiveness on the human plane, and great delicacy in our use of any names or images of God that are in danger of becoming literalized into idols of our own creation and control.[5]

The two dimensions of inclusiveness, namely, language referring to God or Christ and language referring to people, are in fact interrelated. The church has usually been very careful to affirm that God transcends all human categories, and also that such human qualities of Jesus of Nazareth as his Jewishness, his first-century setting, and his maleness are not essential to his being the Christ. What *is* essential in our confession of Jesus as Christ is in that specific human life we learn to know God, and also in that human life God and humankind are reconciled such that (as Paul affirms) "neither death, nor life, nor angels, nor principalities, nor things to come, nor powers, nor height, nor depth, nor anything else in all creation, will be able to separate us from the love of God in Christ Jesus our Lord" (Rom. 8:38–39). However, it is not only what the church thinks and affirms at its best, but how it lives, which communicates its understanding of God. Just as some of the church's images and metaphors for God have a tendency toward literalization, and its christological confession of Jesus as the Christ lapses over into an idolizing of the man Jesus, so these human expressions and understandings become concretized in social structures and relationships. Virginia Ramey Mollenkott reflects on these all-too-human consequences of theological language when she summarizes her own experience of growing up in the church. "If God is always 'he' and imaged as Father, Husband, or Master, then human husbands, fathers, and employers are godlike in a way that wives, mothers, and employees are not. And the stage is set for exploitation."[6] The church in its most careful theological reflection has of course not *intended* any such consequences. Human

fathers are not the models by which we are to understand the father-
hood of God. Nevertheless, in *practice* such connections are made in
people's minds and psyches, and in the church and in the world in which
we live.

If the preceding comments make clear the importance of attentiveness
to language in the church's theology, liturgy, and other literature, it
should be noted that the language of English translations of scripture
must itself be reconsidered. Ambiguities in the task of translation, which
can never be a simple literal rendering of the ancient languages if the
resulting text is to be comprehensible, plus the importance of conveying
as accurately as possible the *meaning* of the biblical witness (with its
vocation to inclusiveness on the human plane and its delicacy in finding
human referents to God), require that a fresh look be taken at the
language in which the biblical stories are cast, lest the words and
grammar themselves blunt the biblical vision. The mandate for such
works as *An Inclusive-Language Lectionary*[7] can thus be found within
scripture itself, and it is confirmed in the church's vocation to faithfulness in our time and place.

CONCLUSION

The controversy that has centered on the issue of inclusive language is
paradigmatic of the way in which the perspectives of feminist theology
push the church and each of us to raise fundamental questions at the
heart of the expression and discussion of our faith, and not simply to
add a new social agenda or to include a new group in our pluralistic
church. Indeed, taken to its logical limits, the critical consciousness of
feminist theology might lead us out of the maze of discussions of the
"ferment" or "tension" in the church, and enable us to affirm the
primacy of our vocation as a "just peace church." By its focus on the
critique of patriarchy, feminist theology participates with the church,
and indeed can help to lead the church, in its struggle to discern the
consequences of "knowing God" for a life of shalom (Isa. 11:6–9). By its
contextual sensitivity, feminist theology can sustain that quest without
giving in to the attempt to identify a new point of belief or practice
which would claim to be the nonnegotiable bottom line of denominational identity. A posture more consistent with feminist theology is that
of "proclamation" or "confession," rather than "discipline" or "orthodoxy." In keeping with our Statement of Faith, feminist theology can
support the efforts of the church to find together "courage in the
struggle for justice and peace," and to know God's "presence in trial and
rejoicing." With the celebration of our diverse gifts, we can move
together toward a fearless proclamation and embodiment of the gospel,

as we learn throughout the church more graciously to "hear each other into speech," as one theologian puts it,[8] and live together toward wholeness in our common life.

NOTES

1. For an excellent anthology of writings by Christian feminists, see Judith L. Weidman, *Christian Feminism: Visions of a New Humanity* (New York: Harper & Row, 1984).

2. See the discussion in James H. Cone, *For My People* (Maryknoll, N.Y.: Orbis Books, 1984).

3. Rosemary Radford Ruether, *Sexism and God-Talk* (Boston: Beacon Press, 1983), 18–19.

4. I am indebted to Yvonne Delk for this image and for her clarification of the experience of pluralism in the United Church of Christ.

5. See the Appendix in *An Inclusive-Language Lectionary,* copyright © 1986, 1987, 1988 by the Division of Education and Ministry of the National Council of the Churches of Christ in the U.S.A. Readings for Year A, Revised, 269–76; Readings for Year B, Revised, 247–54; Readings for Year C, Revised, 255–62. See also Sallie McFague, *Metaphorical Theology: Models of God in Religious Language* (Philadelphia: Fortress Press, 1982), 1–29, 145–92; and Robert Hamerton-Kelly, *God the Father: Theology and Patriarchy in the Teaching of Jesus* (Philadelphia: Fortress Press, 1979), 1–81.

6. Virginia Ramey Mollenkott, "Sexist Language: The Problem and the Cure," in *Language and the Church: Articles and Designs for Workshops,* ed. Barbara A. Withers (New York: National Council of the Churches of Christ in the U.S.A., 1984), 14.

7. An exploration of issues of sexism in biblical language and of biblical translation begun in the early 1970s resulted in an Inclusive-Language Lectionary Committee appointed in 1980 by the Division of Education and Ministry of the National Council of the Churches of Christ in the U.S.A. *An Inclusive-Language Lectionary* was the result.

8. Nelle Morton introduced me to the phrase and the practice of "hearing each other into speech."

12

THEOLOGY OF MISSION

BERTRICE Y. WOOD

When we approach mission theology today we must take into account not only theological discussions in the United Church of Christ that inform our understandings of mission, but also insights of persons in other religious, political, and cultural contexts that bring to our theology an increased awareness of the global situation of our ministry and mission. Mission theology necessarily involves us, as it has involved me in my work with the World Council of Churches, the United Church Board for Homeland Ministries, and the United Church Board for World Ministries, in the ecumenical movement. Its task of working for unity should involve something beyond ecclesiastical unity. Unity is also the goal of the churches' efforts to bring people together across the lines of race and culture and language within and beyond the church. The church is truly ecumenical when it engages in its ministry as an agent of justice and reconciliation in our world, as a sign of the reign of God, and as a sign of a community working to unite people across all that is divisive in the human family. A theology of mission must call the church to support that which serves for the unity of people, as opposed to the domination of one group over another. The task of mission theology is to point us to whatever sources will help us respond to God's call.

While I hold dear the traditions of the United Church of Christ, I sense that we should be listening to others beyond the traditional boundaries of the denomination, beyond the United States, and beyond the cultural arena with which we are most familiar. Some spokespersons for this global perspective are not far-flung at all, but are within the United Church of Christ today as we become an increasingly pluralistic church. There are members of our denomination whose ethnic, cultural, and racial backgrounds have a great deal to offer for expanding our understanding of the global situation and the concerns of persons in our world. Our perceptions of mission are changing. And as our sense of mission develops, it transforms our whole understanding of what it means to be the church of Jesus Christ. It is mission that unifies and binds the church together. That is, mission must not be limited to that segment of the church's program which sends persons to other, less developed countries. Rather, we should see ourselves and all our ministries in unity with churches the world over as they live out their ministry in their communities and in the world at large.

I wish to highlight four accents in contemporary theology that help us understand our church's mission today: (1) New Alignments in Mission; (2) Liberation Theology; (3) the Word of God; and (4) Salvation Theology. My discussion will have to do with one major thrust of the church's mission to the neglect of other equally important topics, such as the interaction of Christianity with other world religions. Interfaith dialogue, long a priority of the United Church of Christ on the world scene, must fall outside the bounds of this essay. In conclusion I will make some suggestions about the significance of the accents with which I deal for the United Church of Christ and some implications for local churches.

NEW ALIGNMENTS IN MISSION

Most North American Christians, when they hear the word mission, think of the church's sending out people on their behalf to engage in evangelism and service. The church has responded for centuries to Jesus' great commission in Matthew 28 to go into the world and "make disciples of all nations, baptizing them . . . [and] teaching them . . ." Insofar as we have conceived of ourselves only as senders and others as receivers, we are challenged today by churches in those countries that have historically been the recipients of Western missionaries. In the 1970s some called for a "moratorium on mission," meaning to reduce North American and European influence in order to realign patterns of partnership for mission among churches in various countries. Church leaders in traditional "receiving" nations have assumed primary responsibility for the life and witness of their churches, for being missionaries in their own settings.

It is often difficult to accept the critique and challenge of Third World churches and Christian leaders. But the critique is not all negative. Third World theologians acknowledge the hard work missionaries undertook to carry the gospel not only in word but in deed into foreign lands. Personal testimonies abound describing the positive impact of missionaries on individuals and communities. Accomplishments in evangelism, literacy, education, health care, economic development, the elevation of the status of women and outcasts, and other areas of mission work demonstrate the presence of God in the missionary enterprise. But the symbiotic relationship between nineteenth-century colonialism and the missionary enterprise is also undeniable. The manner in which Christianity was introduced often exhibited North American and European prejudices at odds with the local culture. The legacy of the colonial era is hard to shake off.

We are entering a new era. The future calls for less reliance on the leadership of mission agencies and more reliance on the leadership of churches in traditionally missionary-receiving countries. Churches throughout the world are invited to celebrate the strong leadership now present in churches throughout the world's diverse communities. Mission is mutually participatory. Today when mission involves the sending out of persons or material support to others, we participate together in discerning how best our efforts might symbolize the church's alignment with God's commitment to peace and justice. Mission today calls for the creation of new forms of partnership among churches. It calls not for certain nations to send out and others to receive, but for all to send and all to receive.

We are now called to listen to the theological reflection of church leaders throughout the world. Most important are some new ways of theological thinking in Third World nations and among certain communities within our nation and our church. To be united in the common mission of Jesus Christ necessarily includes being open to the opportunity to learn from the experience of others.

LIBERATION THEOLOGY

Liberation theology, treated more extensively in other essays in this book, is actually inclusive of many diverse ways people articulate their theological perceptions. It is most closely associated with the theological work of thinkers in both Roman Catholic and Protestant churches in Latin America. I would also place the theological reflection emerging from the American black experience, the thought of Christian feminists, and that taking place in African, Asian, and Caribbean churches within the family of liberation theology. A great deal differentiates these groups from one another, precisely because they are rooted in the communities of people associated with each particular struggle for liberation. But they have in common several approaches to theological exploration.

As the term "liberation" suggests, the primary focus is on the freeing message of the Christian gospel. This gospel was forecast in the liberation of the Hebrew people from Egyptian bondage. The Book of Exodus is an account of God acting to free people to move out of slavery and into new lands, free to respond in worship and service of the God of history. Another commonality of all theologies of liberation is a focus on both the personal and the communal. People are not merely individuals who are fulfilled by a relationship with God, but people are fully human when they live together in justice and peace and relate to God in community. Liberation theology, therefore, has both a spiritual and a political orientation. It offers spiritual renewal and strength, the liberating message of the gospel that opens us to the presence of God within us. It also draws our attention to the message of the gospel, which calls for the transformation of the world. Christians around the world are saying their faith is not satisfied with waiting until the afterlife for freedom from suffering and oppression. The exodus occurred within history. God wills that liberation in our time also must occur within history. Christ is the One who transforms the very concrete realities of the lives of persons and communities.

Third World theologians proclaim that the God revealed in Christ and in scripture has opted for special favor for those who suffer, who are poor, who are oppressed. God supports those for whom the ways of the world have granted less than what the Christian gospel deems just. Rooted in the Bible, this message is not a new gospel. Peruvian Catholic Gustavo Gutiérrez, in his hallmark work, *A Theology of Liberation,* states that although liberation is integral to the gospel it has been a neglected theme in the life and work of the church.[1] While classical theology engages in the pursuit of rational knowledge and doctrinal soundness, liberation theology calls us to proclaim in word and deed God's liberating Word to our world. In a theology of mission knowledge and "praxis" (action for justice) interplay in the ministry of the church. Theology must be socially particular, as it is interpreted and enacted in the context of political and economic life. Global awareness requires that we recognize and celebrate the emerging identities of Christians in contexts very different from our own. These identities are not a threat, much less a negation, of our own Christian identity, but evidence of Third World Christians' response to God's call to be faithful people. Global consciousness demands that we recognize that God's Word comes alive in many different contexts. There need be no contradictions in saying that God's Word takes flesh in the many shapes, sizes, colors, and languages of the world's people.

Theology informed by the biblical theme of liberation does not begin with abstracted theological concepts but with action. Theology is "critical reflection" on this "praxis." The Christian gospel thus speaks to, from, and in particular communities. These may be communities in Latin

America suffering in poverty and amidst human rights abuses, communities sensitized to the struggle of women to be included in all levels of church life, communities in South Africa struggling for self-determination and majority rule, or communities of racial and ethnic minorities in America seeking to affirm the richness of their cultures and their place in society. Robert McAfee Brown, in his very useful book *Theology in a New Key*, challenges North American Christians to listen and respond to the voices of liberation theology. Using the musical analogy, he states that while much of the West's great classical music was written to convey religious themes, new patterns of notes and chord progressions invite us to gain new insights. Similarly, new patterns of religious thought may jar us at first but offer the possibility of responding in new ways to God's call to bring the gospel to all the world.[2] The themes of liberation theology challenge the power-orientation with which North Americans have related to the global arena, including our approach to mission.

THE WORD OF GOD

The United Church of Christ is heir to the Reformation focus on the Word of God as the authoritative source for theological formulations about God, Christ, human nature, and the church. Some who are critical of the theological perspectives of oppressed peoples suggest that such perspectives, while biblical, are not sufficiently informed by economic, cultural, and political analysis. While aware of these realities, Third World Christians are first of all rooted in the biblical revelation of God's will for justice and freedom. Believers always understand the biblical message in their own political and social context. The Reformation itself, for example, is impossible to understand apart from the abuses of the Catholic Church and the conflicts among princes and nations. The Bible is indeed central to any theological understandings, but not apart from the historical moment. Scripturally informed Christians encounter God through the continuity of divine action within the events and struggles of human history, notably in the suffering of the poor and the struggle of the oppressed for justice. Christians eager for the Bible's message and sensitive to the voices of God's people around the globe are best prepared to engage in mission.

SALVATION THEOLOGY

The final accent I would lift up has to do with the meaning of salvation. Concern for the salvation of persons has certainly been one driving force in the missionary movement. But differences in the understanding of salvation divide groups of missionaries and churches into at least two camps. These differences separate those aligned with the modern conciliar ecumenical movement, institutionalized in the World Council of Churches and the National Council of Churches of Christ in the U.S.A., and those affiliated with more conservative or fundamentalist groups.

The difference at its heart is over whether the locus of God's saving grace is in the individual or in the community. "Evangelicals" are generally primarily concerned with the salvation of the individual soul through profession of faith in Christ as personal Savior. On the other side are those, including many voices from the Third World, who insist that God's saving action takes place in the community as well as in the soul, that indeed the community becomes a medium for salvation. Our personal lives are integrally woven together with the life of the whole community. The community helps transform, and the community is to be transformed by God's Spirit. Many Third World Christians argue that mission today must promote the transformation, or salvation, of individuals within their communities, so that communities of faith may become signs of the reign of God already present in human history.

As the United Church of Christ seeks to engage in world and local mission, we are asked whether our own communities, our economic and political systems, our ways of relating to people, are biblically just. Is the United Church of Christ a sign, an embodiment, of Christ? Has our church been so transformed by God that we relate to other nations and peoples in ways that reveal God's will for the world? Is our mission one that shows that we are willing to let go of ecclesiastical, cultural, racial, economic, and political power for the benefit of those who are without power in our world? Can our mission be one that empowers all people to enjoy the blessings of this world, to have food, to determine what they will grow to eat and how they will provide for their families, to determine what their political lives and authorities will be, to determine the importance of their own cultural heritage and experience and pass them on to children, and to grow spiritually? Are we who benefit from the freedom and riches of a superpower nation so transformed and saved from the anxieties of the human condition that our mission may be directed by the God who would remove power from the hands of just a few in order that justice and human wholeness may be shared throughout the whole world? Salvation is in and for the reconciliation of the whole human family with itself and with God. Liberation and salvation are synonyms, different words for the same work of God. If one has a more earthly and the other a more spiritual sound to it, perhaps that is itself indicative of the wholeness of the task of mission. That task is to proclaim in deed as well as in word the signs of the reign of God, which in its days of fulfillment will offer deliverance for all those to whom freedom and justice have been denied.

IMPLICATIONS FOR
THE UNITED CHURCH OF CHRIST

We in the United Church of Christ share a long history of understanding our mission as being holistic, incorporating the individual and the corporate, the spiritual and the physical. Our mission efforts have for many decades sought to embody signs of God's liberating word in very concrete situations in which people suffer in our world. Further, we are a denomination with a history of looking beyond itself to gain self-understanding. I am impressed with the historical accounts of our mission work, including David M. Stowe's very helpful booklet entitled *Year 175: A Brief History of the UCBWM* (New York: United Church Board for World Ministries, 1984). We have long acknowledged our partnership with churches and communities around the globe. Through my experience with the World Board and the Board for Homeland Ministries, I rejoice in our heritage of seeing mission in word and deed and as participation in, rather than the attempted control of, the world. We have understood our advocacy of the oppressed, such as our role in the abolitionist movement in this country, as central to evangelism. Work on behalf of the imprisoned, the poor, and all who suffer has been at the heart, not on the sidelines, of our church's mission.

The time has again come to listen to new voices, some of which may be unsettling. The makeup of our denominational membership is changing to include more diversified cultural groups. We must listen to their voices and to voices emerging in Third World countries. United Church of Christ congregations could well undertake studies of publications of the World Council of Churches, especially its document *Mission and Evangelism: An Ecumenical Affirmation* (1983) and of the Ecumenical Association of Third World Theologians as they develop their own local theology of mission. Because of our tradition and our pluralism as a denomination, we have the capacity and the responsibility at all levels of the church's life to participate in the new dialogues concerning mission and its theology. The theological journey transports us into a global society, which is in our very midst and which invites us into all the world. Local churches may involve themselves directly in world issues through refugee ministry, work among the poor in our communities, and economic and political action in protest against South African apartheid. A global understanding of our faith gives broader meaning even to every act of baptism into the Christian community. When we grapple with issues of biblical authority, such an understanding suggests that adherence to scripture must open us to all it will tell us about human experience and God's will for the world. The result will be a fuller and more just theology for the mission of the church.

The new era in the church's mission is a freeing time. We are free to celebrate and strive to live up to the best of the historical missionary enterprise and free to acknowledege its shortcomings. In this new era we are free to know that we are not the only ones capable of spreading the gospel. We are free to release our old role of seeking to guide the destinies of the churches in other lands and free to work toward developing new alignments of mission partnership. We are free to receive as well as to send missionaries, assistance, and inspiration, especially from churches managing to survive as part of the Christian family under difficult and oppressive circumstances. Mission requires the kind of theology of solidarity espoused by such Latin American theologians as Jon Sobrino and Juan Hernandez Pico.[3] Mission invites our observation of the working of the Spirit in other churches, and movement into trusting relationships in which all are enriched and make some contribution. To be in mission for the United Church of Christ means to be part of the transformation of the world in justice and reconciliation within the human family.

NOTES

1. Gustavo Gutiérrez, *A Theology of Mission,* trans. and ed. Caridad Inda and John Eagleson (Maryknoll, N.Y.: Orbis Books, 1973).

2. Robert McAfee Brown, *Theology in a New Key: Responding to Liberation Themes* (Philadelphia: Westminster Press, 1978).

3. Jon Sobrino and Juan Hernandez Pico, *Theology of Christian Solidarity* (Maryknoll, N.Y.: Orbis Books, 1985).

13

A FAITHFUL CHURCH:
CONCERNS OF THE BIBLICAL
WITNESS FELLOWSHIP

DONALD G. BLOESCH

As one closely identified with the Biblical Witness Fellowship, I would like to share some concerns of this movement regarding the present drift of the United Church of Christ. These concerns are rooted in a deep-seated loyalty to the theological and historical heritage of our church. An important resource in the preparation of this essay has been the Biblical Witness Fellowship book *Affirming Our Faith*.[1]

The erosion of the confessional foundations of our denomination is something to be deplored. It is asserted in the *Basis of Union of the United Church of Christ* that:

> The faith which unites us and to which we bear witness is that Faith in God which the Scriptures of the Old and New Testaments set forth, which the ancient Church expressed in the ecumenical creeds, to which our own spiritual fathers gave utterance in the evangelical confessions of the Reformation, and which we are in duty bound to express in the words of our time as God Himself gives us light.[2]

No impartial observer would doubt that our denomination has relativized this confessional undergirding by appealing to insights derived from the social sciences or current ideologies, which often become a second criterion alongside scripture, or even a higher court of appeal than either biblical or ecclesiastical tradition. This often results from our otherwise faithful concern for social justice, peace, the poor, and women.

For example, whereas Article II in the *Basis of Union* clearly affirms the Trinity, the Statement of Faith adopted by the Second General Synod in 1959 reflects at best a modalistic understanding of the Trinity. The Trinitarian basis is further weakened in the Anniversary Statement of Faith affirmed by the General Synod at Pittsburgh in 1983 where the phrase "God of our Savior Jesus Christ" was substituted for "Father of our Lord Jesus Christ" and where all references to God as Father and Christ as Lord are deleted. I personally perceive an ominous drift toward Unitarianism in our denomination. In light of the incursion of Unitarian beliefs into the Congregational churches in the nineteenth century, it is incumbent on members of the United Church of Christ to be especially alert to this omnipresent danger.

Many United Church of Christ leaders seem to believe that the word "Lord" is sexist because it presumably excludes females and also "classist" because it seems to imply hierarchy in relationships. The title "Lord" has all but disappeared from official church documents. Such an attitude betrays a serious misunderstanding of some of the basic tenets of Christianity. "Lord" in reference to deity connotes a God who radically transcends sexuality, even though God chooses to relate to us predominantly in the masculine gender. When "Lord" is used in reference to Christ or the exalted Jesus, it is only right that this One whom we worship should be elevated above humankind, even though God chooses to realize lordship in the form of a servant.

The confession of Jesus Christ as Lord sharply calls into question the spurious and presumptuous claims of the gods of this world. In an age when Christian faith is being challenged by the lords of technology, when a conflict looms between faith and the principalities and powers that compose the industrial-military complex, it is especially important that the Lordship of Christ be confessed anew.

It is ironic that our denominational leaders have failed to perceive this, given their vigorous warnings against rising militarism. The reason, of course, is not hard to find. They have not been entirely successful in resisting the lure of the ideological temptation themselves.

It is sad to witness the ideological coloring of much United Church of Christ theology as well as social policy. A church should always endeavor to speak prophetically, and this means bringing the Word of God to bear on all vested interests in society. When the church aligns itself with one particular ideology, for example, socialism, laissez-faire liberalism (today's conservatism), or feminism, it then irretrievably compromises the integrity of its witness. This is not to deny the element of truth in all ideologies, for they all protest against some social wrong.

In the opinion of the Biblical Witness Fellowship, our church is identifying itself too closely with ideologies of the left, especially feminism and welfare liberalism. One baleful consequence is the church's inability to give a clear and forthright affirmation of the Trinity. The demand for inclusive language for the deity has resulted in a God beyond the Trinity—an infinite ground of all being, a Primal Matrix or an Eternal Silence (as in Gnosticism).

Another ideology that has apparently infiltrated the policymaking boards of the United Church of Christ is gay liberationism, which upholds a homosexual style of life as a valid alternative to the heterosexual style and even insists on the ordination to the ministry of those who are gay and lesbian. Following the Ninth General Synod the Executive Council recommended that with regard to "a stated homosexual's candidacy for ordination, the issue should not be his/her homosexuality as such, but rather the candidate's total view of human sexuality and his/her understanding of the morality of its use."[3] This statement falls short of the demands of gay liberation ideology, but it nonetheless opens the door to those who advocate a radically different understanding of sexuality than that I believe to be presented in Holy Scripture. I heartily agree with Frederick Schroeder, former president of Eden Theological Seminary: "On the matter of homosexual activity, the testimony of Scripture is unmistakably clear: homosexual activity is sinful."[4]

The divine authority and infallibility of scripture is the issue behind all other issues in our denomination. United Church of Christ president Avery Post has stated that the Bible "has all the limitations of creatureliness: error, hyperbole, contradictions, inconsistencies. It is culture bound."[5] While this may be a fairly accurate description of the Bible's humanity, Post's statement, taken by itself, fails to take into consideration the divinity of scripture, the other side of the mystery of God's self-revelation in accommodation to human language and culture. This sacredness of scripture must not be forgotten. The church is obliged to confess that scripture is not only culturally conditioned regarding its form or language but also culturally transcendent regarding its content or message. Moreover, as Karl Barth many times pointed out, we do not have the divine content except in its innerworldly form, we do not have the gospel of God except in the broken but nonetheless inspired testimony of God's prophets and apostles.

The Dubuque Declaration, drawn up by the Biblical Witness Fellowship, embodies the heritage represented by the four traditions that compose the United Church of Christ when it asserts that the Bible is "the infallible rule of faith and practice."[6] Jesus Christ is the living and revealed Word of God, and the Bible is the written Word. But the two cannot be separated. We have God's self-revelation in Christ in the biblical testimony, and no other interpretation of this revelation can be normative for the church that claims to be both biblical and apostolic. Karl Barth has even ventured to speak of the interpenetration of the three forms of the Word of God: Christ, scripture, and church proclamation faithful to scripture.

Recent theology has sought to take the true humanity of scripture seriously, but in doing so has focused on the diversity of theologies in the Bible and the apparent contradictions between biblical authors. I even sense in some United Church of Christ literature a denigration of the Old Testament (because of its pronounced patriarchalism) and a concentration upon the teachings and ministry of Jesus. What we should try to recover today in the United Church of Christ is the underlying unity of the biblical witness. God did not bring a wholly new revelation in Jesus Christ; instead, the Christ event represents the fulfillment or apogee of God's revelation in the history of the people of Israel. We must here guard against Marcionism, the early gnostic heresy that downgraded the Old Testament. This heresy reappeared in the "German Christians," the group within the German church of the 1930s that sought accommodation with National Socialism, as well as in the theology of Rudolf Bultmann, who saw the Old Testament as merely a preamble to what alone is of vital significance—the Pauline interpretation of the cross.

What Jacques Ellul and others call "the violence against morality" must also be given due consideration in an analysis of present trends in the United Church of Christ. I am thinking of those things that subvert the stability and integrity of the family—abortion on demand, pornography, trial marriages, value-free sex education, no-fault divorce, and advocacy of homosexuality as a valid lifestyle.

By throwing its support behind the pro-choice position on abortion,[7] the United Church of Christ as well as several other mainline Protestant denominations is in effect repudiating the wisdom and counsel of the church through the ages—that abortion entails the killing of human life and is therefore morally wrong. The United Church of Christ position on abortion is also making it increasingly difficult to maintain good ecumenical relations with the Roman Catholic Church as well as with churches that identify themselves as evangelical, all of which see abortion in our country as "the silent holocaust" (in Mother Teresa's words) beginning to approach the barbarity of the holocaust of the Jewish people in Nazi Germany.

On the subject of peace, the United Church of Christ is intimately concerned about this moral issue, and this is indeed to its credit. At the same time, what runs through the peace literature of the United Church of Christ as well as other mainline Protestant denominations is a utopian vision that real peace in this world is a viable possibility. Moreover, one is left with the distinct impression that the hope for peace rests on human diligence and ingenuity, on new methods of peacemaking rather than on the personal return of Jesus Christ. Can there be a permanent or true peace in this world if people are not united by faith with the Prince of Peace? Does not the core of the problem of war rest on the problem of sin in the human heart? The challenge of peacemaking should therefore be a call to evangelism, for unless the human heart is right with God there will always be conflict—with oneself and with one's neighbor. We need to protest in no uncertain terms against our idolatrous dependence on weapons of mass extermination manifested in the uncontrolled armaments race. At the same time, we must not pin our hopes on the ingenuity and wisdom of self-styled experts on peace who tend to believe that all that is necessary for peace in our time is common sense and good will.

Pluralism is a much-celebrated motto of our church, but upon close examination it often proves to be a means of avoiding hard theological decisions. While there can be a certain pluralism in liturgy, methods of evangelism, and even in theology, there can be no pluralism in dogma, in the central affirmations of faith. The apostle Paul reminds us that there is only one Lord, one faith, and one baptism (Eph. 4:4, 5; cf. Phil. 1:27), and the task in our time is to discover what this means and then to live according to it. Pluralism can become a jealous god refusing to tolerate any claims to absolute truth, even when such a claim is made by our Lord (cf. John 8:45–47; 14:6).

Closely related to pluralism is the peril of subjectivism, where the important thing is not what we believe but whether we are sincere in our belief. In this mentality, openness to truth wherever it may be found is prized over dogmatic adherence to particular truths. Life takes precedence over doctrine, character over piety. But the Bible tells us that we are saved from the guilt and power of sin not on the basis of how we live but on the basis of whom we believe (John 5:24; 6:28, 29; 8:21). Our life will most certainly attest and confirm our faith, but if the tree is rotten there can be no good or lasting fruit (Matt. 3:10; 7:16–20; Luke 6:43–45).

Experientialism is another source of confusion and misunderstanding in our church as well as in modern Protestantism in general. Many people, both liberal and conservative, appeal primarily or exclusively to religious or cultural experience rather than to God's self-revelation in Jesus Christ as attested in Holy Scripture. Experientialism leads to subjectivism, which further erodes the objective and ontological foundations of Christian faith. It is not what scripture says or what the ecumenical councils declare but what one personally experiences that is true. But this is not the faith of the apostles or the Reformers but instead the unwritten credo of the Enlightenment.

Another manifestation of rugged individualism is privatism, the stance that morality is a personal issue and that moral issues can be decided only by following one's conscience. Our church has rightly protested against privatism in the area of social justice concerns, such as civil rights, but it has remained strangely silent in the area of personal morality, particularly sexual morality. Are not the commandments against blasphemy and adultery just as binding as the commandment against killing?

In conclusion, I believe that a faithful church will be characterized by a commitment to apostolic doctrine, the evangelical experience, and the Christian life. All three of these are necessary for both soundness and vitality. In every age, however, one needs to be emphasized more than the others because of some imbalance in the church's proclamation. In my judgment, the pressing need today in the United Church of Christ as well as in other mainline Protestant denominations is for purity of doctrine, without which our experience will invariably be misunderstood by ourselves and others, and our life will cease to be a shining witness to the glory of God.

I believe that the rising theological ferment in the United Church of Christ may be a moving of the Spirit calling us to reclaim the apostolic and evangelical heritage of our denomination. We cannot simply return to past positions and repeat the formulations of our fathers and mothers in the faith. We need a fresh appropriation of the gospel, one that will relate to the burning social and spiritual issues of our time but also one that will be in continuity with the faith once delivered to the saints. The Puritan divine John Robinson rightly reminded us that there is yet more light to break forth from God's Holy Word. Yet Robinson did not have in mind a new revelation that would supersede the definitive revelation in Jesus Christ as found in Holy Scripture. On the contrary, he meant that the light given once for all times in Jesus Christ would shine again but in a new way. Robinson entertained the hope that the Spirit of God would bring further illumination concerning the meaning and impact of the one revelation in Jesus Christ. It is misleading to appeal to Robinson for support of "new words from God" in culture and history that clearly violate the plain meaning of the scriptures.

It is not our task to make the Word of God relevant, as liberal theologians are fond of saying. Instead it is to rediscover the abiding relevance already in the Word of God. We do not derive our theological agenda from contemporary culture or history. On the contrary, we derive our agenda from the Bible and then are called to apply it to the pivotal questions and issues of our time.

A truly prophetic church will not be a bandwagon church, in which we embrace the latest theological fad or the most popular social cause. A truly prophetic church will be a witnessing church, one that upholds not its own wisdom of the culture but instead the mystery of the gospel, which will forever be "a stumbling block to Jews and folly to Gentiles" (1 Cor. 1:22–25). A church that argues its case on the basis of a criterion held in common with secular philosophy or cultural wisdom has already abdicated its responsibility to be true to its mission. What the church must do is remain faithful to the revelation once for all given in Jesus Christ and to present this revelation in the language and imagery of its time, but at the same time always returning to "the language of Zion," the biblical testimony in which this message comes to us. What the church needs is not a revised apologetic strategy to reach the cultured despisers of religion but a renewed reliance on the power of the Holy Spirit to persuade and convict in conjunction with the preaching and hearing of the Word of God.

The United Church of Christ might yet become this prophetic church if it makes a sincere effort to sunder its alliances with current ideologies that beguile the modern world. Only in this way will it become free to speak the Word of God again in all of its power and glory. May the Spirit of God guide our leaders to a new vision of the church—a church obedient to the great commission to proclaim the gospel to the whole creation and to teach all peoples to be disciples of the one Lord and Master, Jesus Christ.

NOTES

1. *Affirming Our Faith* (Souderton, Penn.: Biblical Witness Fellowship, 1984).

2. *Basis of Union of the Congregational Christian Churches and the Evangelical and Reformed Church*, Article II, in Louis H. Gunnemann, *The Shaping of the United Church of Christ* (New York and Philadelphia: United Church Press), 208.

3. *Minutes*, Ninth General Synod, St. Louis, Missouri, June 22–26, 1973, 76.

4. Frederick Schroeder, "Ethics: The Basic Issue," *Living Faith* 1 (Winter 1981):5.

5. Avery Post, speech given at Annual Meeting, Ohio Conference, New Breman, Ohio, May 18, 1981.

6. "Dubuque Declaration," *New Conversations* 8 (Spring 1985):17.

7. *Minutes*, Eighth General Synod, Grand Rapids, Michigan, June 25–29, 1971, 58, 131–33.

14

CHRISTIAN DOCTRINE IN
THE UNITED CHURCH OF CHRIST

GABRIEL FACKRE

What *unites* the United Church of Christ? Is it middle-class values and sociological commonalities, as some say? Or is it our ethical commitments and justice and peace concerns? Perhaps it is our ecumenical openness? Maybe the question is itself wrong. Some judge that our congregational polity or our theological heterogeneity belie the name we have taken to ourselves. Better the humorist's slipped "i"—the *Untied* Church of Christ.

While the gentle cynic's comment on our divided state can produce enough evidence to give us pause, our United name does not make a mockery of who we are. Our unities do have to do with ethics and openness. But why that is so, and what it means, are questions that take us to long and deep bondings. They have to do with the *histories* from which we have come, the *decisions* we have made, and the *texts* we have created. Histories, decisions, and texts have to be interpreted, of course. But the beginnings of our unity lie in being *this* hermeneutical community rather than another one. We, the United Church of Christ, live out of these particular histories, decisions, and texts.

What do we make of the histories? The four streams that converge mark us as the only denomination in this country with such diversity that has risked organic union. The experiment is all the more venturesome when the "hidden histories" are taken into account.[1] And what are the warrants for the decisions we have made as a church over the subsequent thirty years? Especially important to consider are those decisions that seem to be refrains of our common life—the UCC as a "united and uniting church" and a "just peace church." The answer to all these questions lies in the *doctrine* of the United Church of Christ. To identify that doctrine we have to give attention to the third of our unities: the texts of the church.

DOCTRINE

Doctrine is the set of fundamental assumptions about "life, death, and destiny" that function in a community of faith. This pattern of belief manifests itself in what we preach and teach, how we worship, where and when we move in mission, why and for what we commit our lives and substance.[2] We do not often attend to these fundamentals with the clarity and passion they merit. However, at critical junctures in our common life we do lift them up for examination. One such historical moment was the founding of the church. Thus in our charters the theological foundations of the United Church of Christ are exposed to view. We shall investigate these texts—the *Constitution and Bylaws of the United Church of Christ* and the *Basis of Union of the Congregational Christian Churches and the Evangelical and Reformed Church with Interpretations*—as they bear on the issues at hand. To the extent that we participate in the church we corporately are, these are the doctrinal ties that bind us.[3] In exegeting our church's founding texts we shall also look to the authoritative, albeit nonbinding, United Church of Christ Statement of Faith commissioned as "testimony . . . not test" and "based in principle upon Article II" of the doctrinal agreements in the *Basis of Union*. In underscoring the importance of covenantal texts as disclosure points of doctrinal identity we shall also refer to some group statements that have emerged in the United Church of Christ theological renewal movement of the 1970s and 1980s.

STANDARDS

Norms

Doctrine begins with prolegomena on the question of standards or *norms* of theological authority: Where do we go to find out what is so? Appropriately, we find guidelines on such standards in the Preamble to the Constitution and in its early articles. The decisive authority in the United Church of Christ charter is *Jesus Christ:* "The United Church of Christ acknowledges as its sole Head, Jesus Christ, Son of God and Savior" (*Constitution*, Preamble). Membership in its churches means accountability to "Jesus Christ, the Head of the Church" (*Constitution*, VI. 14).

Awareness of the historical context of these assertions is important for their understanding. Christian churches in the decades of the 1930s to the 1950s were very conscious of the perils of cultural accommodation. The Barmen Declaration with its firm christological word spoken to the "German Christianity" of the Hitler era was a model confession: "Jesus Christ is . . . the one Word of God which we have to hear and which we have to trust and obey." So too the "isms" on the North American scene, both within and outside the churches, were seen as a challenge to the authority of Christ—nationalism, consumerism, ecclesiasticism, biblicism. Thus the christological norm found its way not only into our *Constitution*, but became lodged in the very name of our faith community—the United Church *of Christ*.

Source

Where do we go to discover this norm? We go to the *source* of Christ's self-disclosure. The United Church of Christ "looks to the Word of God in the Scriptures" (*Constitution*, Preamble). The companion text, *Basis of Union*, says it this way: "The faith which unites us and to which we bear witness is that faith which the Scriptures of the Old and New Testaments set forth . . ." (*Basis*, II). Thus the Bible is authoritative because it bears witness to Jesus Christ, and is to be interpreted in accord with this center. Such a christological cum biblical standard accounts for our self-description as "evangelical Christians" (*Constitution*, Preamble).[4]

Resource

The interpretation of scripture is a controverted question. The United Church of Christ takes a position in the dispute. We have noted the first move it makes, reading the text in the light of Christ. The second is the function of *tradition* in hermeneutics. The *Basis of Union* continues its statement on scripture by speaking about the interpretive role of "the faith . . . which the ancient Church expressed in the ecumenical creeds, to which our own spiritual [forebears] gave utterance in the evangelical confessions of the Reformation. . . ." The Preamble echoes the *Basis of Union*: The UCC "claims as its own the faith of the historic Church expressed in the ancient creeds and reclaimed in the basic insights of the Protestant Reformers." As the scriptures are the source of our understanding of Christ, the historic ecumenical and confessional tradition is a key *resource* in construing its meaning.

But "tradition" is more wide-ranging than its historic sedimentations. It includes the present sisters and brothers as well as the past fathers and mothers. Thus the United Church of Christ "affirms its responsibility in each generation to make this faith its own. . . ." (*Constitution*, Preamble). Or again, "We are in duty bound to express [the faith] in words of our time . . ." (*Basis of Union*, II). Who does this, and how is it done? Here the centrality of the congregation in our polity has implications for the doctrinal process. The hermeneutical community in the United Church of Christ is the *whole* people of God. Basic doctrine from scripture and the historic tradition is interpreted by the "base communities" of the denomination, its congregations (*Constitution*, IV.7.15) when it is functioning as a covenantal congregationalism (*Constitution*, IV.14.16). This "theology from below" does not succumb to the individualism of modern culture but strives for a catholicity of insight weaving the diverse perspectives into a larger tapestry. The *Basis of Union* articulates this vision of a whole that encompasses both the historic tradition and its wide range of contemporary interpreters: "In all our expressions of that faith we seek to preserve unity of heart and spirit with those who have gone before us as well as those who now labor with us."

Setting

In alluding to the contemporary community's role in discerning faith we have already touched upon setting. The contextualizing of the gospel requires an alertness to historical setting. The church is called to make "the faith of the historic Church . . . its own in reality of worship, in honesty of thought and expression and in purity of heart before God" (*Constitution*, Preamble). Or as the *Basis of Union* says, "We are duty bound to express [the faith] in the words of our time." These acts of indigenization are made possible by "the presence and power of the Holy Spirit" given to equip the church for its "creative and redemptive work in the world" (*Constitution*, Preamble). We count on the Spirit to "give us light" (*Basis*) in new times and places.

The Spirit's work in the particular world in which God has placed us, under the Christ of scripture, and through the community of faith, has given us the mission concerns that have marked our church in its thirty-year pilgrimage: *diakonia* and *koinonia*. The distinctive challenges of "our time" have evoked from our heritage a "church united and uniting" and a "just peace church." Already these responses are anticipated in the *Basis* as it speaks in the language of its own time of "the promotion of justice, the reign of peace, the realization of human brotherhood" on the one hand, while asserting on the other that "denominations exist not for themselves" but "as parts of that Church within which each denomination is to live and labor and if need be, die" so that we may respond to the prayer of Jesus "that they all may be one" (*Basis of Union*, Preamble).

SUBSTANCE

Christ the *norm*, the Bible the *source*, the church the *resource*, and the world the *setting* are assumptions about authority in the defining texts of the United Church of Christ inextricable from fundamental teachings about the will and the way of God. Our concept of authority is based on beliefs about certain deeds and disclosures of God. The teachings about these reconciling and revealing acts constitute "the faith" about which both the *Constitution* and the *Basis of Union* speak. This testimony to how reality is viewed subsequently found expression in the Statement of Faith. The *Basis of Union* describes its own articulation of the faith as a "confession" that embodies "those things most surely taught and believed among us," one that links us with "the holy Catholic Church" (*Basis of Union*, II and Preamble). This "substance of the Christian faith" (*Basis of Union*, Preamble) presupposes the doctrinal symbols that were part of the uniting streams, the creeds, confessions, catechisms, and covenants of the Reformed Church in the United States, the Congregational Churches, the Evangelical Synod of North America, and the Christian Connection. As the local church is "the basic unit of the life and organization of the United Church of Christ" (*Constitution*, IV.1) the test of membership is established therein, employing these inherited or other standards. To the thousands of churches so gathered, however, the church-in-council "testifies" to what it believes to be the substance of the Christian faith. To the extent that the *Basis of Union* is what it says it is and the *Constitution* functions constitutionally, the church corporate so governed espouses the substance of faith described in its founding documents. We have noted the concept of theological authority that appears in them. We turn now to the specific teachings presupposed in and developed out of the norm, source, resource, and setting.

In the section of the *Basis of Union* designated "Faith" and in key parts of the *Constitution*, the Trinitarian formula and the ancient triune structure of faith statement are used to express bonding belief. Thus "a local church is composed of persons . . . believing in God as heavenly Father, and accepting Jesus Christ as Lord and Savior, and depending on the guidance of the Holy Spirit" (*Constitution*, IV.8.). This is repeated in the *Basis of Union:* "We believe in God the Father Almighty, Creator and Sustainer of heaven and earth and in Jesus Christ his Son our Lord and Savior, who for us and our salvation lived and died and rose again and lives evermore; and in the Holy Spirit, who takes the things of Christ and shows them to us . . ." (*Basis of Union*, II).

The drafters of the *Basis of Union* and *Constitution* were not conscious of the issues of patriarchal language that now exercise us, and for which on Trinitarian language there is yet no clear resolution. As we struggle with these questions, we cannot overlook the doctrinal *substance* to which they sought to be faithful in their own formulations.

In the language of the tradition, this Trinitarian substance has to do with two understandings of Trinity. First, it has been variously described as "the economic Trinity," "the missions of the three Persons," "the trinitarian history of God." This is the Christian story of what God *has done* in creation, in the covenant with Israel, in the incarnation of Jesus Christ; what God *is doing* in the Spirit's work in the church and the world; what God *will do* to accomplish the divine purpose in the future and finally in consummation of all things. The section on "Faith" in the *Basis of Union* flows in this fashion. And the United Church of Christ Statement of Faith, which is the "ampler statement called for in Article IV, Section F" (*Basis of Union*, II), takes this same narrative direction. In forming the confession of faith around "the divine economy," the UCC documents are following the three acts of the Christian drama delineated in the three-paragraph structure of the ecumenical creeds. Second, it has been known as "the immanent Trinity." This is presupposed in the *Basis*, the *Constitution*, and the subsequent Statement of Faith wherever allusion is made to the status of the Persons. Together with God the Father, Christ is "Lord," "Son of God," "His Son," "the Word of God" (*Constitution*, Preamble, IV. 8. 9; *Basis of Union*, Preamble II). The status of Christ as a full Person of the Trinity assumed in these descriptions is manifest in the Statement of Faith's incarnational assertion: "In Jesus Christ, the man of Nazareth . . . you have come to us and shared our common lot" (Statement of Faith in the Form of a Doxology).

The Holy Spirit is also described in personal terms as one "who takes the things of Christ and shows them to us" (*Basis of Union*, II). Thus the missions of the Trinity are not "parts of God or transient modes, but full Persons." Yet the threefold Being is a triunity, the *Basis* "affirming our devotion to the one God" who "calls . . . creates . . . seeks . . . judges . . . comes to us . . . bestows . . . calls us . . . promises . . ." (Statement of Faith). The mystery of the three in one is not investigated in these terse references, thus inviting us to look both behind us in the confessional traditions for fuller exploration, and forward into newer interpretations of both the narrative and the social Trinity as these have illumined our current concerns for a fully participative life together in both world and church.[5]

Christological affirmations are prominent in the *Constitution*, the *Basis of Union*, and the derivative Statement of Faith. We have already referred to the unity with God in the doctrine of the Person of Christ. The unity with us is there as well in the Jesus who "lived and died" (*Basis*, II). This "man of Nazareth" is one with "us," sharing "our common lot" (Statement of Faith). Here is the Chalcedonian paradox: Jesus Christ, truly human, truly God, truly one.

The work of Christ is joined to the Person, set forth most frequently in the familiar phrase, Christ as "Lord and Savior" (*Constitution* and *Basis of Union, passim*). Or, in historical terms, Christ is the one "who for us and our salvation lived and died and rose again" (*Basis of Union*, II). The Statement of Faith repeats these three phrases of the *Basis of Union*, "the man of Nazareth, our crucified and risen Lord." In these acts, God in Christ is found to be "conquering sin and death and reconciling the world" (Statement of Faith). The outlines of "the threefold office of Christ" can be discerned here: a prophetic work done in the life and teaching, claiming us for "the cost and joy of discipleship" (Statement of Faith); a priestly work on the cross "reconciling the world" that brings "the forgiveness of sins;" a royal work in the resurrection "conquering . . . death."

The work of the Holy Spirit focuses on the church in the *Basis of Union*, the *Constitution*, and the Statement of Faith. We are gathered into the "one holy catholic Church" by the Spirit, "one body in Christ" (*Basis*, II). The Holy Spirit, so bestowed, creates and renews this church of Christ, "binding in covenant people of all ages, tongues and races" (Statement of Faith). The mission of this church is to call to "repentance and faith . . . for witnessing to the saving grace of God . . . for the universal propagation of the Gospel . . . [for] labor for the progress of knowledge, the promotion of justice, the reign of peace. . . ." (*Basis of Union*, II). Stated otherwise, its mission is "to be servants in the service of others, to proclaim the Gospel to all the world and resist the powers of evil" (Statement of Faith).

Outreach is grounded in nurturing the people of God for mission "in the public worship of God . . . the confession of [God's] name by word and deed . . . the administration of the sacraments . . . the upbuilding of the saints" (*Basis of Union*, II). In the language of the Statement this is a life together of being bound in "covenant to faithful people of all ages, tongues and races . . . to proclaim the Gospel . . . to share in Christ's baptism and eat at his table" (Statement of Faith). The *Constitution* takes special pains to mention that "it recognizes two sacraments: Baptism and the Lord's Supper or Holy Communion" (*Constitution*, Preamble).

Throughout the descriptions of mission and nurture are the familiar models and marks of the church—kerygma, diakonia, koinonia, leitourgia, or herald, servant, sacrament, mystical communion.[6] In our church these manifestations of the Spirit come to focus in our basic communities, the gathered churches "organized for Christian worship, for the furtherance of Christian fellowship, and for the ongoing work of Christian witness" (*Constitution*, IV.8). These "local churches of the United Church of Christ have, in fellowship, a God-given responsibility for that Church, its labors and extension, even as the United Church of Christ has, in fellowship, a God-given responsibility for the well-being and needs and aspirations of its local churches" (*Constitution*, IV.14).

The holy catholic church, the body of Christ, continues the ministry of Christ. As a newly phrased paragraph of the *Constitution* says: "The United Church of Christ recognizes that God calls the whole church and every member to participate in and extend the ministry of Jesus Christ by witnessing to the Gospel in church and society" (*Constitution*, V.17). The ministry of the body belongs to the whole people of God. Ordained ministry, called "to preach and teach the Gospel, to administer the sacraments and to exercise pastoral care and leadership" (*Constitution*, V. 20), and thus to "equip the saints," is authorized by the church at large through its appointed judicatories.

To what end is the work of the Spirit in and beyond the church? It is directed to the end of salvation, personal and social. Thus the church is "established for call . . . to repentance and faith" (*Basis of Union*, II), for "the forgiveness of sins and fullness of grace . . ." (Statement of Faith). This personal appropriation of "the saving grace of God in Christ" (*Basis*) is held together with a wider "creative and redemptive work in the world" (*Constitution*, Preamble). Here the sovereign God "judges peoples and nations" (Statement of Faith) and calls us to be in solidarity with this divine action among nations and peoples, resisting "the powers of evil," giving us therein "courage in the struggle for justice and peace" (Statement of Faith).

The climax of the Christian narrative in its UCC reading is "the consummation of the Kingdom of God" (*Basis of Union*, II). Here is "the triumph of righteousness" for which we both "look with faith . . . and work and pray" (*Basis*, II). With it comes "the life everlasting" (*Basis*, II). As the Statement of Faith, Doxological Form, 1981, has it in its crescendo, "You promise to all who trust you . . . eternal life in your realm which has no end. Blessing and honor, glory and power be unto you. Amen!"

We have reviewed the doctrinal touchstones in the defining texts of the United Church of Christ with exegesis of the same by the Statement of Faith. The "substance of the Christian faith" in these texts represents the way our forebears brought the threads of our varying traditions together in the doctrinal fabric of the denomination. Like the earlier discussed concept of authority in these texts, it is an irenic statement seeking to incorporate varied accents and cover the highlights of ecumenical Christian conviction. At work here is the unitive impulse within our church. However, the UCC is not so taken by "togetherness" that it lacks defining edges. Its inclusivity excludes reductionism. Its christological center and triune God cannot be confused with other centers or keep company with other gods. We are the United Church of *Christ*.

The diakonal aspect of our thirty-year journey is also underwritten by these texts. We have to do here with a narrative God moving determinedly in and through the history of people and nations, empowering for the struggles of justice and peace, for resisting the powers of evil, for being a servant in the service of others. A holy love judges the powers and principalities, and exacts the cost as well as gives the joy of disciple-ship. While servanthood is a central feature of our "world-formative" faith,[7] it is not the only mark of our church. The texts keep the doing in partnership with the telling and celebrating, kerygma and leitourgia joined to diakonia, indeed the former rooted in the latter and the latter impossible without the former.

CRAIGVILLE COMMENTARY

Flesh is put on these bare bones of Christian doctrine by the earlier cited historic traditions which have formed us. In closing we mention some subsequent theological textuality that provides an additional inter-pretive framework for our doctrinal convergences.

The search for theological identity in which the United Church of Christ is now engaged (of which this volume is itself a part) has a strong grass-roots character. This is not surprising for a church that prides itself on its local vitalities. In this case, a "theology from below" has taken shape through the initiative of pastors and laity in a theological ferment throughout the church.[8] One of its movements has provided a forum for regular theological encounter for diverse constituencies within the church, striving to locate the unities within the diversities. We draw on the statements of the Craigville Colloquies as indicators of doctrinal convergence that stand in continuity with the official texts of the church just examined.[9]

Colloquies I and II gave active attention to the issue of *norms* of theological authority. Colloquy I, on the fiftieth anniversary of the Barmen Declaration, acknowledged the temptations to cultural captivity in our own churches, the condition to which Barmen spoke. And it struck a similar christological note: "With Barmen we confess fidelity to 'the one Word of God. . . . ' Christ is the Center to whom we turn in the midst of the clamors, uncertainties and temptations of the hour." Colloquy II, addressed specifically to the issue of doctrinal standards, pointed to the same central norm: "Jesus Christ is the primary Word of God, in which we know ourselves judged and reconciled by God, and sent out to be reconciled to our neighbors." So too Colloquy III, focused on the nature of ministry, cites agreement with the Consultation on Church Union Consensus and declares, "Jesus Christ is the minister from whom all ministry derives and to whom it is accountable." Thus the participants in the Colloquies underscore the fact that their faith community is the United Church of *Christ,* and seek to relate that centrality found in its charters to current issues of authority and minis-try.

The three other elements in the pattern of authority in the United

Church of Christ also recur with their characteristic roles. Again echoing the Barmen Declaration, Colloquy I asserts, "We confess Jesus Christ as he is attested to us in Holy Scripture. . . . Christ speaks to us unfailingly in the prophetic-apostolic testimony. Under his authority, we hold the Bible as the trustworthy rule of faith and practice." In a similar vein, Colloquy II affirms the primacy of a christologically interpreted scripture: "The holy God speaks the self-revealing Word in the Holy Scriptures, through the testimony of the Holy Spirit. All our words are accountable to that Word spoken in and through the canon." Scripture so understood as *source* of authority read through the lens of Christ is linked in both Colloquies I and II with the *resource* role of the church and its traditions. Colloquy I: "We believe that the ecumenical creeds, the evangelical confessions, and the covenants we have made in our churches at various times and places, aid us in understanding the Word addressed to us." Colloquy II: "The canon is inextricably bound to the Christian community, known to us both through the stories, creeds and confessions of its history and through participation in its contemporary life." And along with biblical source and ecclesial resource, both Colloquies located these texts in the context of human experience and history. Colloquy I: "We accept the call to relate that Word to the world of peril and hope in which God has placed us, making the ancient faith our own in this generation 'in honesty of thought and expression, and in purity of heart before God.' " Colloquy II: "The authority of Scripture, the authority of tradition and the authority of experience are inextricably bound together . . . new testimonies to God's Word will continue to arise in new historical contexts, and new stories will grow out of our response to the biblical narrative. These testimonies and stories will serve as new earthen vessels to carry the Word of God by which these and all human witnesses are judged."

In the functioning of norm, source, resource, and setting, the Colloquies returned again and again to the two motifs that characterize UCC witness: a *church united and uniting* and a *just peace church*. On authority matters these motifs function as interpretive principles. That is, the hermeneutical community that is aptly positioned to understand the claims of the Christ of scripture, tradition, and human experience is one that is both catholic and committed. Striking the first note, the imperative to be a uniting church, Colloquy II used the figure of a prism: "As light is refracted through a prism to produce a full spectrum of color, so the Word of God is refracted through Scripture. . . . Only when all the colors are gathered in the testimony of the whole community can we begin to glimpse the fullness of God's Word made known to us. As Paul reminds us, all the parts are necessary for the wholeness of the body of Christ" (1 Corinthians 12); and sounding the second note, the struggle for justice and peace, Colloquy I declared that "in the United Church of Christ we believe that the divine initiatives cannot be separated from God's call to respond with our own liberating and reconciling deeds in this world, and thus to accept the cost and joy of discipleship."

CONCLUSION

We began by asking, What unites the United Church of Christ? *Empirically,* we are united by our connection to a singular set of histories and to a series of decisions that manifest our action and ecumenical commitments. *Textually,* we are united by our relationship to defining beliefs that give a theological coherence to the histories we have and the decisions we make. To know and love the doctrinal substance—as ordination papers are prepared, as sermons are preached, as classes are taught, the Bible is studied, decisions are made, and mission is carried out—would provide the theological vertebrae so sorely needed in our body of Christ. And to know that substance would position us for the World Council of Churches' next important ecumenical venture, "Toward a Common Expression of the Apostolic Faith Today"—in which a church "united and uniting" should be expected to give leadership. We do share in that apostolic faith. And we have a special gift to bring to others through our experience of wrestling with it from our varied perspectives. Diversity is not the foe of doctrine. It stretches those who honor it toward catholicity. May we live *out* the enriching unity we have and *toward* a larger unity to come.

NOTES

1. See Barbara Brown Zikmund, ed., *Hidden Histories in the United Church of Christ,* 2 vols. (New York: United Church Press, 1984, 1987), an excellent collection of essays of voices from the United Church of Christ constituencies.

2. For an effort to discern these premises as they function in our liturgy, life, and mission, see "The Confessional Nature of the United Church of Christ," *EKU-UCC Newsletter* 5 (February 1984), 2–15. An earlier expression of ideas in that essay and in this chapter appeared in "Theology and Forms of Confession in the UCC," *The Chicago Theological Seminary Register* 69 (Winter 1979):12–24, reprinted in *Andover Newton Quarterly* 19 (January 1979):176, 189; and *Encounter* 41 (Winter 1980):37–52.

3. How, where, and the extent to which these texts are authoritative is a complex question with its dramatic historical moments (the Cadman court case) and continuing puzzlements. The view assumed here touching Christian belief is as follows: (*a*) The doctrinal affirmations in the *Basis of Union* and *Constitution* were the agreed-upon "essentials" of Christian faith for the formation of the

United Church of Christ. ("In essentials unity" as the lore of several of the
united bodies asserts.) Without this agreement on "the faith . . . held generally
by members of the two uniting communions" (*Basis,* footnote 3), there would
have been no church. They are part of the "basis of union." (*b*) The formulation
of the doctrinal agreements in the *Basis* (and by implication in the *Constitution*
and of course the subsequent Statement of Faith) is "a testimony, not a test of
faith." This means several things—(1) The affirmation of essentials can be stated
in other language that captures the intended meanings. However, these linguistic
formulations are not, as such, tests. This latitude is apparent already in the
constitutional variations in describing one of the sacraments as "the Lord's
Supper or Holy Communion" (*Constitution,* 2). So it might be identified as
eucharist, meal of the kingdom, etc. But the intention is the stable affirmation
that for the UCC this is a sacrament integral to its life. (2) The status of these
formulations as testimony does not preclude the presence of tests of faith in the
churches of the United Church of Christ. They are identified as testimony in
order not to intrude upon the right of a local congregation to adopt its own
regulations for admission, discipline, and dismissal and thus "to formulate its
own covenants and confessions of faith" (*Constitution,* IV.15). A confessional
testimony therefore of the church "is not to be considered a substitute for any
confession of faith which may be used in any congregation today" (*Basis,* footnote
3). (3) Testimony, however, has a positive as well as a negative function. It is a
witness to the congregations as to what the church holds to be so, what the
congregations when they participate in that church will be perceived corporately
to hold to be so, and what the church hopes will be incorporated in the
assumptions of local church confessions. It is, therefore, testimony to both those
in and those beyond the local church of what this church corporate holds to be
true. These confessional testimonies do represent the substance of the faith of
this church. To the extent that a congregation is part of this corporate Christian
body rather than another one, this substance also represents the participating
congregation. This in no way abridges the right of local congregations to express
in their own way what they believe about fundamental doctrinal matters or
current theological formulations. (4) In subscribing to the *Constitution* and *Basis
of Union,* as all officially connected local churches in the UCC have done, these
churches agree that these confessional testimonies represent the doctrinal views
of the church. (Thus in its "Baptism, Eucharist, Ministry" response in 1984, the
General Synod rightly alluded to both the *Basis* and the Preamble to the
Constitution.) (5) A judicatory created by the *Constitution* and grounded in the
Basis of Union is accountable to the intended meaning of the faith testimonies in
these documents.

4. "Evangelical" here refers to the classical Reformation identity of churches
espousing the authority of scripture and justification by grace through faith. For
the relation of this more traditional meaning to recent usage see Gabriel Fackre's
"Evangelical, Evangelicalism," in *The Westminster Dictionary of Christian Theology,*
ed. Alan Richardson and John Bowden (Philadelphia: Westminster Press, 1983),
191–92.

5. See "The Mission and Nature of the Church," the statement of an Office
of Church Life and Leadership task force on ecclesiology: "For Christians, God
is triune. That means the very inner being of God is social. The three Persons

dwell eternally in 'Shalom,' . . . coinhering, related to such intimate *inter*-mission that they are totally present to and in one another. The three *are* one. God is love! (1 John 4:16)." For commentary on the social Trinity, see the work of two UCC theologians, Susan Brooks Thistlethwaite, "God Language and the Trinity," *EKU-UCC Newsletter* 5 (February 1984):16–25; and Royce Gordon Gruenler, *The Trinity in the Gospel of John* (Grand Rapids: Baker Book House, 1986).

6. The dimensions of the church as kerygma, diakonia, koinonia, and leitourgia have emerged in the World Council of Churches' discussion of mission. Avery Dulles has developed the models of the church as herald, servant, sacrament, mystical communion, and institution in *Models of the Church* (Garden City, N.Y.: Doubleday & Co., 1974). For an attempt to correlate dimensions, models, and the traditional marks of the church as one holy, catholic, and apostolic, see Gabriel Fackre, *The Christian Story*, rev ed. (Grand Rapids: Wm. B. Eerdmans, 1984), 159–71.

7. The Reformed tradition so identified by Nicholas Wolterstorff in *Until Justice and Peace Embrace* (Grand Rapids: Wm. B. Eerdmans, 1983), 3–22.

8. For a chronicle of these developments see Gabriel Fackre, "Theological Soul-Searching in the United Church of Christ," *Mid-Stream* 24 (April 1985): 155–64.

9. For Colloquy I, see "The Craigville Colloquy Letter," *New Conversations* 8 (Spring 1985):7–10, together with commentary by participants, 11–15, 33–42, 48–55; Colloquy II: "Craigville II Theological Colloquy Witness," *United Church News* (November 1985):6; Craigville III: "A Witness to Our Brothers and Sisters in the United Church of Christ from Craigville III Theological Colloquy," *United Church News* (December 1986):10.

15

LIBERATION THEOLOGY AND
THE UNITED CHURCH OF CHRIST

M. DOUGLAS MEEKS

Like all churches throughout the world, the United Church of Christ is discovering that, far from being a passing phenomenon, liberation theology is a way of doing theology that is important for the future of the denomination. Liberation theology, however, is not a monolith. Even though I shall refer to liberation theology as a single trajectory, it is more accurate to speak of liberation theologies, diverse theologies, sometimes conflicting, that have been developed in various parts of the world, which nevertheless have important family ties.

In addition to Latin American liberation theology, Asian and African, black and feminist, Native American, Chicano, and Asian-American theologies consider themselves "liberation" theologies.[1] In Europe many of the themes of liberation theology have been found in the movement called "political theology." Other groups in North America have begun to find liberation theology crucial to their life. These groups include urban workers, the elderly, the disabled, the marginalized, and advocates of different life styles. A large number of United Church of Christ persons are deeply involved in one or more of these liberation theologies. In fact, the first person to develop liberation theology specifically in the North American context is a UCC theologian, Frederick Herzog, whose book, *Liberation Theology*, was published in 1972.[2]

In this essay I shall refer to the originating thrusts of Latin American liberation theology, but the primary focus will be on the relevance of liberation theology for the United Church of Christ. One of the basic assumptions of liberation theologies is that you cannot import theology from one cultural and socioeconomic situation to another. Latin American liberation theology imported ready-made to North America would seem not only strange but also unfaithful to its own methodology. There are, however, some basic similarities that liberation theologies keep learning from each other which give them a strong kinship. How would these similarities appear in the context of the United Church of Christ?

The UCC is a young church still struggling to find its theological identity. When the UCC came into being, it united three major strands of the Reformation—an extremely difficult undertaking. The attempt to mediate these traditions looked arduous and uncertain from the beginning.[3] Many in the church thought it best to realize the union by looking to the future and to engage in common mission tasks in the present. But the UCC is now learning out of experience that it cannot live faithfully in the present without retrieving the tradition. Liberation theology offers a way in which the church can critically remember the past, reject what is distorted and yet receive the tradition-mediated promises that give the denomination a future in God's mission in the world. It is not surprising that many people in the UCC are open to liberation theology, for though it recovers much that has been suppressed in the tradition, liberation theology does represent a break with modern theology and opens up new ways of doing theology.

It is also true that the public commitments of the United Church of Christ to justice and peace find critical and substantive support in liberation theologies, for which justice and peace are not ancillary matters but the very heart of theology.[4] Justice and peace are the heart of theology, however, not simply for ethical and strategic reasons but because they belong to God's own character. Occasionally the UCC has been tempted to make justice and peace its issues merely to construct its own identity. By developing its own liberation theology the UCC might be able to find its identity shaped by the being and work of God in the world.

The UCC has sometimes spoken a good game of justice and peace in pronouncements and programmatic visions but in actuality has found that there are not many people to carry out these pronouncements and visions in society. Liberation theologies work at the conversion of individual persons and the formation of actual communities that can bear these projects in the world.

TURN TO THE POOR

Liberation theology represents a dramatic paradigm shift, a "Copernican turn," in Christian theology. It is too early to say whether the shift is, as some claim, as dramatic as the Protestant Reformation. But it seems rather clear that all existing theologies have been influenced by the move away from the hegemony of certain dominating tendencies in European and North American theology over the last two hundred years. The new way of doing theology is characterized by the claim that Christian theology should begin with the experience of the poor. Beginning with the model of Friedrich Schleiermacher's dialogues with the "cultured despisers of Christianity" in the early nineteenth-century salons of Berlin, Protestant theology has been dominated by white, affluent, academic males. The experience of the poor, people of color, and women has been theologically marginalized. Those who have so far been the authors of liberation theology were themselves trained in the theological centers of Europe and North America. But they have identified with people who, in the eyes of society, were "non-persons."[5]

A primary concern of liberation theologians is the liberation of theology itself.[6] This requires first the conversion of the theologian. The theologian is to live a life accountable to those for whom Christ died: the poor, the oppressed, the sinners, and the dying. Theology is not to be imposed from above by an infallible magisterium or an unquestioned sourcebook of tradition. Rather, theology is to be done from below, from the locus of oppression in which people find themselves and directed toward the transformation of the conditions of oppression. Theology finds its proper context where God is involved in the suffering of the world.

Latin American liberation theology began with an analysis of the conditions of dependence, poverty, and injustice in which the vast majority of the people live.[7] Why are people hungry, landless, diseased, illiterate, poor, tortured, and fearful? The analysis in Latin America, as in other contexts, led to uncovering systems of oppression in which the church and its theology have also become entangled and often supportive of dominant political policies. Through the periods of colonialism, neocolonialism, and dependence on the multinational corporation economy of the United States, the church's theology in Latin America has had its part to play in the domination and repression required to keep two hundred years of imperialism alive. If Christian theology must always ask the question, *Cui bono?* (For whose good is theology done?), the answer of liberation theologies is, For the sake of the poor and oppressed who are struggling for their freedom and dignity.

This answer is not an ideological response. It comes from the character of God as known in Israel and Jesus. A name of this God is "Immanuel" (God with you). This God is characteristically with slaves, the oppressed poor, orphaned, and widowed, with those who are sinners, and with those who are most subject to death. Liberation begins with the poor because God is with the poor. We come to know God precisely by coming to know God's involvement in the struggle of the poor for freedom.[8] However much Moses at the burning bush might desire a fully developed metaphysics of the divine being who is sending him to liberate slaves in Egypt, the enigmatic reply "I will be who I will be" suggests that Moses will come to know God only in the concrete historical events of struggle for freedom in Egypt. As the poor irrupt in history, and the way we are living historically is called into question, a new experience of God is occurring.

For this theological reason liberation theology speaks of the "privileged option of the poor," "the disturbing presence of the poor," and "the power of the poor in history." No sound liberation theology thinks of the poor and poverty in one-dimensional terms. Even in Latin America, where economic dependence has been the focus, liberation theologians emphasize the additional dimensions of poverty and oppression. The cries of poverty and oppression are heard in the economic, political, cultural (for example, racism, sexism, ageism, the degradation of the handicapped, meritocracy), natural, and personal spheres of life. The cry of the poor is the cry for bread, for freedom to determine one's future, for the right to name and story not defined by society's racist and sexist projections, for the right of nature to its own environment and its access to what it needs to live, and, finally, the cry for personal meaning and hope in life. Liberation theology has taught us that these dimensions of poverty and oppression are interrelated. If one is poor in some of these areas, one is likely to be oppressed in the other areas.

The United Church of Christ needs a liberation theology that brings together all of these spheres. That theology should make clear that most of us are "oppressed" at some time or another in one or more of these dimensions.[9] Sometimes one is oppressed, sometimes one is an oppressor, and all of the time we are all caught up in oppressive systems. Liberation theology identifies the radicalness of God's liberation by beginning with those who are most greatly oppressed.[10] God in Jesus Christ begins with those whom the New Testament calls the 'am aretz, the ochlos (the crowd), the ptochoi (the poor)—the mass of hungry, politically unorganized, nameless, sick, and hopeless people who gather around Jesus. They are the people in whose presence Immanuel is present. God begins with these people because they are most subject to the threat of death, sin, and evil. God seeks to redeem the whole creation, but God begins with these people because it is among them that God's own glory and power are most denied and threatened. If God's righteousness, God's power, is to be demonstrated in the world, it will have to be here where it is most fundamentally contested.

And thus liberation theology begins with God in the poor and the poor in God because it is only there that we shall find the God who creates everything out of nothing, who makes a people out of the nullity of slavery, and who liberates from the power of death the just one, Jesus, in the shape of whose righteousness we are promised a future without death for the whole creation.

SIN AND SALVATION

God's involvement in all of the dimensions of oppression and liberation means that sin and salvation must be understood in new ways. Sin is not only thoughts and acts impeding the attainment of a spiritual salvation in afterlife. Sin is a historical reality, a fundamental alienation from God and humanity. That sin is embodied in social structures that turn people into commodities, objects to be exchanged and manipulated. It is the evil and violence that distorts humanity and destroys the creation. God's redeeming work in history must, then, include freedom from oppressive systems, even if this freedom will never be realized fully in history.

PRIORITY OF PRAXIS OVER THEORY

Beginning with the poor disrupts and transforms previous ways of being Christian and leads to a new method of doing theology. The starting point of traditional theology is philosophical assumptions about knowledge, the existence of God, and the personal experience of the believer. Christian theology starts with an active commitment to the liberation of the oppressed. Instead of theology as abstraction from history, liberation theology expresses the community's actions in God's involvement in history.

Liberation theology eschews dichotomies and dualisms, which it considers instruments of domination. One central dichotomy it criticizes is the split between secular and sacred history. God is at work in the history of the only world there is, the world God loves with God's whole life (John 3:16). History as locus of theology leads to praxis as the orientation of theology.

Liberation theology also criticizes the theory-practice dichotomy. Knowledge of the gospel is not an abstract, propositional knowing but an obedient doing. There can be no understanding of the gospel apart from doing it. To know God is to do God's will; to know God is to do God's justice. Liberation theology thus speaks of *orthopraxis* rather than *orthodoxy*, enhancing the classical definition of theology, "faith seeking understanding," with "faith seeking obedient doing."

The North American tendency to interpret praxis as sheer practice is mistaken. Praxis is an unending reciprocity between action and reflection within the community. Praxis is practice that includes the intervention of God's word and the critical reason that arises out of God's word confronting the contemporary situation of suffering. The exaltation of practice may be simply the intensification of unfaithful practices, that is, a way of continuing the status quo.

REMEMBERING THE PROMISES IN A
DISTORTED PAST

If theology in the Western world has often been entangled with and supportive of domination, then theology must discover a way of criticizing its own distortions. This constant self-criticism should begin with a criticism of its sources. Christian theology always finds its sources in Christian tradition and human existence; it must always put text and context together in such a way that we become obedient to God's action in history. The way Christian theology has retrieved and used its sources has led to its own contribution to domination. Some North American interpreters have gotten the impression that liberation theology recommends that we forget about the Bible and the tradition and emphasize the immediacy of our experience. Nothing could be further from what liberation theology maintains. Its objective is to retrieve or reclaim our theological sources critically.

Liberation theology holds that all theology requires constant ideological critique of our own situation. Are we living with and upholding ideologies that make it impossible for us to read and understand the dangerous memories and the promises of the Bible for our time? Are we so much caught up in the logic of the market and its compelling insistence that life and future depend on the accumulation of wealth that we cannot receive the logic of the gospel? The practical life of solidarity with the poor has the power to rupture our unreflected acceptance of the ideologies by which we hold our world together; it gives us a perspective from which to criticize the interests and power configurations of our social location. Liberation theology refuses to cordon off a private dimension of human experience that is assumed to be religious and thus structurally inclusive of the divine. Human experience is fundamentally political.

What then of the source of Christian theology in Bible and tradition? One of the great problems within the UCC is the difficulty of coming to grips with the Bible. The Bible seems alien and silent in many places of this church.[11] But where the Bible is silent, the church simply conforms to the world around it. The church says nothing new to the world. Understandably, the world loses interest in the church when it hears only what the world has already said. Only God's promises remembered in the scriptures give the church its distinctive identity and a message that will be new to the world every time it is faithfully proclaimed.

Why is the Bible silent in much of the church? One reason for the silence is that the Bible is full of "dangerous memories" that call our present way of living into question. To allow these dangerous memories a place in our present removes the amnesia and anesthesia by which we learn to live oblivious to the suffering around us and in the global household. The rupture of history, of our oppressed and oppressive way of being in the world, begins with the disturbing memory of suffering. Only then can there be another interpretation of history and of the Bible than that given so far by the wealthy victors.

Another reason for the Bible's silence is that we have the sense that even the Bible has been distorted by the ideologies of the times and places in which its traditions were formed. Many of the biblical texts mediating God's word are deformed by exploitative, racist, and sexist ideological assumptions. Liberation theology clings to the biblical texts (for in the end they are all we have) and seeks to identify false ideologies within text and traditional interpretation, letting the text speak through the particularity of time.[12] If the Bible is both to demonstrate and transform Christian norms, there must be a hermeneutic circuit among text, traditional interpretations, and the interpreter in the present context.

These hermeneutic methods of critiquing are not so sophisticated that they cannot be followed by lay people. The means of criticizing and interpreting the Bible and the history of theology are not meant to keep the Bible and theology from ordinary Christians.[13] The work of clergy and scholars should be aimed at enabling lay people to read the scriptures in a new way. All liberation theologians assume that the Bible can be read and interpreted in a nonideological and nondistorting way by the gathered community. *The Gospel in Solentiname* depicts the way Nicaraguan peasants learned to read the text of the Bible and the context of their own situation through a critique of ideology and a hermeneutic based on their own experience of liberation.[14]

JESUS THE LIBERATOR

Given liberation theology's emphasis on history as the locus of God's redemption, it is not surprising that it focuses on Jesus instead of on many of the christological abstractions of the tradition.[15] This is not an attempt to find the "Jesus of history" but rather to take seriously the presentation of Jesus in the New Testament narratives as the beginning point and criterion for understanding God, God's eschatological relation to the world, and the church's life in the world. Some liberation theologians tend to become reductive in their concentration on Jesus. But, on the whole, liberation theologians understand the whole life and future of the triune God out of the relationships that come to expression in the Jesus narratives.[16] Theologians typically understand Jesus in his Jewishness, claiming that it is impossible to understand the Jesus movement without the framework of the messianic and apocalyptic traditions. The exodus is particularly important to the interpretation of God's radical embodiment in Jesus.

Jesus is understood in relation to the *basileia*, the reign of God's righteousness. The preaching, parables, miracles, and controversies of Jesus are all interpreted as expressive of God's righteousness, God's power for life against the forms of death, sin, and evil manifested in the human structures that distort and destroy human life.

Christology cannot be reduced to concepts or to a theory of how we are historically related to Jesus who is supposed to remain in the first century or mythically situated in heaven. Everything in the church and its mission in the world depends on the real presence of Jesus in the present. God's resurrection of Jesus from the dead means that Messiah Jesus is at work in our present, seeking to bring the homeless into the household God seeks to create.

SPIRITUALITY RECAST

It often comes as a surprise to many people that liberation theology stresses spirituality so thoroughly. This was the case already with the first major book of Gustavo Gutiérrez.[17] Closer to home, it has been the tireless effort of Frederick Herzog to remind the UCC and other North American denominations of the centrality of spirituality. The most important liberation theology statement to come out of the UCC is "Toward the Task of Sound Teaching in the United Church of Christ," published by the Office for Church Life and Leadership in 1978. The statement includes a "Liberation Affirmation" which has the character of a declaration/confession. It can be found in the appendix of Herzog's book, *Justice Church*, which is an example of liberation theology contextualized in the UCC's struggle to move beyond the deadening captivity to North American denominationalism.[18] The affirmation culminates in the "recreating of people through the Spirit" and defines the church as the "people responding in obedience to God's Holy Spirit as empowering Presence in history."[19]

Liberation theology calls for a spirituality that is neither privatized piety nor ethereal escapism. Rather, it points to the concrete ways in which the Holy Spirit works in the personal lives of baptismally covenanted Christians to create the church. It is working with new interpretation of the means of grace embodied in word, baptism, eucharist, and the charismata, the gifts of the Holy Spirit for ministry. The church cannot expect to be the locus of God's conversion of people without freeing baptism and the eucharist from the deadening ritualization and privatization that have made them impotent to form the life of the congregation. Remembering our baptism is the means by which we enter into covenantal cooperation with God's liberation struggle in the world. At the Lord's Table we learn a radically alternative logic for distributing what people need for life and life abundant. The congregation gathered around the alternative *oikonomia tou Theou* (economy of God) finds time and place in which to become and practice an economy different from what society offers.

Spirituality is the Holy Spirit *justi*fying us through God's grace, freeing us from dominating views of justice and rights so that we may be sanctified, empowered for living God's economy in the public household where there is almost no "good news for the poor." God does not expect people to go into the public household for the sake of the poor without freeing them and empowering them for this task. Thus liberation theology leads as a matter of course into hymnody, liturgy, prayer, witnessing, comforting, counseling, tears, and celebration—all those things necessary if we are to keep our promises to be God's people of justice in the world.

MODEL OF THE CHURCH

The UCC is similar to the other old-line denominations in North America in suffering a deep anxiety over declining members and finances. What will make the church grow? It is tempted to follow the "successful" growth models of multinational corporations. But it is beginning to discover that this way leads neither to growth nor to faithfulness. It is beginning to take seriously the question of how the church of Jesus Christ actually comes into being.[20] One factor that is gradually bringing the UCC into this consciousness is an awareness of the discrepancy between what it pronounces about its involvement in society and the little actual impact it has often had in changing the oppressive conditions of our society. In this situation the UCC might find new hope for its own experiment in ecclesiology by working through its own liberation ecclesiology in dialogue with that of Latin American theology.

Liberation ecclesiologies follow the simple biblical realization that the mission of God in the world needs people to bear it. Unless there are converted people in a transformed church, we are not really participating in God's transformation of the world. Thus liberation theology begins in the life and work of people. Its aim is the new formation of the church, in solidarity with the poor, for the transformation of the world.

Even in liberal churches in North America the conception of the church is not much different from individualistic "soul-saving." In the more liberal church this has to do with understanding the church as "vacation" or therapy, a way of compensating, unburdening, and isolating the individual in face of the dehumanization that takes place in the public world of production and consumption.[21] The church belongs to that part of culture we call "the pause that refreshes." Belonging essentially to the private world, the church serves the public world by helping people cope with dehumanization in the public household and by providing a stable, unchanging institution in a society where all institutions of the political economy are in constant flux. When it performs these functions, the church does not exist for the conversion of people, much less the transformation of society.

The new model of the church in liberation theology is embodied in groups called in Latin America the *comunidades eclesiales de base* (base ecclesial communities).[22] Estimated to number more than seventy thousand in Latin America, these base communities gather once or twice a week to hear the word of God. Participants know that the church of Jesus Christ is *creatura verbi*, creature of the living word of God. But from the beginning no one is a passive recipient of the word. Rather, everyone is given the chance to be an active interpreter of the word. Out of exegesis and interpretation of the people comes a sense of the text as a living, creative presence. The key is that the gospel is always confronted by the concrete situation and problems of the people in the community. The Bible is not merely a consoling message or a source of private meaning in life. It is light for the problems of the community; it is leaven for the action of the community.

The concept of the base community could revitalize the life and witness of our denomination. These groups could be fostered within the congregations but also include people from outside. In the context of the UCC, communities would gather around mutual interpretation of the Bible by bringing to it community concerns such as the illness, unemployment, family crisis, or joy of a community member. The scriptures would be read out of this experience. But the exegesis would not be privatized, for if the community of believers remains closed in on itself, then it has disregarded its covenanted character to live for the sake of the world. Through local base communities, congregations could more faithfully become churches of the poor, among the poor.

Thus, this first stage of interpretation leads the community to take account of the social questions of their surroundings: the question of schools, health-care delivery, the repair of the community's infrastructure, the welfare system. These questions in turn lead to gaining a perspective on the political economy in which we live. Christians are called to read and understand not only the biblical text but also the text of the world. The way our society is organized must also be understood. This task should not be left to the social scientists any more than interpreting the Bible should be left to biblical scientists. Finally, the biblical and social interpretation of the community should lead to the participation in various movements, organizations, and parties that work for changing and moving legal, economic, political, and social structures toward greater justice.

Liberation theology has already influenced the United Church of Christ in many ways, notably in the social justice programs of national instrumentalities and agencies. But the greatest promise of this movement lies in the rebirth of our denomination at the local level, as congregations of committed believers act and worship in solidarity with the poor in our midst. This is truly to serve Jesus Christ.

NOTES

1. For an introduction to liberation theology see Philip Berryman, *Liberation Theology* (Oak Park, Ill.: Meyer-Stone Books, 1987); and Robert McAfee Brown, *Theology in a New Key: Responding to Liberation Themes* (Philadelphia: Westminster Press, 1978). A more technical introduction is Rebecca S. Chopp, *The Praxis of Suffering: An Interpretation of Liberation and Political Theologies* (Maryknoll, N.Y.: Orbis Books, 1986).

2. Frederick Herzog, *Liberation Theology* (New York: Seabury Press, 1972).

3. This story can be followed in Louis H. Gunnemann, *The Shaping of the United Church of Christ: An Essay in the History of American Christianity* (New York: United Church Press, 1977); and idem, *United and Uniting: The Meaning of an Ecclesial Journey* (New York: United Church Press, 1987).

4. See Susan Thistlethwaite, ed., *A Just Peace Church* (New York: United Church Press, 1986); and Audrey C. Smock, ed., *Christian Faith and Economic Life* (New York: United Church Board for World Ministries, 1987).

5. As Frederick Herzog puts it, "Theology which does not take the world's poor into account from the word 'go' isn't Christian theology" ("Birth Pangs of Liberation Theology in North America," in *Mission Trends No. 4*, ed. Gerald H. Anderson and Thomas F. Stransky [Grand Rapids: Wm. B. Eerdmans, 1979]:34).

6. Juan Luis Segundo, *The Liberation of Theology*, trans. John Drury (Maryknoll, N.Y.: Orbis Books, 1976).

7. An early example of this is the still-standard text, Gustavo Gutiérrez, *A Theology of Liberation: History, Politics, and Salvation*, trans. Caridad Inda and John Eagleson (Maryknoll, N.Y.: Orbis Books, 1973).

8. See Gutiérrez, *Theology of Liberation*, 189–208.

9. See Jurgen Moltman and M. Douglas Meeks, "The Liberation of Oppressors," *Christianity and Crisis* 38 (25 December 1978):316ff.

10. M. Douglas Meeks, "How To Speak to God in an Affluent Society," in *Is Liberation Theology for North America?* (New York: Theology in the Americas, 1979), reprinted in shorter form in *The Witness* (October 1979):8–9.

11. This was one of the major issues of the discussion in an entire issue of *New Conversations:* "Toward Theological Self-Understanding in the United Church of Christ," *New Conversations* (Spring 1985).

12. One of the best examples of working in this way is Elisabeth Schüssler Fiorenza, *In Memory of Her: A Feminist Theological Reconstruction of Christian Origins* (New York: Crossroad, 1983).

13. Letty M. Russell shows how the question of sources and authority can be contextualized in the situation of the North American congregation in *Household of Freedom: Authority in Feminist Theology* (Philadelphia: Westminster Press, 1987).

14. Ernest Cardenal, *The Gospel in Solentiname*, 4 vols. (Maryknoll, N.Y.: Orbis Books, 1976).

15. See Jon Sobrino, *Christology at the Crossroads*, trans. John Drury (Maryknoll, N.Y.: Orbis Books, 1978); and cf. Frederick Herzog, *Justice Church: The New Function of the Church in North American Christianity* (Maryknoll, N.Y.: Orbis Books, 1980), 30–51.

16. Liberation theology "uses narrative as a basic form or structure of theology to retrieve the Christian tradition, to narrate the dangerous memories of suffering, and to effect conversion and transformation. In liberation theology the centrality of narrative is the attention to the radically historical and hermeneutical character of life and to the narrative structure of Christianity. Narrative speaks of suffering in a way that theory cannot; it matches the structure of experience and the nature of Christian tradition" (Chopp, *Praxis of Suffering*, 141).

17. Gutiérrez, *Theology of Liberation*, 255–308; see also idem, *We Drink From Our Own Wells: The Spiritual Journey of a People*, trans. Matthew J. O. O'Connell (Maryknoll, N.Y.: Orbis Books, 1984).

18. Herzog, *Justice Church*, 139–48.

19. Ibid., 147.

20. Leonardo Boff, *Ecclesiogenesis: The Base Communities Reinvent the Church*, trans. Robert R. Barr (Maryknoll, N.Y.: Orbis Books, 1986).

21. See M. Douglas Meeks, "Hope and the Ministry of Planning and Management," *Anglican Theological Review* 54 (April 1982):147–62.

22. For a brief account of Latin American base communities see Leonardo Boff, *Church: Charism and Power: Liberation Theology and the Institutional Church*, trans. John W. Diercksmeier (New York: Crossroad, 1985).

16

LESBIAN AND GAY:
THE GOSPEL AND THE CHURCH

ALICE O'DONOVAN

In 1972, on the fifteenth anniversary of the United Church of Christ, William Reagan Johnson, an openly gay man, was ordained to ministry by the Golden Gate Association of the United Church of Christ. At the close of the Ecclesiastical Council that approved his ordination, Johnson said, "I celebrate that today you have given me the opportunity to do the work that I know I do best."[1]

Nearly two decades later, Johnson has yet to realize that opportunity. Few openly lesbian or gay clergy persons have been called to pastoral ministry by United Church of Christ congregations.

Some Christian denominations have simply closed the door of ministry for their openly lesbian or gay members. In 1986, John McNeill was expelled from the Jesuit order after forty years because he publicly advocated ethically responsible homosexual relationships; he recently broke a ten-year order of silence in order to protest the Vatican document "The Pastoral Care of Homosexual Persons."[2] A similar incident involved the defrocking of Rosemary Denman, a United Methodist minister, because she is a lesbian.[3]

The Task Force on Changing Patterns of Sexuality and Family Life of the Episcopal Diocese of Newark stated: "We believe that the [Episcopal] Church should be as inclusive of homosexual persons as it is of heterosexual persons. . . . Criteria for membership, for participation in church committees, choirs, education, vestries, etc. and for ordination should be no different for any given group."[4] This report of the Task Force has become the focus of much publicity and controversy.

These glimpses of people and their churches grow out of a complex matrix of human experience; ignorance and knowledge, history, polity, theology, and ethics. The question that continues to lie before us both individually and corporately is this: Are lesbians and gay men fully human persons, entitled as such to first-class citizenship; or, are lesbians and gay men somehow less than fully human, and intrinsically morally inferior to the rest of sinful humanity?

The lives of lesbians and gay men are living testimony to the effective power of structural oppression, namely, racism, classism, sexism, and heterosexism. These forms of systemic oppression depend upon the notion that one group of people is somehow less than fully human; and therefore, members of the group in question deserve to be ruled (oppressed) by others.

Historically, humanity has drawn upon religious and sexual myths to reinforce the structures of oppression. A few examples? Biblical myth of Eve the temptress, the curse of Ham, Sodom and Gomorrah, and Jews as killers of the Christ have been used to fuel the fires of sexism, racism, heterosexism, and Auschwitz. Jews, women, blacks, and gays have been described as subhuman, inferior, and sexually perverse. In addition, the victimized group is often portrayed as being particularly dangerous to children, a pernicious myth that extends to the present day.

A bill to protect the civil rights of lesbians and gay men was introduced into the 1987 session of the Connecticut legislature; and after much political maneuvering it eventually lost in the House of Representatives by only one vote. This was in spite of the fact that twenty-five people testified in favor of the bill while only three persons testified in opposition. Some of those testifying were subjected to remarks like these from legislators:

> One of the biggest problems facing homosexuals is that if they're school teachers, parents fear that homosexual school teachers, you know, are less professional, that they will attempt to establish liaisons with their students.

> Suppose I had a strong, or you or any members here had a strong sexual orientation for animals? Would I be permitted under this particular bill to do whatever I choose and not be discriminated against for that?[5]

In recent years, Christian churches have attempted to draw a distinction between sexual orientation and sexual behavior, that is, between being and doing. Orientation has most often been understood as a reality beyond the moral control of the individual, and behavior as within the moral control of the individual. The United Church of Christ Task Force for the Study of Human Sexuality applied the distinction this way.

> In considering ordination we would suggest that sexual orientation in and of itself not be a criteria for determining a candidate's qualification, although an association might establish standards of behavior which apply to all candidates. Some of us on the Task Force make a distinction between

sexual orientation and sexual behavior. Those members believe that sexual
orientation, which refers to orientation of a person's feelings toward the
same sex, the opposite sex, or both, is not a moral issue. However, they
believe that sexual behavior does have moral significance.[6]

The Vatican document "Pastoral Care of Homosexual Persons" states
that homosexuality "must be seen as an objective disorder," that individual homosexual actions are "intrinsically disordered" and that "a person
engaging in homosexual behavior therefore acts immorally."[7] Other
denominations have taken similar positions, and have often held that the
celibate lesbian or gay man may be accepted as a generally moral person,
while those lesbians and gay men who engage in sexual activity are
intrinsically immoral, even "excluded from the kingdom."

This distinction between behavior and orientation raises several questions: Are sexual sins *the most important* category of human failing? (What
of greed, racism, and militarism, which claim millions of human lives
annually?) Is human sexuality limited and circumscribed by genital
sexual relations, or is human sexuality a more comprehensive reality? If
genital sexual behavior between persons of the same gender is always
immoral, meriting exclusion from the kingdom, is the lesbian or gay
man excluded from salvation by grace through faith? Are we required
to earn salvation through the "work" of celibacy? Virginia Mollenkott,
coauthor of *Is the Homosexual My Neighbor?* has written:

> The church must preach a consistent gospel of grace rather than backslid-
> ing into a message of works where this minority is concerned. When any
> church teaches that homosexual persons must live celibate in order to be
> first-class Christians, that church is adding to John 3:16 by asking that
> homosexual people believe in Jesus *and also* sacrifice sexual relationship,
> or reorient it.[8]

I would suggest that it is certainly appropriate for the church to
provide criteria by which human behavior may be evaluated for its moral
quality. First among such criteria is love, and the recognition that where
love is absent, justice also is absent. And justice is absent in all relationships based upon an inequality of power, that is, coercion. It matters not
whether the coercion is based upon economic power, greater intellectual
capacity, disparate age or maturity, greater physical (or military)
strength. It matters not whether the relationships are between nations,
corporations, or persons. It matters not whether the relationship is
contractual as between labor and management, or covenantal as between
wife and husband. Where coercion is present, where there is abuse of
power, love and justice are absent.

It therefore follows that if coercion is present in any sexual relationship, that relationship must be viewed as morally flawed, regardless of

the genders of the participants. This reality is exemplified by the statement "Wives are often just one man away from welfare." Prostitution, sexual molestation of children (a crime perpetrated primarily by heterosexual males upon female children), and sexual harassment in any setting fall into the same category of relationships characterized by coercion.

Moral sexual relationships, like any other relationship, are those characterized by love, that is, justice, mutuality, respect, "joy, peace, patience, goodness, gentleness, faithfulness, self-control" (Gal. 5:22–23). Such qualities are not dependent upon the gender of those in relationship.

The relationship of the church at large, and of the United Church of Christ in particular, to its lesbian and gay members (and women, persons of color, the handicapped, the old, and Native Americans) is a relationship characterized by coercion. First-class citizenship is systematically denied to persons in these several categories. The very existence of the Recognized Special Interest Groups is evidence of immoral relationship, evidence that the church responds with a resounding No! to the question, Are lesbians and gay men fully human?

The church is the home of hypocrisy is the charge leveled by those outside the church. Heterosexism, racism, and sexism are several reasons why such a charge is accurate. However, it is possible that the church can look to its scriptures, listen for the voices of the prophets and the voice of Jesus echoing across the centuries, and repent. It is possible that the church can turn from its sinful ways and commit itself to the gospel of love, the gospel of justice.

The making of justice—the realization of the gospel—is going to mean making some changes, some radical changes! It will mean answering the question with a resounding Yes! It will require the ordination and placement of clergy on the basis of merit and gifts for ministry rather than race, gender, age, or sexual orientation.

The realization of the gospel will require the blessing of all relationships where the intent of the partners is faithful commitment to one another and where the basis is love. It will require that churches distinguish themselves from the norms of society, and declare that since "God so loved the world," all are welcome. It will also require that the church become an advocate on behalf of lesbian and gay persons, that the lives of lesbians and gay men be celebrated, and the deaths of partners mourned, just like everyone else, no more, no less!

Even as I write these words, I can hear voices saying, But that will mean conflict in our churches! and hear knees knocking like castanets! I hear other voices, calm voices, smug voices, saying, Oh yes, but don't forget our polity. Congregational autonomy, you know! We can't force a

church to hire anyone, or do anything it doesn't want to. And some-
where between those who tremble and those who are smug, I hear
someone else saying, We must hear all the points of view, we must stay
neutral, we can't alienate anyone.

Bishop Desmond Tutu concluded his message to the fourth anniversary of the All Africa Church Conference with these words, "When two
persons are engaged in a conflict and one of them is considerably
stronger than the other, to be neutral is not just and fair and impartisan
because to be neutral is in fact to side with the powerful."⁹

Neutrality is an illusion. When we hear a call for neutrality by someone
who will not stand solidly with the victims of oppression, we must ask,
How is that person's self-interest served by the maintenance of the status
quo? Tutu is correct; a call for neutrality is always an alignment with the
powers that be.

Neutrality is never invoked apart from conflict, and there is little that
can strike fear more deeply into the heart of a pastor than church
conflict. The reasons for such fear of conflict in churches lie in faulty
methods of conflict resolution (for example, fire the pastor) and the
principle of congregational autonomy, which means that no real job
protection exists for the pastor or other church employees. Present
reality being what it is, few issues generate conflict any faster than the
issue of ordination of openly lesbian and gay persons to the ministry of
the church.

Homophobia is a real and potent force in our society and churches
today. The fear that pastors and other church leaders express is not a
groundless terror, but rather a realistic acknowledgment of the possible
cost of solidarity with lesbians and gay men. The church needs women
and men, ordained and lay, with sufficient conviction of the gospel's call
of love and justice, people with sufficient courage who are willing to pay
that price on behalf of lesbians and gay men. Similarly, lesbians and gay
men must also find that same conviction and courage in order to forgo
the tenuous security of invisibility.

The General Synods often speak clearly on behalf of lesbians and gay
men, and take stands demonstrating courage and welcome. However, it
is a constitutional reality that the General Synod never speaks for the
denomination; in fact, no voice exists that can speak for the denomination. It is also a constitutional reality that the Synod can only recommend
actions to local churches; "the autonomy of the local church is inherent
and modifiable only by its own action."¹⁰

Various conferences have also spoken clearly on behalf of gay persons.
However, like the General Synod, a conference cannot require a congregation to act justly; it cannot require that gay clergy be hired.

A serious question must be asked: Does the principle of congregational autonomy contribute to the process of creating justice or hinder the process? It is possible to recall situations in which the contribution of a congregation to the justice process has provided real leadership for the larger church and society. It is, however, a sad fact that such congregations have been the exceptions rather than the rule. I would suggest that when churches support civil rights legislation, affirmative action legislation for women, blacks, or gays, but have no intention of hiring women, blacks, and gays, then a serious credibility problem is created.

It is no longer acceptable to hide behind congregational autonomy in order to avoid doing what is right and just. Rather, it is time for congregations to seize the opportunity for moral leadership, and commit themselves to real justice and credible witness. It is time for conference placement officers working with search committees to advocate lesbian and gay candidates.

Some congregations have stepped into such moral leadership. As of January 1989, more than twenty United Church of Christ congregations across the country had publicly declared themselves "Open and Affirming." This means they issued a public statement of welcome to lesbians and gays and committed themselves to nondiscrimination in volunteer and professional placement. A few congregations have hired openly lesbian or gay clergy.

Lesbians and gay men constitute one of the largest groups of people who have been subjected to "church abuse." The church has tried many techniques to accomplish the agenda of exclusion of gay people. These techniques have included murder, slander, silence, and public denunciation.

The one thing that has not been tried is to transform the agenda. Genuine welcome, real pastoral care, and affirmation can alleviate suffering, as well as add wholeness and integrity to the life of the congregation. Authentic ministry with and for lesbian and gay persons might well be a whole new arena for evangelism and church growth.

It is a lively truism that "Until all are free, none are free." Like many others, lesbians and gay men are not free to love, work, and worship as persons of full integrity and humanity; therefore, no one is truly free. I have argued that the roots of such oppression are the same roots that feed other human malignancies. I am convinced that social justice is essential to our continued existence, and that the United Church of Christ is called to this ministry. I am well aware that our congregations are too small and too autonomous to accomplish all that is needed. We must find ways to witness as members of the body of Christ even as we work within the restrictions of congregational autonomy. The enemy is real and powerful; great courage and great faith are required.

Let us claim the promise set before us: "You promise to all who trust you, forgiveness of sins and fullness of grace, courage in the struggle for justice and peace."[11]

NOTES

1. W. Evan Golder, "Ordaining a Homosexual Minister," *Christian Century*, 28 June 1972, p. 716.

2. *New York Times*, 10 December 1986, section B, p. 1.

3. John Ellement, "N. H. Methodist Conference Faces Issue of Ousted Lesbian Minister," in *Boston Globe*, 22 May 1987, p. 25.

4. Report of the Task Force on Changing Patterns of Sexuality and Family Life, Episcopal Diocese of Newark, 1986.

5. *Proceedings*, Judiciary Committee, 1987, vol. 4, p. 37. Representatives Edith G. Prague and Francis X. O'Neill, respectively.

6. *The Report of the Task Force for the Study of Human Sexuality to the Fourteenth General Synod*, 1983, 14.

7. Congregation for the Doctrine of the Faith, "The Pastoral Care of Homosexual Persons," *Origins* 16 (November 1986): 379.

8. Virginia Ramey Mollenkott, "Overcoming Heterosexism," in *Breaking the Silence, Overcoming the Fear: Homophobia Education* (New York: Presbyterian Church, U.S.A., n.d.), 17.

9. Desmond M. Tutu, *Hope and Suffering* (Grand Rapids: Wm. B. Eerdmans, 1983), 39.

10. *The Constitution and Bylaws of the United Church of Christ*, IV.15.4.

11. United Church of Christ, Statement of Faith.

17

THE GIFT OF AUTHORITY

FREDERICK R. TROST

On May 30, 1836, George Wendelin Wall and Joseph Rieger arrived in the new world.[1] They traveled immediately from New York City to Hartford, Connecticut, where they were welcomed by the Congregationalist who taught English to these German-speaking missionaries. In October, they were given two boxes of books and Bible tracts by the congregation and they departed by way of Pittsburgh for the Ohio River to travel by steamer to the western frontier of Missouri. Though they began their journey together, Rieger arrived two days later because, recalling the commandment to keep the Sabbath day holy, he preferred to wait in Cincinnati until after the Lord's Day. Wall had no such qualms and arrived in Missouri two days ahead of his friend.

Here were two brothers in Christ, each baptized, each trained in the Basel Mission House in Germany, each called by God to the western frontier of America, each a servant of the Word, each carrying Bible tracts from the Congregationalists in New England, each understanding the commandments to be divine law, but choosing to interpret the words "Remember the sabbath day, to keep it holy" in different ways. I mention this seemingly insignificant event because I believe it offers an insight into the spirit of many whose faith eventually shaped the life and work of the United Church of Christ.

Among the various traditions that gave birth to this denomination is the one represented by Rieger and Wall, *Der Deutsche Evangelische Kirchenverein des Westens*, predecessor to the Evangelical Synod of North America. We remember Wall and Rieger and other pillars of the *Kirchenverein* not so much for their sermons or theological acumen, but for their bold attempts to live the love of Christ they sought to preach.

A few years ago a building lovingly called "the Castle" at the Bensenville Home near Chicago was razed. For more than a half century it had housed orphans and older adults as one of the mission projects of the Evangelical Synod of North America. When the cornerstone was cracked open, a parchment was found inside with the words "*Die Liebe Christ dringet uns also*" ("The love of Christ compels us"). It is true that the Evangelical Synod was not absorbed in mighty theological battles over Christian orthodoxy, but it did possess theological conviction. At its heart was the confession that "Jesus Christ is Lord," and this faith was accompanied by an unassuming piety that found expression through ministry in the world. The Bible was at the center of that faith and the attempt was made simply to live in the light of biblical truth, not argue and fight over its contents. As the story about Wall and Rieger shows, there was room for more than one interpretation of the meaning of scripture, while the witness of the prophets and apostles remained central.

In matters of faith the scriptures were to be trusted, and as guides to interpretation of scripture the *Kirchenverein* turned to three historic confessional statements: the Reformed Heidelberg Catechism, the Lutheran Augsburg Confession, and Luther's Small Catechism, with the understanding "insofar as they agree; but where they disagree, we adhere strictly to the passages of Holy Scripture bearing on the subject." Thus we see in the *Kirchenverein* not a *Lehrgemeinschaft*, a fellowship built on doctrine, but a *Liebesgemeinschaft*, a fellowship built on love. The confessional statements, as important as they are for the church, must give way when in conflict to the authority of scripture. Thus there was room in the *Kirchenverein* and later in the Evangelical Synod for those who understood the scriptures literally and those who did not; for those who understood Christ's presence in the bread and the cup in classic Reformed or Lutheran ways and those who believed differently. There was room in this Christian community for diversity, but always gathered around a common center, around the One who gives life to the whole body, whose life, death, and resurrection redeem a lost creation, the One who summons the church in every generation to joyful obedience under the guidance of the Holy Spirit.

There were those who feared that such a conciliatory position in the *Kirchenverein* would lead to unbridled subjectivism, in which everything in matters of faith is left to individual conscience. This was not, however, to be the case, because the Lutheran and Reformed confessional documents, while not infallible, were received as authoritative. They were seen as a gift to the fellowship built on love, the ultimate authority of which resided in scripture, which was to be treated with reverence and honor, with prayerful responsiveness to the Holy Spirit. Where this was done, these mothers and fathers of the United Church of Christ believed the gospel would so nourish the souls of the faithful that all would see the light of Christ in them, to the glory and praise of God. The church is always a community of believers, knit together by the love of Christ, as attested by scripture and the sacraments.

But let us probe more deeply this concept of the church as a fellowship built on love. It is not insignificant that the first major controversy in the church, described by Paul in 1 Corinthians 11, was not over the nature of the sacraments or the meaning of Jesus' words, "This is my body which is for you. . . . This cup is the new covenant in my blood." Rather, the misunderstanding that divided the early church centered on a breakdown of neighborliness. Justin Martyr wrote that "the rich among us come to the aid of the poor." But at Corinth, this understanding of the Christian community was mission. The decisive question for Paul about the Eucharist (thanksgiving) had little to do with what was said about the bread and the cup, and everything to do with whether there could be a true Eucharist when the poor were overlooked. This question was decisive for Augustine as well, who emphasized in his *Christian Doctrine* that whoever seems to have understood the divine scripture in such a way that the double love of God and neighbor is not built up has not yet understood the Bible. George Wall and Joseph Rieger with their varying interpretations of the fourth commandment surely would have agreed with Augustine. This question was later at the center of the birth of the pietistic movement in the seventeenth century, and indeed strongly influenced the development of the *Kirchenverein*.

While Wall and Rieger and those who served with them did not believe the church should engage in fierce disputes over doctrine, they did believe that the church cannot be understood apart from the Bible, and that a fellowship built on love will turn again and again to the scripture in its quest for truth about the nature and will of God. Since the teaching of the *Kirchenverein* on the nature of God and the church was deeply indebted to the Protestant Reformation, it accepted as crucial the place of the Bible in the center of worship and mission. The Bible was understood not as an authority, or as one testimony among many, but rather as *the* authority and testimony to the gracious activity of God with us.

For the *Kirchenverein* and later for the Evangelical Synod of North America, the Christ the church is called to serve is not the Christ of our words and sentiments, but the Christ of Word and sacrament. A minister of the Word of God therefore does not "preach what is right in his [or her] own eyes, without foundation in divine Scripture."[2] These spiritual forebears of the United Church of Christ echoed the assertion of Huldreich Zwingli at the Disputation of Berne in 1528 that "the holy Christian church, whose one Head is Christ, is born of the Word of God, and heareth not the voice of a stranger." In the twentieth century the

Theological Declaration of Barmen (1934) reaffirmed this crucial point in these words: "Jesus Christ, as he is attested for us in Holy Scripture, is the one Word of God which we have to hear and which we have to trust and obey in life and in death" (8:11). This does not eliminate the possibility of hearing the screams of God amid the terrifying events that mark the age, or seeing the tears of God in the hunger, poverty, and misery through which Christ is again crucified in our time. The *Kirchenverein* and later Barmen both rejected the "false doctrine, as though the Church could and would have to acknowledge as a source of its proclamation, apart from and beside the one Word of God, still other events and powers, figures and truths, as God's revelation" (8:12).[3]

This is precisely the temptation that has accompanied the church throughout the twentieth century—our tendency to turn from the God whose nature and heart are disclosed in Jesus Christ and to bow instead before a myriad of puny, comfortable, tolerable gods of our own making. For this reason, sound teaching rooted deeply in the prophetic and apostolic traditions is so necessary in the church. Sound teaching that takes seriously the incarnation of justice and reconciliation in Jesus Christ is crucial to our worship, community, mission, purpose, our very being as a people of the Word.[4] This is more easily said than done, for where this God is welcomed into our lives, we are met by the Christ whose crucifixion is reenacted daily in a thousand different ways, whose broken body and miraculous resurrection are not merely memories from the ancient past but contemporary events that complete us into the shaping of the private and public history of our time. To risk opening the scripture, listening there for the Word of God, involves our "recognizing God once more as God, a task alongside which all cultural, social and political duties are child's play."[5] Little wonder that sound teaching is often tempered, softened, or even rejected among us.

There are many words in the world, but there remains only one Word, one thing needful, indispensable to the life of the church. The special and wonderful insight of Joseph Rieger, George Wall, and others of the *Kirchenverein* saw that the mind of Christ can be discerned where there is a faithful search of the scriptures, a willingness to listen to the witness of the church's confessions of faith, a prayerful determination to seek the truth that nourishes Christian conscience, and a loving concern for neighbors. Among the many words that flood our days and amid the many changes in the church's life—new music, new liturgy, new demands, new expressions of faith, new temptations, new follies, new variations on ancient themes—the *Kirchenverein* believed that certain fundamentals remain in place. To open the Bible and listen to the Word of God is to risk confrontation with God who addresses us as a still, small voice, or as thunder. To look for the blood of Christ poured out in the world is to see the truth about ourselves, our nation, our era, and our world. The truth brings us to our knees in order to resurrect us again, shaking us in our calm, calming us in our distress, shattering the idols we create, setting us free to live in grateful obedience.

What of the Bible? What has the church thought about its authors and the work of the Holy Spirit? Is it a human document or is it divine? Can God take a few barley loaves and some fish (human words and human speech) and feed the multitude? Or are the words of the Bible, down to the last syllable, of heavenly origin, like manna that nourished the people in the wilderness? Within the United Church of Christ, just as in other denominations, there is no perfect agreement on these issues. But Christians have never been of one mind when it comes to such questions. The early church believed God to be the author of the Bible, but this belief had various interpretations. Clement of Alexandria interpreted Matt. 5:18 to mean that not a single "iota, not a dot" of all God has spoken shall pass away or be found in error. Gregory of Nazianzus wrote that every slightest line and stroke of scripture is due to the minute care of the Holy Spirit. Irenaeus believed that what the witnesses to God's truth have said, God said; thus those who hear them hear God. But Gregory the Great was seen as going too far in suggesting that what the witnesses say is not human speech at all, but divine dictation. Athenagoras insisted that the Holy Spirit has done much more than inspire the prophets; the Spirit of God literally had moved their mouths and snatched away from them their own thoughts, so the divine "song" might be heard like a flute player breathing music into the instrument. In the teaching of Hippolytus, the Holy Spirit speaks through the prophets and apostles as on a zither or a harp. But what then of the whole sense of mystery? May not a mechanical act come to replace the earlier sense of profound grace in which, as Jesus is born in a humble manger, so God takes even the stuttering words of the biblical writers and causes them to serve a divine purpose? This was the view held by Theopholus, who insisted that the inspired writers were not mere mechanical organs or wind instruments, but persons gifted by moral and personal excellence, called to be vehicles of the revelation of God.[6]

Throughout Christian tradition there have been different understandings, not of the belief that scripture is divinely inspired, but of how and in what way. Luther and Calvin insisted, with the Reformation recovery of the Bible at the center of the church's life, that scripture is divinely inspired and that it all points to Jesus Christ. But they have reservations about the clarity with which parts of the Bible are able to point to the cross and the resurrection. "All scripture," Luther wrote, "receives its light from the resurrection."[7] This can be understood only as the Spirit of God works in our hearts and reveals the truth of this enormous mystery. That Jesus, the revelation of God, should take the form of a servant (being born in a stable with the breath of cows and sheep to keep him warm) is a truth so astonishing that only God could open the eyes of the Gospel writers to it and inspire them to proclaim it. Surely scripture is inspired, the Reformers believed. God lifts up the hearts of the biblical writers and removes the blinders from their eyes, so they might perceive and know what otherwise must remain hidden. God inspires. God speaks, but through frail human instruments.[8]

To read the scriptures and to recover them at the center of the church's life, whether we come to them through John Calvin, Martin Luther, and Jonathan Edwards, or through Dorothea Soelle and Rosemary Radford Ruether, or alone and naked and on our knees with utterly empty hands, can be a dangerous thing. The only thing more dangerous is for those of us in the United Church of Christ to disregard the Bible or set its witness aside. We may approach the Bible from Jerusalem or Corinth, Wittenberg or Geneva, Soweto or Managua, or from points in between. Finally, however, the Bible must be approached with reverence, joy, questions, fear, excitement, expectation, tears, hope, gratitude, and prayer. This is a lesson we can learn from Wall and Rieger, and from the many faithful witnesses who have preceded us in the Congregational Christian and the Evangelical and Reformed traditions and all the rich heritage we share in the United Church of Christ.

The authority of scripture in our denomination is not primarily a matter of dogma, nor is it an issue of polity.[9] Neither is the authority inherent in scripture a question of tradition nor of the critical insights provided by the Councils of Nicaea and Chalcedon. The authority of scripture is rooted in a determination presented to us by the fact that in Jesus Christ "the Word became flesh and dwelt among us, full of grace and truth" (John 1:14). The authority of scripture is reflected in the audacious confession that Jesus Christ is Lord, a confession that is impossible apart from the work of the Holy Spirit. Thus in every generation the integrity of the church's words and deeds depends on the gracious answer to our prayer, "Come, Holy Spirit."

As Wall and Rieger carried their Bible tracts down the Ohio River to St. Louis, they knew that the authority of scripture is not something the church invents. It is rather a gift that nourishes and enlivens the Christian congregation. It is an authority not to be feared but welcomed; not suspect, but treated as a friend. Where biblical authority is present, the prayer of the faithful will be that of the publican: "God, be merciful to me a sinner" (Luke 18:13). Where biblical authority is present, resurrection from the dead is experienced as wonder. Resurrection is a teaching to be memorized, nor so much an article of faith to be confessed, but an *event* that renews the conviction of the church. The congregation kneels in the shadow of a cross, alongside the weary and heavy-laden, and despite doubt and despair—like Mary on the first Easter Day—rushes from the tombs to the world to proclaim the awesome truth, Christ is not dead! Christ is risen! The authority of scripture is a force that takes root, assumes stature, and becomes real as it points to the gracious intervention of God in history. The God of scripture is not a god we can shape with our hands or mold according to the longing of our hearts, but is instead the God before whom we tremble and rejoice. The authority of scripture lives in the proclamation that the grace of God is greater than our unfaith, that the generosity of God is greater than all our doubt. The benevolence of God is more determined than the might of all the giants of the earth. The justice of God is more powerful than the murderous legions that devour the life of the world. Though we bear a thousand griefs and are wounded by a thousand transgressions and are captive to a thousand regrets, we proclaim in word and deed with those who came before us, Thanks be to God, who gives us the victory through our Lord Jesus Christ.

NOTES

1. Georg(e) Wendelin Wall (1811–67) was born in Wurttemberg, Germany. At the age of nineteen he entered the Basel Mission Institute (Germany) which was training pastors for the Western frontier of the United States. Joseph Rieger (1811–69) was born in Bavaria and raised as a Catholic. At the age of twenty-one, he began his studies with the Basel Missionary Society. Wall and Rieger were among the earliest members of *Der Deutsche Evangelische Kirchenverein des Westens.*

2. From the invitation issued in 1523 by the Council of the City of Zurich to a theological disputation on the nature and significance of Holy Scripture.

3. The Theological Declaration of Barmen (8:12), in Arthur C. Cochrane, *The Church's Confession Under Hitler* (Philadelphia: Westminster Press, 1962). In my view those in the United Church of Christ are correct who urge *not* that we affirm the confessional statements of the Reformation (or of Barmen for that matter) as definitive for our time, but that we listen to them in our search for truth while making our way through the theological and political thickets of our time.

4. More than a decade ago, the Office for Church Life and Leadership of the United Church of Christ convened a theological seminar to think through the faith and ministry entrusted to us. This resulted in the publication of the document, "Toward the Task of Sound Teaching in the United Church of Christ" (1977). It is a statement with which one may or may not agree. That is not the point. It should be read and reread in our congregations as we struggle with our vocation as Christians.

5. See Karl Barth, *The Word of God and the Word of Man* (New York: Harper & Brothers, 1957), 24. Originally part of a lecture on "The Righteousness of God"

which Barth gave in January 1916 in the city church of Aarau. Quoted in Eberhard Busch, *Karl Barth* (Philadelphia: Fortress Press, 1976), 89.

6. See Karl Barth, "The Doctrine of the Word of God," in *Church Dogmatics*, I.2 (Edinburgh: T & T Clark, 1956), 514f.

7. In the seventeenth century, the human element, so important to Luther and Calvin, disappears altogether. The flute player of Athenagoras returns. G. Voetius goes so far as to suggest that the New Testament was inspired not in the authors' native Aramaic or Syrian, but in Hellenistic Greek. Every last syllable is conceived in heaven, including Paul's comment in 2 Timothy 4 about the coat he left behind in Troas. Should there be found even the smallest error in the Bible, Lutheran orthodoxy of the seventeenth century teaches it is no longer wholly the Word of God, since God is incapable of making a mistake.

8. In April 1936 Dietrich Bonhoeffer wrote a letter to his brother-in-law and friend Rudiger Schleicher, in which he mentions the urgency of the church recovering the scriptures (and with them Jesus Christ!) at the center of its life. "In the Bible, it is God who speaks to us. . . . Naturally, one can also read the Bible like any other book, from the perspective of textual criticism, for instance. There is nothing to be said against that. But that will only reveal the surface of the Bible, not what is within it. When a dear friend speaks a word to us, do we subject it to analysis? No, we simply accept it, and then it resonates inside us for days. The word of someone we love opens itself up to us the more we 'ponder it in our hearts' as Mary did. In the same way, we should carry the Word of the Bible around with us. We will only be happy in our reading of the Bible when we dare to approach it as the means by which God really speaks to us, the God who loves us and will not leave us with our questions unanswered." See Dietrich Bonhoeffer, *Meditating On the Word*, ed. David McI. Gracie (Cambridge, Eng.: Cowley Publications, 1986), 43f.

9. Some may take issue with me here. For an important discussion of the relationship between order and polity in the United Church of Christ and the accountability of all who confess Christ as head of the church, see Louis H. Gunnemann, *United and Uniting: The Meaning of an Ecclesial Journey* (New York: United Church Press, 1987), 160f.

18

THE UNITED CHURCH OF CHRIST
TOMORROW

ROGER L. SHINN

I love the United Church of Christ. I am its minister, and it is my church. I neither yearn nor lust for some other church. I am grateful for the union that produced it and that opened my life to wider horizons. Why do I bother to say this? Because I am going to ask some critical questions, perhaps make some critical assertions about the United Church of Christ. If you believe love should be uncritical, you may soon be thinking that I do not love this church. But my experience has been that to be a member of the United Church of Christ is, almost by definition, to be a critic of it. To be uncritical is to be the real oddball in this church. Perhaps to be uncritical is to be un-christian.

At the conclusion of a book contemplating past and present, we address the future of the United Church of Christ. Ours has always been a future-oriented denomination. And yet, unforeseen events in church and society have often taken us in unplanned directions. To accept this topic, then, requires some brashness. I may have no other qualification to write on this bold subject, but I think I have the brashness.

TOMORROW

One word in my topic is tomorrow. What hopes and fears cluster around that word! To get a fix on our place in world history, let us look for just a minute at our past. Our formal birthday was June 25, 1957. And what a year 1957 was!

That was the year when Sputnik I and Sputnik II sent a chill into American society. It was the year Albert Camus won the Nobel Prize in literature and Dr. Seuss wrote *The Cat in the Hat.* It was the year Trevor Huddleston in South Africa published his book *Naught for Your Comfort,* words as poignant today as when he chose them. Leonard Bernstein brought *West Side Story* to the theater, and Jack Kerouac wrote *On the Road,* introducing the word beatnik into our language. Nineteen fifty-seven was the year President Eisenhower sent troops into Little Rock.

Before the United Church was a year old, the United States had sent its first satellite into space. During our second year Eisenhower sent Marines into Lebanon, a reminder now that history sometimes does repeat itself. John XXIII began his papacy, and to our surprise we learned to love him. Castro overthrew Batista in Cuba. General De Gaulle became president of France. Eisenhower submitted to Congress a budget with a surplus of $70 million. A major university put all its four thousand students on probation after snow-fight riots.

Who at that time guessed that this world, in barely more than a quarter century:

- Would experience a sequence of assassinations: John F. Kennedy, 1963; Malcolm X, 1965, Martin Luther King, Jr., and Robert F. Kennedy, 1968?
- Would see America deeply involved in the longest and most frustrating war of its history?
- Would observe Vatican II, welcomed by Protestants as enthusiastically as by Catholics?
- Would find the Christian church producing Nobel laureates in peace: Albert Luthuli, 1960; Martin Luther King, Jr., 1964; Mother Teresa, 1979; Desmond Tutu, 1984?
- Would find Iran—and some other countries that most Americans could not locate on a globe—disturbing the life of this and other nations?
- Would find U.S. industry unable to compete with foreign imports, but U.S. agriculture making this nation the world's greatest exporter of food?
- Would puzzle over the rise of exotic cults and political activism of right-wing fundamentalists?
- Would see churches and other social agencies in America operating soup kitchens and shelters for homeless on a scale unlike anything since the Great Depression long ago?

How little we then knew of today! How little we now know of tomorrow! Wolf Hafele, a German scientist, has called this the "age of hypotheticality," the age of great hypothetical adventures of which nobody knows the outcomes. Of course, every age has its hypotheticalities, its unknown futures. But we are running experiments on a global scale, at great speed, unlike anything in the past.

We read various scenarios of the human future. One is of nuclear war and the nuclear winter that may make the northern hemisphere, perhaps the whole globe, unlivable for human beings, most animals, and most food crops. Very different is the scenario of ecological exhaustion, ending our wasteful style of civilization. T. S. Eliot told us that the world might end "not with a bang but a whimper." He did not then know about the nuclear warfare or ecological collapse that now give his words more catastrophic meaning.

Very different is the scenario of John Naisbit's *Megatrends,* with its world of high tech, decentralization, participatory democracy, cooperative networking—with scarcely any notice of militarism, ghettoes, and the economic despair of those who may be constituting a permanent underclass; with scarcely any notice, also, of the church.

I have volunteered to be brash—but not too brash. There is much we do not know.

THE UNITED CHURCH OF CHRIST

Now we come to the other term in my title: the United Church of Christ. What does tomorrow mean to us in this church?

I propose that our future, like our past, will be a search for faithful freedom. I can think of no other phrase that so well states the issue that we struggle with, the kind of Christian life and community we treasure. Faithful freedom is what we seek.

We have been searching for it. We can claim gratifying moments in the quest. We cannot claim success. Faithful freedom is not a goal that can be achieved, as some goals, for example, a membership target or a financial goal, can be achieved. Faithful freedom means a perennial quest, with days of thanksgiving for some acts, days of perplexity as we keep searching.

Faithful freedom cannot be legislated, but some legislative structures can express and support it. Like love, it cannot be guaranteed by any structures, but can find expression and nourishment in some structures of family and community.

Faithful freedom requires a pilgrimage. We always risk slipping into structures of accountability that cramp freedom, or into assertions of freedom that are careless of faithfulness.

Faithful freedom calls us to walk a precarious path, a path that calls for constant renewal, for *metanoia,* the New Testament word that we pallidly translate "repentance" but that H. Richard Niebuhr described as "permanent revolution."

We might compare faithful freedom with water. How do you keep it in circulation? Not by containing it in a bottle that preserves it intact, and not by letting it drain out and disappear. There is another possibility, known in scripture and experience: "a spring of living water."

As a teacher, I see the appeal of the United Church of Christ to theological students. Every year I listen to some who are thinking about becoming members; I don't remember any wanting to leave for other denominations. In recent conversations one student was looking for more freedom, another for more substance than in their present denominations. Both thought they might find it in the United Church of Christ.

THREE ISSUES:
BELIEF, POLITY, ACTION

I ask you to think with me about the working out of faithful freedom in three issues that we meet all the time: issues of belief, polity, and action.

Belief

We are a church that loves those New Testament words: "You will know the truth, and the truth will make you free" (John 8:32). I suppose all of us believe that. We just don't agree on which truth will make us free.

Our Constitution (1984 edition) states our ambivalence. Paragraph 8 defines the local church as "composed of persons who, believing in God as heavenly Father, and accepting Jesus Christ as Lord and Savior, and depending on the guidance of the Holy Spirit, are organized for Christian worship, for the furtherance of Christian fellowship, and for the ongoing work of Christian witness." That is a heavily doctrinal definition, deliberately trinitarian in form.

Then soon we come to paragraph 15, which affirms "the autonomy of the local church" with a long list of rights that cannot be limited—note the sweeping language—"now or at any future time." The rights include, among many others, the right "to formulate its own covenants and confessions of faith." Do these have to be trinitarian? Do they have to agree with paragraph 8? Apparently not. The local autonomy is stated without qualification.

Paragraph 8 is written in theological language. I suppose the lawyers looked at it, as they scrutinized every sentence in the Constitution, but the language is not theirs. Paragraph 15 is written in legal language; the lawyers apparently took over there. They did it with knowledge of the lawsuit that made the union such a difficult ordeal.[1]

These paragraphs appear to be the result of a bargaining process. I have no inside knowledge, but anyone who has ever tried to analyze the sources of the Pentateuch is likely to recognize signs of diverse authorship. And anybody who has attended a General Synod is likely to see signs of a familiar negotiating process. Two groups champion different themes. Unable to work out a real agreement, each tolerates the other, provided it can get its own theme in.

This resolution, or irresolution of the conflict, sets up future debates, going on now. These are not necessarily destructive. The New Testament has diversities of theology within it, and every church has. Uniformity is impossible and undesirable. But it is not our temptation. We must be concerned about the possibility of polarization with a vacuum in the center. I say the possibility, not the necessity.

But there are worries. The faculties of our United Church–related seminaries have felt a concern. They instituted a theological journal, *Prism,* intended to encourage theological discussion within the United Church of Christ. A journal will not solve the problem; it may be the typical way professors meet a need. But a journal can help, and I hope this one does.

Polity

Similar issues arise in polity. We can look at this in three areas.

Autonomy of the local church. The issue of belief, which we just looked at, now appears in relation to organization. Congregations can drift in and out of the United Church of Christ. They do not often do so, but sometimes they do. I suppose I am partly responsible for some departures; that is, I have worked to persuade the General Synod to endorse some proposals that have led to indignant withdrawals of one or two churches.

If I had my choice, I'd prefer a somewhat firmer covenant among our congregations. But I'm not terribly worried about this issue. If a congregation wants to leave and we enforce a legal tie, what have we gained? The real unity must be rooted in loyalty. But I don't think you know what a church is if your vision is limited to the experience of only one congregation.

I recall a conversation with Eugene Carson Blake back in 1960 or 1961. He had proposed the Consultation on Church Union (COCU), which is still alive and vigorous although in a somewhat modified form. Blake expressed his hope that the UCC would be interested. I said that our constitutional provision for autonomy of the congregation might make difficulties for us in any further church union. His reply was that he took hope from our frequent statement that we wanted to be a uniting as well as a united church. So I ask, Do we?

The Autonomy of Conferences. Here a comparable issue arises. An article in the November 1985 issue of *Keeping You Posted* took up the matter. It quotes paragraph 159 of our Bylaws: "A Conference consults on a regular basis with the Stewardship Council, acting on behalf of the General Synod, to reach mutual agreement upon the percentage, or the dollar amount of the undesignated gifts for Our Church's Wider Mission to be retained for its own support." Legally, that is curious language. A law can require consultation; it cannot require agreement. The result is that the Conference has the power.

The article continues by saying that over the years an increasing share of the money has been retained by Conferences for their mission programs. I do not say that this change is wrong. I see great value in all congregations and Conferences being conscious of their responsibility to be engaged in mission; I do not want mission to be a responsibility only of national agencies. I also understand that the consultations between Conferences and national bodies have become much more earnest than in earlier days. My memory of the early years, differing a little from what I read in *Keeping You Posted,* is that Conferences simply kept what they needed of mission funds. If contributions fell short, the national church took the blow. We are making progress toward a more covenantal relationship. But the Conferences still have the power.

Instrumentalities. Again the same issue arises. The "recognized" instrumentalities have great autonomy. Constitutionally, they are far older than the UCC; their charters go back in history. One day the United Church of Christ appeared and "recognized" them. They, not the president or the Executive Council, are the power centers of the denomination. The boards and agencies have large budgets, with income from both the benevolent contributions of Our Christian World Mission and their own endowments.

A symbolic issue has been the matter of salaries. The General Synod has no control over the salary grids of boards and agencies, even though the General Synod votes the budget and supports them. There have been some tense moments in General Synods, when delegates have asked to know about salaries. Only after considerable pressure did General Synod get the information it wanted. Many members of General Synod were surprised and displeased to find that some agencies set some staff salaries above the salary of the president of the UCC. One effort, some years ago, to coordinate salary schedules met great resistance and it lost. I do not set great store by this issue. The whole matter of salaries and status has nothing to do with the Sermon on the Mount. But if we human beings take such things seriously, as obviously we do, we have to ask what our polity means in this regard.

Similar issues arise in respect to programs. The General Synod has little direct power to implement programs. The boards and agencies do that, and they may even compete with each other. I think we are making some progress in achieving greater cooperation, not by coercion but by conversation and agreement.

Action

We are known as a "liberal" church. What does that mean? The votes of our General Synod and Conferences and the statements of our church leaders are strong on social issues of race, poverty, peace, and human rights. We may be the foremost American denomination in articulating support for progressive social policies.

But what does this mean to our membership? I pick one example, chosen simply because I have some data—the issue of armaments. When the House of Representatives passed a resolution (1981–82) supporting a nuclear freeze, somebody analyzed voting patterns in relation to religious affiliation. Most church bodies had taken stands supporting or at least congenial to the freeze. How did congressional representatives vote? Here is the record of support in Congress: Jews, 82 percent. Catholics, 78 percent. Protestants, 57 percent.

My impression is that at that time, prior to the Catholic Bishops' Pastoral Letter on peace, the Protestant churches had the strongest recorded support for arms limitations. Why did not Protestants in Congress lead the pack? Probably because Protestants are so acculturated in America as to have little religious identity, to be little influenced by their affiliation. Jews usually know they are Jews; whether they go to synagogue or not, they have a Jewish identity. Catholics know they are Catholics. Protestants often barely have a Protestant identity. I have no separate data on UCC members of Congress, but I'd be surprised if they varied much from the Protestant average.

I do not imply that politicians should take orders from their churches. I might complain if I thought a Catholic politician were doing that. But I suggest that their religious insights might have some influence on their political judgments. The evidence points to a low Protestant identification.

If you examine the social attitudes and behavior of UCC members at large, my guess is that you will find these more closely correlated with sociological classification than with positions of General Synod. We are in danger of fading into the landscape.

Let me give an example drawing together several of the issues of belief, polity, and action. It comes from General Synod IV, Denver 1963. Issues of racial justice were at the forefront of the Synod. At that time I was president of the Board for Homeland Ministries (BHM) and therefore a delegate to the General Synod with voice but without vote. The Directors of the BHM were scheduled to meet immediately after the General Synod. On our agenda was a proposal that the BHM grant no more funds to mission churches that discriminated racially or neglected to take a stand for racially open membership. The plan would not break covenants with churches already being funded, but would apply to all new ventures.

Early in the Synod a delegate moved from the floor that the General Synod instruct the BHM to adopt the policy that, in fact, it already expected to adopt. That provoked a constitutional crisis with heated discussions on the floor and after hours in corridors and rooms. I could not get excited. Why, I asked, should not we in the BHM welcome a vote of the General Synod supporting our policy? Would not that increase its moral authority? It is unconstitutional, I was told. It might give the General Synod the idea that it could instruct the BHM to do something else some other day.

On the floor the moderator ruled the motion out of order—as constitutionally it surely was. Many delegates bristled at the ruling, but they accepted it. Then the motion came from the floor that the General Synod recommend the same policy to the BHM. That motion was in order. It was debated at some length, with BHM directors supporting it. In the debate no one spoke to justify segregation. Whether some delegates were segregationists in their hearts, I cannot judge. What I know is that many delegates opposed the motion as an intrusion on the autonomy of the congregation. Clearly, the General Synod could not require congregations to desegregate, but it could recommend that benevolent money not go to segregated churches. Even that, said some delegates, was an offense against autonomy. In fact, so many took that position that the motion was defeated. Then in a strange and providential way, one woman who had voted to defeat the motion moved for a reconsideration. Later she said she did not know why she had done so. Her motion carried. There was further floor debate, and this time the motion passed. The directors of the BHM adopted the policy a day or two later. I report the events because they illustrate so well the problems of faithful freedom in relation to belief, to polity (including autonomy of the BHM and of congregations), and to action.

LOOKING AHEAD

Now, at last, let us look again at tomorrow. I repeat my earlier warning: We know little of the future. But perhaps we can raise some questions that are likely to be important despite our ignorance of tomorrow. I have three.

1. Will the UCC get a surer sense of Christian identity or will we fade into the cultural landscape?

This issue of identity comes up often among us. I hear it in different ways in New England, in Pennsylvania, in the South, in the Pacific states.

But it keeps coming up. Will our actions flow from a shared faith, or will our faith be the "sacred canopy," in Peter Berger's phrase, that covers an identity and action that we get from other sources? Do we decide what we want, pretty much as anybody does, then expect the church to support us? Or do we let our faith guide us in deciding what we want?

Identity in the United Church of Christ will certainly include a high appreciation of freedom. I concur in that. But Christian freedom cannot simply mean that we all assert, Nobody can tell me what to believe or do. We are not a bridge club, a football team, or an automobile agency. We are a church, and a church is centered in a faith. Such faith cannot be imposed from outside or above. But freedom that is not faith-filled, faithful, is not Christian freedom.

2. Will we maintain an ecumenical loyalty?

We think that we have an ecumenical loyalty. Often I am pleased when I see our contributions of leadership in the National Council of the Churches of Christ and the World Council of Churches. But I am ashamed when I see our budgetary contributions to these bodies. Our low contributions are related to our polity. The General Synod and Executive Council have little money; contributions to ecumenical work must come from boards and agencies that have the same specialized interests.

Beyond money, the ecumenical issues are not simple. I have some convictions that I won't surrender for the sake of bland ecumenicity, even if that makes me an obstructionist. Think of *Baptism, Eucharist, and Ministry,* the World Council of Churches document adopted in Lima, Peru, in 1982. It was hailed around the world as an immense achievement, overcoming obstacles that have prevented Christian unity for centuries. While we in the UCC hear the applause and join in some of it, we have our stubborn questions. We are—rightly, I think—sensitive to some contemporary issues that muffle our applause; for example, the ordination of women. We cannot prescribe policy to other churches. But we cannot keep silent about our convictions. And we have trouble even talking with churches if they do not recognize the ordination of the women who represent us in the conversations.

I think of another example. Many Christian conversations are going on across confessional lines. Lutherans, for example, are talking with Roman Catholics and with Reformed groups. Do we belong among the Reformed churches talking with the Lutherans? After all, we are part of the World Alliance of Reformed Churches. But one Lutheran leader, dismayed at paragraph 15 of our Constitution—the paragraph giving every local church the right to formulate its own confession of faith—

wonders whether we have a firm enough Reformed identity to enter into
the conversations. President Avery Post could reply with paragraph 8
and its doctrinal description of the local church. The Lutherans are not
convinced.

Our ecumenicity is related to our identity. One of our inhibitions to
ecumenical acts is our own uncertainty about identity. Proposals for
closer relations with other churches—most recently, the Christian
Church (Disciples of Christ)—are sometimes thwarted by our inner
uncertainties: How can we move closer to other churches when we don't
know who we are? Don't we have to slow down until we get our own act
together?

It could be that some great ecumenical activities are aborning now
and that we will get stuck in a cul-de-sac and miss the action. I don't
think so, but I'm concerned.

3. Will we learn to listen to our dissenters within, yet not be immobi-
   lized?

We do not expect unanimity on many issues in the United Church of
Christ. But often we move to a fairly broad consensus, then hear it
challenged by dissenters on the left and on the right—as we usually use
those terms. Do we meet dissent by freezing it out of the conversation
rather than drawing it into conversation? I hope we will do the latter,
learning to listen as well as talk. I recognize the opposite danger—that
we so encourage the conversation that it becomes the escape from doing
anything.

We are a church that encourages the flourishing of interest groups.
We have our Biblical Witness Fellowship, our Christians for Justice
Action, our Craigville Colloquies, our Charismatics, our Spiritual Development Network, our caucuses, our many special conferences. Will these
enrich us or immobilize us? Will they contribute to common mission or
thwart it? Will we be a United Church of Christ—with a unity that
transcends our differences—or will we be an agglomeration of people
vaguely reflecting a middle- and upper-middle-class Americanism?

Conclusions

I have been asking some questions that trouble me. I think they are
inherent in the responsible freedom that we seek. We might avoid such
questions by an enforced conformity or by an indifference that lets
every faction do its own thing without the pain of interaction that joins
the issues. I believe God calls us to a higher and harder way. I pray that
God will give us the grace to walk in that way.

I ask these questions in what may be an epochal time of testing for

American churches. We may be at the point where we must learn that our beliefs and practices as Christians, which seem ridiculously easy in our society, can be costly.

Once it was a victory for Christians to learn that they did not have to go to war against people who had a different doctrine of the Mass or the Lord's Supper, that they did not have to burn heretics, that they could live as neighbors with those who did not share their belief in Christ. That more generous understanding of human community was a true insight. But its truth could be profound or bland.

Now may be the time to learn that some heresies demand exposure. Vicious heresies are at work in the world: idolatries of race, nation, ideology, mammon. In 1934 some German church leaders recognized such heresies in the Barmen Declaration, in which they denounced Nazi falsification of faith. In September 1985, some South African Christians recognized heresies in the Kairos Document, rejecting apartheid as "a false offer of salvation" that is "hostile to Christianity."

Is our time of trial coming? Are we being called to confront a government that asks us to commit more and more of our resources to an arms race, less and less to the needs of suffering people?

Are we being called to denounce economic policies that, in the words of Nobel economist Franco Modigliani, "have no compassion for the poor or handicapped, and none for future generations either?"

Are we called to denounce an Immigration and Naturalization Service that winks at food producers who encourage illegal immigrants to harvest their crops, but prosecutes church people who try to protect immigrants whose lives are threatened by governments at home?

I do not want to be dogmatic. I do not want to turn every disagreement into a fight. I recognize that people of good will can differ on public issues of our time, that my opponents in public debates may have arguments that I need to consider. But there come points where opinions become idolatries and heresies to which we must object. And there come times when we must move from discussions to deeds.

We must not despise the opportunities provided by our constitutional form of government in the United States. Representative government, freedom of speech, a Bill of Rights are so precious an inheritance that we need not rush to civil disobedience whenever we dissent from the dominant tides of government and the popular will. But times come— and we had better be prepared—when we have to accept the cost of our convictions.

Then, as now, is the time to remember the prayer in Harry Emerson Fosdick's hymn that we sing so often in the United Church of Christ:

> Grant us wisdom, Grant us courage,
> For the living of these days.

NOTES

1. Some Congregational–Christian churches sought court action to block a denomination-wide decision on the union, claiming the autonomy of each local congregation. See Louis H. Gunnemann, *The Shaping of the United Church of Christ* (New York: United Church Press, 1977), 46.

19

INTO A NEW CENTURY

DANIEL L. JOHNSON

Toward the close of the twentieth century, "Y2K" was the nearly-apocalyptic fear that all computers all over the world would crash when midnight ended 1999 and began 2000, possibly rendering non-functional most, if not all the electronic networks and systems of civilization. The stock market, transportation, communication and media systems, banking, access to stored data, could all come to a nightmare halt. No one could say with certainty that such a major disaster would not occur. But midnight came and went without much of a glitch anywhere, and life as we know it went on.

Readily we became accustomed to saying "2000" instead of "19-something", but September 11, 2001 remains a date which immediately challenged life as we know it. If we thought the age of anxiety was over with the dawn of a new century, we were wrong; once again the neat classification of eras and epochs by decades and centuries proved more imaginary than accurate. If prior to September 11, 2001 Jewish-Christian-Muslim relations had been an important theological pursuit, after 9/11 it has become an urgent necessity to understand the religious extremism and attendant fear which has erupted anew on the world stage, together with manipulation of such fear for political purposes. At the same time it is now more important than ever before to distinguish between the conventional, faithful practice of each of the world's major religions on the one hand, and extremist distortions of the same religions on the other hand.

Now that we are into a new century, it still seems strange to speak of the Christian theological giants of our times—Karl Barth, Dietrich Bonhoeffer, Paul Tillich, H. Richard and Reinhold Niebuhr, Martin Luther King, to name just six—as belonging to "the previous century". That term still feels as if we are speaking of the nineteenth century. But we now live in a time just recently foreseen as "the future", and the twenty-first century is present-day reality. Without so much as a Y2K ripple tomorrow arrived simply with the tick of the clock.

In the last half of the previous century, the United Church of Christ evolved and developed from an ecumenical vision to the denomination it still struggles to become. The first seventeen chapters of this book provided insights into that development up to 1990. With the accelerated pace of change studied notably by Kenneth E. Boulding and Alvin Toffler, these most recent sixteen years in the life of the United Church of Christ have seen remarkable change and adaptation to new realities. Already some of the perspectives and stances of the original chapters of this book seem to reflect the realities of the past century more than the present. For example, Randi J. Walker critiques this book's 1990 attempt to understand the United Church of Christ by analyzing theologically our four predecessor denominations. Walker explores the post-1957 development of the UCC, suggesting that large numbers of members no longer maintain active memory of the previous component traditions. But given the continuing regional differences within the UCC, I believe her point is debatable. Countless times in my New England pastoral ministry I have had to remind church members that our denomination is now the United Church of Christ, and often I found it necessary to explain what that means to members who know quite well what Congregational means.

In the national setting, we have lived and struggled our way into the realities of a new denomination since 1957. And it is in the national setting that any denomination holds together. For example, General Synod delegates and visitors experience the theology and identity of the United Church of Christ in as nearly complete an expression as possible.

The UCC national setting is now structured differently than it was in the first formative years (see earlier editions of the pamphlet History and Program). A cumbersome, overlapping and competitive structure of offices, boards, instrumentalities and agencies were downsized and streamlined, beginning in 2000, into four "covenanted ministries"—the Office of General Ministries, Justice and Witness Ministries, Local Church Ministries and Wider Church Ministries. The purpose of the restructuring was to develop a more collegial use of human and financial resources while preserving essential historical autonomies within covenantal accountabilities (see current edition, 2007, History and Program). However, as of this writing difficulties in the restructured national setting have emerged, and once again it may have become necessary to rethink and perhaps redesign the national offices. The national structure created in the 1957 union attempted to bring together and blend the different polities of two (previously four) denominations. The attempt was only partially successful. Edward LeRoy Long, Jr. notes that "At the time, many doubted such a union was possible—combining, as it did, elements of presbyterian and congregation-

al polities—but it has resulted in a major body with strong denominational identity and a highly functional example of effective associational congregationalism." But Long's positive assessment may in fact signal part of
the continuing structural problem: if associational congregationalism is
really the polity of the UCC, the other more presbyterial polity which was
brought into the union has been sharply attenuated or modified. The
preservation of essential historical autonomies, while simultaneously maintaining covenantal accountabilities, turn out to be complicated and even
competing agendae not made easier by downsizing and streamlining the
national setting. Clearly the UCC is still a work in progress, with continuing polity complications.

One of the challenging tests of our polity came with the negotiations,
beginning in the early 1970s, toward Full Communion among four denominations—the Evangelical Lutheran Church in America, the Presbyterian
Church USA, the Reformed Church in America and the United Church of
Christ. Full Communion was finally achieved in 1997, overcoming historic
church barriers dating from the Reformation. But progress toward this
remarkable ecumenical achievement raised serious and difficult questions
about the polity of the United Church of Christ. Our polity makes nearly
impossible a central, authoritative voice to speak officially for the UCC to
other denominations, or even within the UCC. This reality is driven home
with every General Synod pronouncement and resolution, which never can
claim to speak *for* the UCC, only *to* the UCC. Polity is not the only reason
for our lack of a central authoritative voice.

Diversity is valued and protected at every setting of the UCC, as part of
the legacy of autonomy. While diversity can and does lead to serious, and
sometimes church-dividing differences and debates, freedom of belief and
expression remain major features of UCC life. In such a context of diversity, how can any one position on any perplexing issue be identified as correct or official? So the ecumenical question for us has become, Who can
speak officially *for* the United Church of Christ in an ecumenical forum or
context? It is an internal question as well whenever the General Synod,
Conferences and Associations "call upon" local congregations to consider
difficult and urgent matters of social justice. To "call upon" is very different
from directing or mandating.

Various attempts have been made in the most recent twenty years to
understand and address the perplexing quest for an authentic UCC voice.
Beginning in 1985 the annual Craigville Theological Colloquies (see pp.
147-149) have sought a theological centerline in the UCC which might be
able to speak with authority, but "from below" rather than from "on high",
functioning as a grassroots gathering. Clergy and laity from all over the
country gather at Craigville on Cape Cod each year, to study and address
current concerns, questions and controversies in church and society. At the

end of a week's work of intense discussion and consensus-building, a Witness Statement is produced, to be shared throughout the church. The Craigville witness spawned "Confessing Christ" in 1994, an organization of clergy and laity struggling to understand and define theological orthodoxy in the midst and mix of pluralism. Confessing Christ holds regional meetings, and publishes study documents and a newsletter. The Mercersburg Society was founded simultaneously with the Craigville Colloquies, and the Mercersburg Society also meets regularly, striving to recall, reclaim and recast the nineteenth century ecumenical vision of Mercersburg Professors Philip Schaff and John Williamson Nevin for the present-day church. Papers are presented and discussed at Society meetings, exploring Christological, liturgical and ecumenical dimensions of Mercersburg Theology. *The New Mercersburg Review* is a regular periodical of the Society, together with a newsletter. The Order of Corpus Christi, spawned by the Mercersburg Society, is a formal order of clergy and laity committed to catholicity in the liturgical life of the church, in hope and witness to Christian unity. Also the Biblical Witness Fellowship (see pp. 132-138), the "loyal opposition", continues to publish a conservative newspaper sharply critical of UCC leadership, stances and trends. The BWF seems to prefer criticism over departure. Though occupying various and differing places along the theological spectrum, these groups and movements seek an authoritative recovery of Christian orthodoxy when heterodoxy seems to weaken the church.

At the same time within the UCC some vigorously resist any attempts to discover a centerline or define an authoritative orthodoxy. The traditions of freedom of belief, freedom of the pulpit, and local church autonomy do not necessarily keep easy company with attempts to identify orthodox standards. And always part of the UCC spirit insists on a radical openness to diversity, progress and change, with remarkable sensitivity to the demands of justice amid the many seductive bondages of the times. As Oliver Powell observed of the UCC Statement of Faith, "And, who knows, to keep faith with where people will be tomorrow may require us to amend the Statement from time to time in order to keep it close to the ever shifting human situation." Oliver made that point in 1975, and indeed we have revised the Statement of Faith twice so far, since then (1976, 1983). Both revisions were attempts to modify or eliminate the patriarchal bias of the original Statement, a bias only dimly perceived prior to the 1970s.

The New Century Hymnal, introduced in 1995, identifies with both the quest for Christian orthodoxy and radical openness to progress and change. The newest hymnal of the United Church of Christ recovers much of the Reformation underpinnings of UCC hymnody, psalmody, history, theology, and liturgy, and it includes new hymns and many hymns from minority traditions previously overlooked or ignored. At the same time almost all of the patriarchal bias (see. pp. 120-123) and archaic language of older hymns is eliminated. The creators of the new hymnal, a project authorized in 1977 by General Synod 11 and the then United Church Board for Homeland Ministries in 1989, listened widely and carefully to thousands of expressed grassroots needs from UCC people. The goal was to create a truly inclusive hymnal. The Hymnal Committee was offered this memorable challenge from Robert J. Batastini, General Editor of GIA Publications, Chicago, one of several invited guest consultants: "Create a new hymnal not just for the United Church of Christ as it now is, but also for what it might yet become." Large numbers of congregations are purchasing and using it, and *The New Century Hymnal* is loved by many. But it is also resisted by many, mostly because of textual alterations necessitated by the justice issue of inclusive language (opponents who marginalize the justice issue sometimes enjoy calling it "intrusive" language). In these sharply polarized times in church and nation, perhaps a hymnal which identifies with opposing priorities in an attempt at inclusivity can only fall short of the full inclusivity intended. Such is one of the current ironies of the United Church of Christ, a denomination whose polity cannot mandate use of a new hymnal, as could and did the Episcopal Church with their new Hymnal of 1982.

In the new century a new UCC initiative was launched to increase denominational visibility and recognition. Even a half-century since the birth of the United Church of Christ, public awareness of the UCC remains problematic. In New England "Congregational" remains easily recognizable as a denominational name, dating from the seventeenth century. In Pennsylvania and the Midwest "Evangelical and Reformed" continued well-known denominational traditions dating from the seventeenth and eighteenth centuries. But from 1957 on, the name "Evangelical and Reformed" was abandoned in favor of "United Church of Christ", a new name which "former" Congregationalists added to signboards, bulletins and letterheads. But one is often obliged to explain all of that when asked, "United Church of Christ—what's *that*?" Partly to address this public identity crisis, "God Is Still Speaking" became a new UCC public slogan, proclaiming faith in God's continuing watchfulness and involvement in today's world, over against the religious distortion that God's word is immutably imbedded in the past. Along with the slogan was a large stylized comma, reflecting Gracie Allen's memorable advice, "Never place a period where God has placed a comma." Large outdoor red-and-black banners adorned church buildings all across the land, affirming the still-speaking God. At the same time television commercials were produced and broadcast in major market areas (not without controversy when some networks at first refused), displaying and demonstrating the radical hospitality and openness of UCC congregations. Public response was noteworthy; visitors phoned church offices with questions, and they came to worship where the big red-and black banners were displayed.

Openness when defined as "Open and Affirming" of people of homosexual orientation came to a head at General Synod 25 in Atlanta in 2005. The "God Is Still Speaking" television commercials made it clear that people of various identities and orientations are welcome in UCC congregations. But given the widespread diversity on all issues throughout the UCC, such welcome and hospitality needed General Synod support. After much study and preparation, a resolution was passed by the GS 25 delegates in support of homosexual marriage. The justice issue of legal marriage rights for same-gender partnerships equal to those of male-female partnerships was studied, debated and finally affirmed by vote. Again throughout UCC conferences, associations and congregations, much was repeated about General Synod's inability to speak for the whole UCC or to make its resolutions and pronouncements mandatory for all settings of the denomination. Even so, some local congregations lost members, and the UCC lost some congregations. But a new boldness going beyond Open and Affirming understandings and commitments is emerging, and the UCC in every setting finds itself encouraged to take with new seriousness this new public stance. A challenge to the General Synod 25 resolution did not overturn it two years later at General Synod 26 in Hartford.

No review of the most recent years of the United Church of Christ would be complete without grateful celebration of *The Living Theological Heritage* series of seven volumes, published from 1995 through 2005. This massive collection is the comprehensive historical work of Barbara Brown Zikmund, Series Editor, and it goes a long way toward meeting the "ecclesiological and theological deficit" sometimes identified as a UCC problem. *Ancient and Medieval Legacies, Reformation Roots, Colonial and National Beginnings, Consolidation and Expansion, Outreach and Diversity, Growing Toward Unity,* and *United and Uniting* are the seven encyclopedic volumes of primary materials augmented by the editorial commentary of twelve church scholars. One would be the richer for a thorough chronological reading from Volume One through Volume Seven. But even short of that comprehensive commitment of time and learning, use of *The Living Theological Heritage* as a resource for specific references to people, dates, events, documents and developments is of immense and lasting value.

As noted in the Preface, one of the significant dynamics currently reflecting, shaping and reshaping UCC life together is the annual gathering in Cleveland of UCC seminary polity teachers. While basic theology and polity legacies continue to anchor UCC identity in history and tradition, our denomination is always unfolding in new directions and gaining new insights. Comparing notes and exploring new texts and methods annually among the polity teachers keeps the denominationally-specific preparation of future ministers authentic, coordinated, informed and creative. It makes a difference if one is a UCC student at a "seminary of the United Church of Christ" or at one of the "historically related seminaries" (see the current UCC *Yearbook* for the distinction). That is one reason why regular formal conferences among all UCC history and polity professors helps to keep the curriculum and discipline consistent and current throughout the UCC. Addressing the study of polity in the seminaries, Edward Long offers this insightful observation:

> Despite the importance of governance for understanding the churches in all their institutional diversity, most theological education ordinarily focuses attention on the study of doctrine. The usual seminary curriculum treats the polity course as a matter of logistical or operational concern— something necessary professionally but not intellectually important. The course in polity is usually taken (sometimes begrudgingly) to qualify for a leadership position within one specific denominational or ecclesiastical group. But if it is true that patterns of governance determine how ecclesiastical systems work, a far better understanding of churches as institutions can come from increased awareness of the forms of governance and of the logistical and ethical problems that arise within ecclesiastical groups by virtue of the ways they are governed. Understanding polity should not be merely an exercise in parochialism but a fundamental branch of theological study that can provide the depth and breadth of understanding necessary to deal with vexing issues in ecumenical cooperation. The study of polity should be an intriguing exploration of fundamental theoretical and functional differences. . . . Efforts to create working relationships among mainline churches frequently flounder, not so much over differences about doctrine, but over differences about governance.

See, above, the particular relevance of Long's reasoning to my comments on the difficult Lutheran-Reformed negotiations toward Full Communion.

In 1999 Charles Shelby Rooks observed in his additional updating ninth chapter in Louis Gunnemann's 1977 *The Shaping of the United Church of Christ*, "The United Church of Christ is a Christian community that understands itself never to be finally shaped. It is always and forever being shaped." The observation calls into question this or any effort to update *Theology and Identity*, which except for this new chapter is a collection of perspectives on the United Church of Christ at various places along the journey up until 1990.

We are now at mid-century in our denominational life. At our fiftieth anniversary are we more "who we really are" than in 1957? Robert S. Paul raised significant questions about who we really were even in 1957. Paul was a member of the early UCC Theological Commission about which I commented in the Preface. In his book *Freedom with Order,* Paul writes:

> When the UCC came into existence in 1957, it did so without
> any detailed doctrine of the church or commitment to any
> particular polity. . . . few persons doubted that the UCC either
> could or would then address itself to working out the theological
> basis on which this new and exciting expression of Christian
> unity had been established. There was, after all, essential agree-
> ment in all matters of theology between such people as the
> Niebuhrs and Elmer Arndt on the one hand and Douglas Horton,
> Gerald Cragg, and John Bennett on the other. . . . Give us a
> little time, it was assumed, and we shall soon produce an
> ecclesiology to match our ecumenical conviction about the nature
> of the church. But this theological undergirding never took
> place.

Paul's early regrets, like my own, reflect gaps in the early phases of our denominational work. But if Randi Walker's and Shelby Rooks' much later assessments are accurate, the theology and identity of the UCC has evolved by a less formal process. And it is significant that twenty-five years after the birth of the UCC the World Council of Churches document *Baptism, Eucharist and Ministry* (1982) also discovered much ecumenical theological consensus among nearly all of the separated denominations of Christianity, but major polity issues remained divisive (again, Long's point).

In the ecumenical excitement attending the birth of the UCC, there was hope that instead of merely blending and compromising four predecessor polities, the new United Church might explore and develop nothing less than a new way of being the Church of Jesus Christ which could become a city set on a hill. Such a hope and vision shaped the early priorities and commitments of the uniting leaders. That was how we saw ourselves in 1957, that was who we were or what we might have become.

In the fifty years so far of our journey, as so many other analyses of the UCC attest, social justice urgencies have claimed and demanded our atten-tion and energy, also because of who we were and continue to be. For a sea-son it seemed almost irresponsible to our national UCC leaders to devote time and energy to ecclesiastical, structural matters when cities were burn-ing, racial conflicts reached critical mass, warfare was increasingly protested, gender injustice could no longer be ignored, poverty and economic imbalance injured the humanity of all God's children, and substance abuse threatened to sap the vitality of new generations. The UCC and our predecessor denominations have courageously faced into the social crises of the United States and the world, and we can be expected to continue to do so into the future.

But unfinished ecclesiastical business comes home to roost. Again Robert S. Paul: ". . . What was the United Church of Christ? *Why* had it a ministry? *How* did we relate what we were doing to the name of Jesus Christ and his gospel?" Ironically it was our ecumenical imperative itself which brought us back to the need to order our own house, as the negotiations toward Lutheran-Reformed Full Communion made clear. If we are to have a legitimate place at the ecumenical table, we must know very well who we are and what gifts we bring; and if we are to develop strong and faithful witness within the midst of our own diversity, we must know very well who we are and what gifts we are given. We must recognize and claim our particular role within the Body of Christ. Some would welcome us to the table if we would embrace an episcopal polity. Some would welcome us to the table if we would own one orthodox creed. Some would welcome us to the table if we would muzzle our witness for economic, racial, gender and linguistic justice. Some within our own house would be surprised and delighted if we would take a right turn on theological and political issues. If we continue to reject these and other options, we must know *why* we reject them, while at the same time affirming those who accept them as our sisters and brothers in Christ. Such is part of the burden and role of the United Church of Christ. Seeing how and why we are different from other denominations is, paradoxically, one step on the ecumenical road toward a unity in Christ which could make differences far less important. Seeing how and why we are not typically right-of-center on political and theological issues, at a time in the United States when radical right-of-center values have come to dominate the political landscape, is a 14 step toward clarity of identity (and perhaps further membership losses) within our own house.

However it is one thing to contemplate denominational membership shrinkage theoretically, and quite another thing to continue to take the risks which indeed cause the loss of members. The United Church of Christ, in fifty years so far, has not retreated from the risks of witness to social and economic justice. Such is, after all, who we are.

Membership shrinkage obviously results in financial loss. In 1957 we claimed a total membership of more than two million. Now, as of this writing, we are at a little more than half that number. Mission giving "from below", to borrow a Craigville expression, when reduced in local church settings results in budget cuts at all settings of the UCC. We also currently observe a generational shift in attitudes about mission and the money it takes to support it. Older generations willingly contributed to the institutional church as a matter of identity and responsibility. Younger generations now may address themselves to significant emergencies, such as Hurricane Katrina, ongoing working partnerships with the people of Honduras, or various local projects to meet human need; but financial support of denominations seems no longer the priority it once was. Thus two major realities—membership loss due to risk-taking social witness, together with attritional factors, and generational reduction in patterns of institutional identity and loyalty—signal critically important implications for the next fifty years of the United Church of Christ.

Clearly the United Church of Christ is on a journey, with much unfinished business yet to address. Heady and exasperating business, as Oliver Powell said so well. In the mix of UCC experience there is at once joyful loyalty and competing agendae, and there is nothing new about that either in the UCC or in all the centuries of Christian history. At our fiftieth anniversary, are we becoming more who we really are than we were in 1957? Are we chastened and instructed by hard internal and ecumenical challenges, yet still committed to the vision of one holy catholic and apostolic Church of Jesus Christ? Are we able to resolve unfinished polity issues and move on to better efficiency and institutional clarity? Can we affirm the priority of Christ's mission over institutional survival? Are we willing to foresee what the United Church of Christ might yet become? Whether or not we are now more UCC than ever, we continue to work and witness to the truth of the Gospel of Jesus Christ from the unique perspective of a denomination that yearns to be more than it is, a denomination that indeed yearns, witnesses, works and prays for the visible unity of the whole Church, "that they may all be one".

NOTES

1. Boulding, Kenneth E., *The Meaning of the Twentieth Century* (New York, Harper and Row, 1964).
2. Toffler, Alvin, *Future Shock* (New York: Bantam Books, 1970, 1971, 1984, 1991).
3. Post, Margaret Rowland, *History and Program* (Cleveland: United Church Press, 1986, 1991, 2007).
4. Long, Edward Leroy, Jr., *Patterns of Polity: Varieties of Church Governance* (Cleveland: The Pilgrim Press, 2001), 122.
5. Powell, Oliver, *A.D. Magazine* (New York) September, 1975.
6. *The New Century Hymnal* (Cleveland: The Pilgrim Press, 1995).
7. General Synod 25 Resolutions. Http://www.ucc.org/synod/resolutions/past-general-synod.html
8. Zikmund, Barbara Brown, *The Living Theological Heritage*, Volumes 1-7, (Cleveland: The Pilgrim Press, 1995–2005).

9.   Long, Patterns of Polity, viii-ix.

10.   Gunnemann, Louis H., and Charles Shelby Rooks, *The Shaping of the United Church of Christ,* rev. and enlarged ed. (Cleveland: United Church Press, 1999); see chapter 9.

11.   Paul, Robert S., *Freedom with Order: The Doctrine of the Church in the United Church of Christ* (New York: United Church Press, 1987), 51-52.

12.   Paul, *Freedom with Order,* 52.

United Church Press

BOOK NOTES

History and Program Revised & Update

MARGARET ROWLAND POST,
THOMAS E. DIPKO, ED.

The best-selling booklet shares the history of the UCC, background on its predecessor bodies, explanation of its emblem, and Statement of Faith.

ISBN 978-0-8298-1763-8 **$5.00**

Confessing Our Faith

An Interpretation of the Statement of Faith in the United Church of Christ

ROGER L. SHINN

This resource includes the description of the process that led to the adoption of the Statement of Faith by the UCC in 1959.

ISBN 0-8298-0866-3 **$13.00**

The Evolution of a UCC Style

Essays in the History, Ecclesiology, and Culture of the United Church of Christ

RANDI J. WALKER

Focuses on the development of themes that define the UCC.

ISBN 0-8298-1493-0 **$30.00**

Freedom with Order

The Doctrine of the Church in the United Church of Christ

ROBERT S. PAUL

This book encourages a discussion of the doctrines of the UCC that will faithfully express the historical traditions and the ecumenical imperatives that formed the denomination.
ISBN 0-8298-0749-7 **$13.00**

A History of the Evangelical and Reformed Church

DAVID DUNN, ET AL.

The only detailed, illustrated, single-volume history of the two churches that in 1934 joined together to become the Evangelical and Reformed Church and, in 1957, became part of the United Church of Christ.
ISBN 0-8298-0855-8 **$20.00**

The Living Theological Heritage of the United Church of Christ

BARBARA BROWN ZIKMUND, SERIES EDITOR

A series of documents, statements, and commentaries that chronicle the history, faith, and practices of the United Church of Christ. Hardcover.
Volume 1: Ancient and Medieval Legacies
ISBN 0-8298-1064-1 **$60.00**
Volume 2: Reformation Roots
ISBN 0-8298-1143-5 **$60.00**

Volume 3: Colonial and National Beginnings
ISBN 0-8298-1109-5   **$60.00**
Volume 4: Consolidation and Expansion
ISBN 0-8298-1110-9   **$60.00**
Volume 5: Outreach and Diversity
ISBN 0-8298-1111-7   **$60.00**
Volume 6: Growing Toward Unity
ISBN 0-8298-1112-5   **$70.00**
Volume 7: United and Uniting
ISBN 0-8298-1113-3   **$70.00**
Complete 7-Volume Set–Save $90
ISBN 0-8298-1461-2   **$350.00**

PRISM

A Theological Forum for the
United Church of Christ

LEE BARRETT, III, AND ELIZABETH NORDBECK, EDITORS

This journal, published two times each year, is sponsored by the seminaries of the United Church of Christ. It's purpose is to offer serious theological reflection from a diversity of viewpoints on issues of faith, mission, and ministry.

The Shaping of American Congregationalism: 1620–1957

JOHN VON ROHR

A comprehensive history of Congregationalism from the story of Plymouth Rock to the birth of the UCC.
ISBN 0-8298-0921-X   **$30.00**

The Shaping of the United Church of Christ

An Essay in the History of American Christianity

LOUIS H. GUNNEMANN

Expanded by Charles Shelby Rooks How the UCC took shape in the mid-20th century and has grown into a denomination striving to become a multicultural and multiracial church.
ISBN 0-8298-1345-4   **$22.00**

United and Uniting

The Meaning of an Ecclesial Journey

LOUIS H. GUNNEMANN

This book provides historical perspective and a call to recover the original vision for a greater understanding of the denomination.
ISBN 0-8298-0757-8   **$17.00**

United Church of Christ

Who We Are, What We Believe

This popular leaflet interprets the UCC and is suitable for distribution to your congregation.
U3000   **$0.30 each; $25.00 per 100**

Who Do You Say That I Am? Christology and Identity in the United Church of Christ

SCOTT R. PAETH, ED.

This collection of essays focuses on the role of Christology from various perspectives in the United Church of Christ— how it developed and the part it plays currently in shaping the direction and mission of the church.

978-0-8298-1702-6   **$28.00**

All items can be ordered by phoning our customer service center at 1-800-537-3394 or visiting our website at www.unitedchurchpress.com

All prices subject to change without notice.